Many Cultures
One Market

Many Cultures One Market

A Guide to Understanding Opportunities in the Asian Pacific American Market.

by Robert Kumaki
and Jack Moran, Ph.D.

Many Cultures · One Market:
A Guide to Understanding Opportunities
in the Asian-Pacific-American (APA) Market

©2010 Bob Kumaki
All Rights Reserved. Published 2010.
Second Printing: June, 2011
ISBN: 978-1-887229-40-1

Published by The Copy Workshop
A division of Bruce Bendinger Creative Communications, Inc.
2144 N. Hudson • Chicago, IL 60614
773-871-1179 • thecopyworkshop@aol.com

Editor: Bruce Bendinger
Production Editor: Patrick Aylward
Cover Design: Gregory S. Paus
Producer: Lorelei Davis Bendinger

To my dad, Jim Kumaki
1922–2010

Contents

Foreword:
The APA Gambit

In the game of chess, a *gambit* is a calculated opening move. The player risks one or more minor pieces in order to gain an advantage in position. That is the essence of the strategy for marketers who wish to gain advantage in the Asian Pacific American arena. This book will not only introduce you to a market of growing importance and affluence, it will reveal to you opportunities with a relatively low cost of entry and the potential for high ROI. We believe that a growing number of smart marketers will recognize the advantage of targeting this segment as part of an overall plan.

This book is a beginner's guide for those who wish to know more about this fascinating market.

Opening Moves

Even more than chess, I enjoy another game of strategy – the Asian game of go. Go is played with black and white stones on a grid. *Fuseki* is the opening stage in which the entire board is taken into account. The opening moves are critical.

Go starts with an empty board – think of it as zero-based budgeting. The goal is to capture territory, not pieces as in chess, with the least number of stones possible. Unfortunately, as in the game of chess, too many marketers start with a full board and work on eliminating pieces until only a few remain, rather than starting from an empty board and basing strategy on an overall goal – with a restrained and thoughtful use of resources designed to maximize return.

We believe that in the pursuit of ROI, the smart marketer should make some small but intelligent moves in their marketing plan to make the opening gambit of reaching out to the APA market.

We see this market as, for the most part, unknown and uncharted territory, and an empty part of the board.

The APA market is both simple and subtle. It offers, we believe, a new world of growing opportunity.

We invite you to make your opening moves as you discover this dynamic segment of the American marketplace.

Acknowledgements

Thanks first and foremost to my co-author and daily collaborator, Jack Moran. I've never worked with anyone who has the level of intellectual curiosity and enthusiasm for the human experience that Jack has. Almost a dozen years ago, Jack and I conceived this book together. And through continual exchanges of news clippings, books, e-mails and random ruminations, our book is complete. It was Jack who came up with the brilliant insights in Chapters 7, 8 and 9.

Thanks to all who have read the book in its early incarnations, particularly Linda Garrison, Director of Marketing for Chicago's famous Steppenwolf Theater and my former boss at Ogilvy & Mather; Sarah Patterson of Leo Burnett, one of the few real British Account Planners in the U.S.; Bala Ramakrishnan, President of PentaTwo Consulting; Mark Rukman, Planning Director at Young & Rubicam; Jim Haefner, former head of the Department of Advertising at the University of Illinois and one of my first advertising teachers; and Ken Kabira, former CMO of McDonald's-Japan and now Managing Principal of TrueWorks Branding.

To Katie Daniels, Scott Wheeler, Teresa Wiedel and Katherine Vogel formerly of AZN-TV for allowing us to use the rich data accumulated in working with them; Karen Wang, longtime friend and perhaps the most seasoned APA media professional in the country; Joe Cappo, former publisher of Advertising Age and tireless supporter of the future of advertising; and to my publishers Bruce and Lorelei Bendinger, Patrick Aylward and the team at The Copy Workshop, who showed me that this book could be more than just a consultant's calling card.

Thanks to all the members of the APA community who lent their images for this book.

Former head of Sony Pictures, Chris Lee once told me that when white actors receive an award, they thank their agent; when black actors receive an award, they thank God; and when Asian actors receive an award, they thank their parents. So thanks to my parents for (sort of) understanding when I dropped out of pre-med to follow my heart into advertising.

Finally, to my wife Mary, for everything – especially Elizabeth.

Bob Kumaki
Chicago

I. Introduction
Why a book on Asian Pacific American Marketing?

THE ANSWER IS SIMPLE. Before, there was none. Now there is one. This is the first current resource that provides up-to-date information and insight on one of the most interesting and dynamic sectors of America's multi-ethnic market.

While a number of marketing texts, specifically several multi-cultural marketing books, explore the Asian Pacific American (APA) market as part of a broader explanation of minority markets in the U.S., there is currently no single book-length treatment of the APA market and the range of marketing opportunities it contains.

One result is that while many companies have African American and/or Hispanic American marketing programs, relatively few have marketing programs directed specifically at Asian Pacific Americans. Yet, for many marketers, these vibrant and affluent markets represent major opportunities – for the combined buying power of Asian Pacific Americans (an estimated $500 billion)[1] rivals that of these two larger groups, despite being significantly smaller than either in terms of population.

For many marketers, Asian Pacific Americans represent a key opportunity. Both demographically and geographically, Asian Pacific America is a dream target: young, upscale, extraordinarily well-educated and, in general, geographically concentrated. But though the demographics may be clear, this target market is far less well-understood psychographically – a shortcoming this book intends to remedy.

A Different Approach/A Different Result

For a variety of reasons, few marketers in the U.S. have much real knowledge about the Asian Pacific American market. In a few cases, this is due to lack of data, but in the main, it is lack of insight.

This is particularly true when marketers are exposed to table after table of demographics that offer little or no interpretation as to what those numbers really mean. As we move through this book, we hope to provide you with a different perspective – one that provides useful insights that will help you get to that common goal of all companies – an improved ROI.

What will make this book different from other currently available texts is a combination of what the book is and what it is not.

A Book for Marketers

First and foremost, this is a book for marketers. It is not a book on social services, civil rights or politics. While some of these issues will be brought up to illustrate points or help explain why the APA market reacts as it does, we do not take a stance on issues such as political representation, immigration, hate crimes or bilingualism. The arguments we'd make on social issues are not necessarily in line with good marketing principles, nor are they our area of expertise.

Second, this is a book to help marketers develop strategies – not just tactics. In our experience, many texts designed to help explain minority markets provide plenty of demographic tables but few cultural cues. They do not address how to *think* about the marketplace, but rather take a "How-to" book approach.

For example, we've seen one book that lists "dos and don'ts" for the market that cite stereotypical generalities as gospel (e.g. "Koreans are hard workers[2]," " When advertising and promoting to Filipinos, it's a good idea to incorporate humor[3]," "the color red is good luck[4]"). They also offer as insight obvious statements that are true in any category such as "word of mouth is important[5]."

Actionable Insights

One of the key stumbling blocks in allowing more marketers to reach out to the APA target has been a lack of both qualitative *and* quantitative data. The insights we provide are all based on both types of data, in a combination of both primary and secondary research, done within and outside of the target sphere. In helping you develop actionable insights, we focus well beyond demographic segmentation and discuss cultural clustering, perceptual mapping and profiling, as well as other tools to provide a comprehensive meta-analysis of the APA market, giving a holistic description. Our goal is to allow for an understanding of the primary drivers that explain marketing behaviors and how these behaviors play out in the American context, along with practical, efficient means to implement your marketing plans.

An American Perspective

This is a book on Asian Pacific *American* marketing, not *Asian* marketing. To some, this may not seem like much of a distinction, but the change in emphasis defines the target in immigrant terms with immigrant issues. Worse yet, it overemphasizes marketing influences related to what's going on on the Asian continent, rather than here in America.

Moreover, it ignores the very different situation of long-term Americans, particularly those of Chinese, Filipino and Japanese ancestry whose families may have been in the U.S. for over five generations.

Author's family – 19th Century.   *Author's family – 21st Century.*

This misuse is pervasive. At an APA marketing conference we attended in Chicago, presenters were interchangeably using APA with Asian while focusing predominantly on recent immigrant topics. You will find that even though this group represents a wide range of heritages, they are – at their heart – very American. For one of the authors, heritage aside, home is not Hiroshima, Japan, but the North Shore of Chicago.

What's more, as you will see, a common set of strategies is having a continual positive impact on this market – one that grows with each generation.

Multi-Cultural? Not Exactly

This is not a book on multi-cultural marketing. While both of the authors have considerable experience with African American and Hispanic American markets, we are not experts in those fields, nor is multi-culturalism the focus of the book. We may use corollaries from other marketers in these areas to illustrate points, but not comment on how they are accepted in other target markets.

For some marketers wishing to enter ethnic markets, this will make the process slightly more difficult, as the conventional wisdom and common practice is to lump all ethnic markets under on banner of "Multi-cultural," treat them the same (with exceptions for language and skin color) and allocate marketing support based on population size. Our goal is not to take away support for any particular target, but rather to shine a light on overlooked opportunities.

A True Mass Market

That said, this is not a book for separatists. Within the APA market, the usual rhetoric is that the market is too complex for anyone but "experts" who are ethnically born to the market to understand ("It takes a Chinese person to understand Chinese people," etc.). Taken to the logical extreme, this means all marketing programs must be segmented beyond all massification into discrete sub-units, and, as a result, only local level programs are efficient. "To this, we politely say, 'Bunk!'"

Under this reasoning, no person who is not of Hispanic heritage can ever hope to become a Hispanic marketing expert, there is no such thing as a Gay/Lesbian market, and only New Yorkers are interested in the Yankees.

Along the way, we hope to eliminate some of these marketing myths. While we make no claim that the APA market is completely homogeneous, you will see that there are sufficient commonalities to examine the target as a *true mass market*, and one deserving the attention of many companies.

Some Brief Bits of Biography

Perhaps our perspective is shaped by our personal background. You can read our business biographies later, but we think it's appropriate to note that the authors represent a unique combination of professional, academic, community and ethnic background:

- over 25 years of both general market and APA market experience
- experience as a marketing practitioner and social scientist
- experience as a marketing practitioner and APA activist
- APA, not Asian, ethnic heritage

We believe it is a range of background and experience unique in the field and will result in a uniquely useful perspective.

A Brief Bit of Philosophy

Race makes people do crazy things – sometimes with the best of intentions. Ethnic targeting does not erase the need for good marketing principles. Rather, it is one more tool in a smart marketer's skill set.

The APA Identity
Who are Asian Pacific Americans?

If we are to truly understand this group in *marketing* terms, which is the purpose of this book, we must think in terms of mass target marketing. Proponents of online or social media may flinch at this statement, but we'll address that later. While there are probably goods and services out there with a target market of a few hundred e.g. the latest Bentley Continental Flying Spur, most marketers must look at numbers as large as possible in order to maximize their sales potential and to get efficiencies of scale in their programs.

That said, just as marketers have created an Hispanic Marketplace that combines those of Mexican, Puerto Rican, Cuban, Chilean and other backgrounds, so can marketers think in terms of a combined Asian Pacific American target.

In the following chapters, we will define APAs as anyone having origins on any part of the Asian landmass including the Indian subcontinent and Pacific Islands, but excluding the former Soviet Union and far western Asian countries such as Iran, which are more closely associated with the Middle East.

APA = Over Two Dozen Distinct Groups

If this is still too vague, the U.S. Census offers some clarity. They account for over two dozen different Asian and Pacific Islander groups.[6]

Asian Indian	Filipino	Malaysian
Bangladeshi	Hmong	Okinawan
Burmese	Indonesian	Pakistani
Cambodian	Japanese	Sri Lankan
Korean	Thai	Chinese
Laotian	Vietnamese	Fijian
Guamanian	Hawaiian	Palauan
Tahitian	Samoan	Tongan
Tibetan	Nepalese	Northern Mariana Islander

A few of these groups are quite small and, no surprise in a multi-ethnic place like America, many have a combination of Asian and other ethnic heritages – including the sister of the current President of the United States.

The US Census accounts for over two dozen different Asian and Pacific Islander groups.

Note: The 2000 Census was the first time that individuals could self-identify as more than one race or ethnicity. This presents a difficult situation in that we need to avoid double- or triple-counting multiracial individuals. However, for the purposes of this book, we will gladly include anyone who self-identifies as even part APA, with none of the social judgments of being "one of us" or not being "APA enough."

There will be a major update when 2010 Census data becomes available – we predict some fairly dramatic and interesting results.

APA – Why use the term?

When immigrants from any country have come to the United States, they identified themselves as part of their country of origin e.g. Irish, Japanese, Russian, Brazilian etc. and not part of a larger group, at least until they became citizens. Thereafter they were proud to be American as apple pie, sometimes even denouncing their national heritage. Or, in the case of of German and Japanese Americans, literally going to war. As the Civil Rights Movements of the 20th century grew, members of different ethnic/gender/religious groups saw the advantages of working together, or at least claiming to work together, as a mass group in order to effect social change through political or economic power.

As with African Americans and Hispanic Americans, so too, has a mass label been given to persons of Asian ancestry. In this text, we will use the term Asian Pacific American or the APA acronym for all references to this group. This term is distinctive in several ways:

- It clearly separates persons of Asian ancestry living in the United States from those who are "just visiting," such as students and Asian business executives. That is, an Asian vs. an Asian American. One of the authors, born and bred in Chicago is an Asian Pacific American. His friend from Nippon Steel, here on a three-year work visa is an Asian living in America.

- It provides an inclusive term for all persons of Asian or Pacific Islander heritage, while excluding Western Asians e.g. Iranians etc., as described above.

- It recognizes other unique Pacific ethnic heritages. For the first time in 2000, the U.S. Census allowed people to identify themselves as Native Hawaiians and Pacific Islanders (NHPI) separately from Asian Americans. The justification for this was that many of those claiming NHPI background had a dramatically different socio-economic experience from the rest of Asian Americans. However, for the purposes of this book, APA was chosen to be as inclusive as possible.

- It avoids the also inclusive term "Oriental" that is at once antiquated, racist, ethnocentric, non-specific, without an appropriate counterpart, and used more for inanimate objects. Terms and cultural values evolve – today, this term is, quite frankly, distasteful to a great many APAs.

- APA is "acceptable" to all. While not universally embraced, neither is it shunned by any particular group to any great degree. Just as some Hispanic Americans may prefer Latino and those of African ancestry may prefer Black or Afro-American. Hispanic and African American seem to be acceptable to the vast majority of Americans. So too, will we use APA as the accepted description.

Finally, it just takes too darn long to write Asian Pacific American every time we use it. From now on, APA.

Understanding the APA Opportunity

By offering new insights into the APA population, we hope to help you understand the APA opportunity with an eye to entering or expanding the marketplace for your company.

Here are some of the things we will provide in the following chapters:

- the most complete demographic and psychographic profile on APAs created to date, most from readily available secondary data sources
- a view of why your company probably does not have an APA-targeted marketing program in place, and a quick exercise on what you might be missing
- a short U.S. history lesson on APAs and the impact of sociopolitical movements on the APA population
- a short treatise on ethnic marketing in general and why marketers cannot take a cookie cutter approach to developing APA marketing plans
- a unique approach to understanding and sorting your way through APA subcultures
- a new paradigm for thinking about the APA marketplace that simplifies the complexities and offers a clear, concise approach to address the target
- an understanding of the huge non-APA crossover opportunity
- a fresh approach to reaching APAs via mass media, events, and organizations

Cultural Considerations

Throughout this book we will offer "Cultural Considerations" – short essays, lists and ruminations on the state of APA culture, some of the forces that affect it, and how it's manifested in the marketplace. We think they're both entertaining and instructive.

Cultural Considerations: A conversation with an APA

A conversation between an average APA and an "American."

American: *Your English is so good! Where did you learn to speak so well?*

APA: *Right here.*

American: *Where are you originally from?*

APA: *Chicago.*

American: *No, I mean where are your parents from?*

APA: *Southern California.*

American: *No, I mean where were they born?*

APA: *Southern California.*

The "American" walks away thinking the APA is a jerk who's just being difficult. In actuality, what's difficult is the inescapable feeling by the APA that he or she is not being taken seriously as an American, not just as an American citizen, but as an American.

Is this any different and should it not provoke the same outrage as when someone says of a Black person, "He speaks so well"?

Comedian Chris Rock riffs:

"Colin Powell could never have been president. The best thing white people could ever say about him was, 'He speaks so well. He is so well spoken.'

'Speaks well' is not a compliment. Why would people say that to Colin Powell? Did he have a stroke? He's a f@#$ing educated man. What did people expect him to sound like?"[7]

A Simple Idea

This book has been built upon a simple idea. The idea is that every successful marketing plan or program, whether targeted towards an ethnic group or not, is based upon some universal marketing principles. There is nothing new to this.

What is new is how we will strip away extraneous noise and misinformation to help companies see this multi-faceted segment with the kind of clarity marketers need to identify opportunities and make good decisions.

With that in mind, you are about to embark upon an exciting marketing journey – one that takes you into the heart of 14 million[8] hard-working Americans with money to invest and spend.

It will be simultaneously familiar and brand new, as you discover solid gold nuggets of opportunity scattered across the American landscape.

Chapter by chapter, we'll show you where they are, how they got there and, with the addition of your own insight and marketing skill, how to make the most of this powerful market – Asian Pacific Americans. APA.

II. Background

An Asia-centric vs. Euro-centric Perspective

EVERY DAY, we touch something made in Asia. It might be the electronics we use, the clothes we wear, or the cars we drive. But how many of us know anything about Asia or its people beyond the menu of the local Chinese take-out?

For obvious reasons, most Americans have a Euro-centric view of the world. Even African- and Hispanic Americans, when discussing global issues will have this perspective. Asia is simply not on the minds of most Americans – unless there's a North Korea nuke threat, a recall of lead paint-contaminated Chinese toys, or a tsunami hitting the South Pacific.

A Global Challenge. A Global View.

As globalization grows, so will the challenges – both good and bad.

Former Secretary of Education Rod Paige notes "We are ever mindful of the lessons of September 11th that taught us that all future measures of a rigorous K-12 education must include a solid grounding in other cultures, other languages and other histories."[1]

Other Cultures. Other Histories.

America's growing APA population has a role to play in helping to achieve a global perspective. But it won't be easy.

The 2006 National Geographic-Roper Public Affairs Geographic Literacy Study finds that the most recent graduates of the U.S. education system are "unprepared for an increasingly global future" and "far too many lack even the most basic skills for navigating the international economy or understanding relationships among people and places that provide critical context for world events."[2] For example:

- Fewer than 30% think it's important to know the locations of countries in the news, and just 14% believe speaking another language is a necessary skill.
- Two-thirds didn't know that the earthquake that killed 70,000 people in October 2005 occurred in Pakistan.
- Forty-seven percent could not find the Indian subcontinent on a map of Asia.
- Although the U.S. has been "occupying" Iraq for almost seven years, only 37% can find Iraq on a map[3]
- Sixty percent did not know that the border between North and South Korea is the most heavily fortified in the world (30% thought the most heavily fortified border was between the U.S. and Mexico)
- 74% think English is the most commonly spoken native language in the world (it's Mandarin)
- Although 70% could locate China on a map, 45% said that China's population is only twice that of the United States.[4]

In terms of language, the statistical picture is even more thought-provoking. According to the U.S. Department of Education:[5]

- More than 200 million children in China are studying English, a compulsory subject for all Chinese primary school students. By comparison, only 24,000 of approximately 54 million elementary and secondary school children in the U.S. are studying Chinese. There are almost four times as many Chinese students studying English as all U.S. students combined.
- Only 31% of American elementary schools (and 24% of public elementary schools) report teaching foreign languages. Of those schools, 79% focus on providing introductory exposure rather than achieving overall proficiency. This is the so-called "food, fun and festivals" approach.
- Only 44% of American high school students are enrolled in foreign language classes. The most commonly offered (and taken) foreign languages are still Spanish, French and German. Of

these 69% are enrolled in Spanish and 18% in French.[6]

- Less than 1% of American high school students *combined* study Arabic, Chinese, Farsi, Japanese, Korean, Russian or Urdu. More students study American Sign Language than any Asian-based language except Japanese.[7]

We're not suggesting you run out an enroll in a language course, but, as you read this chapter, you might think about broadening your global perspective. Then again, the rest of the world seems to be thinking about us.

As with most things, it helps to understand the current situation if you go back to the source. To understand APAs, it's going to help to know a little about Asia first, even if the APAs you're looking at have been in the U.S. for five generations.

Here's a different way to begin to understand Asia and Asians in a simple Euro-centric context. The hard stuff will come later.

Geography

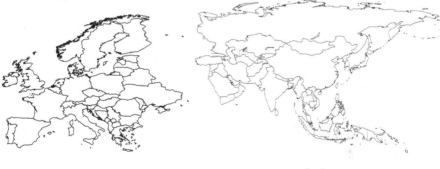

| Europe | Asia |

The map of Europe is probably more familiar. While there are significantly more countries in Europe than in Asia (47 vs. 29, as we define them), the Asian landmass is more than four times larger (4 vs. 17.1 million square miles). And, Asia's population is six times larger (512 million vs. 3.3 billion).

The Asian continent stretches across 10 time zones. Europe covers three. The bulk of Europe's climate is considered temperate. Asia's climates run the extremes from torrid heat to arctic cold, from torrential rain to arid desert. Practically all of Europe may be considered "developed," whereas Asian development ranges from the cutting edge technology of Tokyo to the nomadic subsistence of Mongolia.

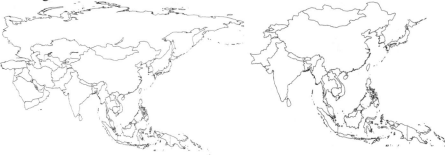

Geographic Asia   **Ethnic/Cultural Asia**

From a cultural perspective, we need to separate "geographic Asia" from "ethnic/cultural Asia." As noted in the Introduction, we will also exclude the Middle East from our definition. There's also one small group in transition – with the breakup of the former Soviet Union, countries such as Kyrgystan and Tajikistan are redefining their place in the geopolitical make-up of the Asian continent. Since the populations are primarily Turkic, some indications are these countries will look west toward Turkey and Europe. Then again, the growing economic power of India and China may have its own gravitational effect.

"Chopsticks Cultures"

Another way to frame Asian countries and their relationship to each other is via what we call "Chopsticks Cultures." Simply put, there is a basic divide between Asian cultures that use chopsticks and those that do not. There are very real sociological differences between the two.

Europe: North vs. South

Max Weber, of the German Historical School of Economics, in his book, *The Protestant Ethic and the Spirit of Capitalism*, defined the "Protestant work ethic" as a means of explaining the national prosperity of Northern European countries.[8] The countries of the North e.g. Germany, England, Scandinavia, were portrayed as Protestant, materialistic, cerebral, living for the future, and focused on work, where work was seen as duty for the benefit of the society as a whole.

Asian: Chopsticks vs. Non-Chopsticks

The stereotypical view of the "chopsticks cultures" of Japan, China and Korea correlates with this region in much the same way.

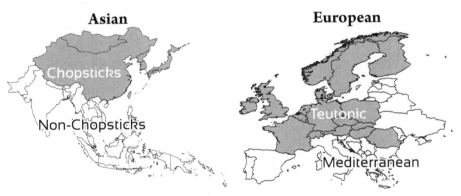

Chopsticks v. Non-Chopsticks   **Teutonic v. Mediterranean**

Southern Europe (e.g. Spain, Portugal and Italy) was seen as Catholic, less materialistic, sensual, living for today, and focused on the Catholic idea of doing good works, not necessarily working for the common good. The "non-chopsticks cultures" of India, the Philippines and Thailand correlate with this group.

> Note: Yes, although you will find chopsticks in virtually all Asian food-focused restaurants in America, some Asian cultures use forks. At a recent dinner at one of the more popular Thai restaurants in Chicago, one of the authors asked the server, "Why are you placing chopsticks on the table? Thai people generally don't eat with chopsticks."

The reply was, "Everyone expects all Asian people to use chopsticks, so instead of customers getting mad at us not having them, we just put them out as a matter of course."

Forks, by the way, were invented by the Chinese over 4,000 years ago and brought to Europe via the Middle East in the 12th Century, when most Europeans were still eating with their hands.[9]

Or maybe different cultures act differently just because people in warmer climates tend to eat spicier food. Who can say if any of these are correct? But it's interesting that both Asia and Europe have cultures with greatly different levels of performance.

Weber's theories were widely criticized in the 20th century, as they mostly revolved around the cultures and history of Europe and did not take into account societies that exhibited "Protestant ethics" but had never been Christian, such as Japan. However, for our purposes, it remains another fascinating, if somewhat inexact, way of looking at Asia.

Language

Language differentiation becomes much more apparent in comparing Europe to Asia when you realize that not only are the languages themselves different, but the writing of those languages varies dramatically as well. Some note that this symbology promotes the development of a radically different way of thinking and learning compared to Western cultures. We'll discuss that later.

Asian Iconic +   European Latin/Cyrillic

Germanic, Italic, Slavic

Virtually all of modern Europe is based on one of three Indo-European language roots – Germanic, encompassing German, English, Dutch, and most Scandinavian languages; Italic, the root of French, Italian, Spanish, and Portuguese (the Romance languages); and Slavic, covering Russian, Bulgarian, Serbo-Croatian, Polish and others; plus modern Greek. With the exception of Greek, all of these languages use Latin or Cyrillic symbols.

Different Languages, Different Writing

Asia has quite a few more language families. There are a significantly larger number of language roots in Asia – Sino-Tibetan (Mandarin, Cantonese), Dravidian (Tamil), Austronesian (Tagalog), Austro-Asiatic (Vietnamese), Mongolic (Mongolian), Japonic (Japanese), Tai-Kadai (Thai, Lao), and Indo-Aryan (Sanskrit, Hindi, Urdu). Each of these has its own family of languages and dialects, but each also has its own system of writing and symbols. In addition, the colonial heritage adds English (India, Pakistan, and Hong Kong), French (Vietnam, Cambodia, Laos), Dutch (Indonesia), and Spanish (the Philippines).[10]

Religion

Historically, with the exception of Jews and a few pockets of Balkan Muslims, Europe may be considered primarily "Christian" or at least supporting a "Christian Ethic." Asia, on the other hand, is comprised of Buddhists, Muslims, Hindus, Taoists, Shinto, Shamanists, and Christians, all with an underlying Confucian ethic.

Prior to the 20th Century, religion and politics went hand in hand. Christianity grew along with European political and economic expansion. This was not always good news as it often led to the destruction or at least diminution of aboriginal Asian cultures and religions. Witness the destruction of "heathen" language and culture in Polynesia, Australia and the rest of the South Pacific.

Asian Multiple Belief Systems   **European Christian Dominance**

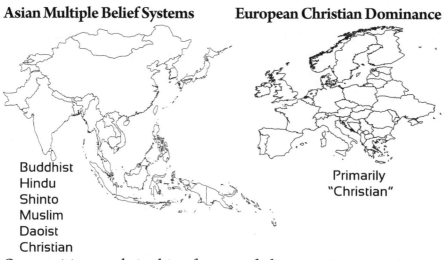

Buddhist
Hindu
Shinto   Primarily
Muslim   "Christian"
Daoist
Christian

One positive result is this often eased the transition into American culture of peoples from significant Christian outposts in Asia, including South Korea, Vietnam, the Philippines, and Indonesia among others. When immigrating to the U.S., they brought "their" religion with them, and found themselves very much at home.

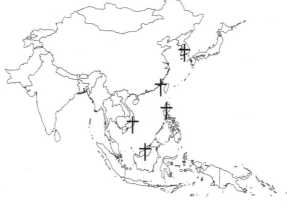

Colonialism

It hasn't just been religion. Asian countries have been significantly influenced over the past two centuries by various European countries. British outposts in India, the French in Southeast Asia, the Spanish and Americans in the Philippines, and the Dutch in Indonesia have left their mark on the cultures of those countries.

But, long before the Europeans, there was another cultural power – China spread culture, technology and often political rule from one end of Asia Pacific to the other. The Chinese influence is profound, even if countries were not physically conquered. In addition, emigrated Chinese in Asia, across countries such as Singapore, Thailand, Indonesia, and the Philippines, provide another powerful influence in Asian culture – particularly Asian business culture. New America Foundation senior research fellow Parag Khanna espouses that the new global order of the 21st century and beyond will once again see the major superpowers consisting of the United States, the European Union and China along with a host of second tier "swing states."[11] Each of these three strong cultural influences has been around for quite some time.

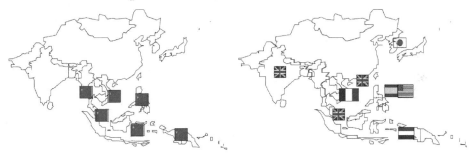

Implications for Marketers

So what does all this have to do with marketing to APAs? Our comments for this chapter will be short, simple and to the point.

- Unlike most other examples of target marketing, marketing to APAs must be understood within a global context. Add an Asian-centric perspective.
- China has had a profound influence across most of Asia.
- Asia has very different cultural variables – such as language, writing, religion, and even the way they eat.
- Despite those differences, some cultural variables are surprisingly similar – such as European influences and, in many cases, Christianity.

Cultural Considerations: A Guide to APA Names

Can you tell what nationality someone is just by their name? Sometimes. It may not be difficult (for some) to figure out that Sakamoto is a Japanese name or that Chang is Chinese. But what about Lee? And it can become quite complex. What about Remandaban? Tran? Ramakrishnan? Here are some general guidelines for those not adopting Anglicized usages.

Ethnicity	Name Order	Special Considerations
Chinese	surname, first name (However, it has become common to adopt a "Western" name – in which case the practice of first name, surname is usually, but not always, adopted)	There may be a "generational" name that all same-sex siblings share. Further confusion added when you see Wade-Giles spellings e.g. Mao Tse-tung (the European colonial influence) vs. Pinyin spellings e.g. Mao Zedong, which also uses letter X for those phonemes that do not exist in English. Common names include Chan, Wong and most of all, Lee.
Filipino	first name, surname	Unless they're Tagalog names, most Filipinos have Spanish surnames from the colonial era using the Castillian pronunciations. This presents a real challenge in trying to identify Filipinos in a phone book or database. An unusual affectation is that the tough guy bouncer at the local Filipino bar may go by the name of Junior or Baby.
Indian	first name, surname	Initials may be an important part of a person's identity. Women may use their father's first initial as a middle name. Religion is usually easy to identify by last name. Patels are mostly Hindu, Khans are usually Muslim. Someone with Singh in their name is almost always Sikh.

Japanese	surname, first name	Women's names often end in "ko" which means child. More forward thinking women often drop this usage in the professional workplace. Even good friends may use the honorific "san" after last names however, the extreme opposite is true also, when good friends may use "chan" (a diminutive used mainly for children) after the first name, even if the person is elderly. Shimizu, Tanaka, and Watanabe are common Japanese names. The author's last name, Kumaki, is not.
Korean	surname, usually 2-part first name	Married women in Korea usually don't take their husband's surname. Korean women in the U.S. do. If you're confused, look for a hyphen to let you know it's a first name. Similar to the Welsh (Smith, Davis, Williams), Koreans have a relatively small number of surnames. The four most common Korean names are Kim, Lee, Park (variant Pak, Bak) and Choi.
Thai	first name, surname	In the U.S., Thai people are usually known by their first name. This is because it's not uncommon for Thai surnames to be a dozen or more letters long. In addition, many Thais with Thai names are ethnically Chinese. A number of years ago, Chinese living in Thailand were required to adopt Thai names.
Vietnamese	surname, middle name, first name	It's common to refer to someone as Mr. First Name. Most people with the middle name Van are men, most with middle name Thi are women. Over half of the population has the surname Nguyen. Points if you can correctly pronounce Nguyen

What's in a name?

Plenty, if you live in the state of Texas. In his testimony before the Texas House Elections Committee, Ramsey Ko, of the Organization of Chinese Americans, stated that many Asian ethnic groups have difficulty voting because their legal forms of identification often carry a transliterated name along with a commonly used English name.

These adopted English names appear on driver's licenses, school registration cards and other forms of ID, while official voter rolls may only have the Asian name.

U.S. Representative Betty Brown suggested that voters of Asian descent should all simply change their names! She commented, "Rather than everyone here having to learn Chinese – I understand it's a rather difficult language – do you think it would behoove you and your citizens to adopt a name that we could deal with more readily here? Can't you see that this is something that would make it a lot easier for you and the people who are poll workers if you could adopt a name just for identification purposes that's easier for Americans to deal with?"[12]

There's a thought. Let's tell Geraldo Rivera to change his name to Jerry Rivers! However, it points out just one of the many cultural reference points that is emerging as the U.S. becomes more multi-cultural.

Bonus Question #1: What's the most common surname in the world? If you guessed Smith or Jones, you're a Eurocentric. It's Lee (variant Li, Ly), with over 108 million.

Bonus Question #2: What do the names Akaka, Cao, Chu, Faleomavaega, Inouye, Matsui and Wu have in common? They are all members of the U.S. Congress (Faleomavaega is a non-voting member from American Samoa).

III. Blind Spots
Why aren't there more APA Marketing Programs?

THERE EXISTS IN ALMOST EVERY corporate bureaucracy at least one person whose job it is to say "No."

It's not just a simple "I'm the boss" kind of "No." It's subtler than that. It's more of a "No, and here's my marketing rationale." These are the conscientious nay sayers who can always find a reason for not trying out a new, different program. It's been said that no one has ever been fired for just repeating what the Company did last year.

Getting to "Yes" with an APA program – at least in the beginning – may involve more than the usual amount of up front work.

For a start, it's always easier to support a "Why we shouldn't" than a "Why we should," particularly if the answers to those questions are based on any sort of capital expenditure.

But it's more complex than that. Some of the more typical responses for not supporting an APA marketing program include:

"the absolute size of the market is too small"
"there are too many languages"
"they're hard to reach with mass media"
"we already reach them with our media buy"
"they don't need marketing support. They're the 'model minority'"
"the African American and Hispanic markets are more important"
"we don't have any products geared towards Asians"
"we can't measure the media"
"we can't reach them with a single message"
"we have no minority set-aside program for them"
"there aren't any Asians who live around here"

*"there's no such thing as an Asian American market – I know
that there are Hispanic and African American markets"*
"if they wanted our attention, we'd be hearing about it"

How many of these have you heard?

Blind Spots at Work

This sort of thinking isn't restricted to small or unsophisticated companies. They're easy blind spots to have – and most marketing budgets are already straining to cover the items that have already been approved. So it's no surprise that we've heard these responses from Senior Management in Fortune 500 companies. We've even heard from the CEO of an *Asian American advertising agency* that *"There isn't such a thing as an Asian American, but if we all stand together, it's pretty close"* [1]

But the real blind spot, the real reason that so many companies do not have specific APA targeted programs is that most companies simply do not see the opportunity. What's more, even if they do glimpse an opportunity, most companies do not have APA programs because:

- they have no expertise in the marketplace
- they do not know where to find expertise
- there is no desire to look for expertise
- there is no internal champion for such a program
- all of the above

So it's easy to understand why there is no realization of the APA target potential. There are challenges to be met.

Challenge #1: Simplify

It's hard to identify opportunities in a cluttered landscape. Every description of the APA market we've ever read contains the word *complex*. However, as with many subjects, conventional wisdom can miss a few things.

In the APA marketplace, there are indeed issues of language, generational imprints, and immigration status among a host of other variables a marketer must review. But, as you will see, there are a number of factors that unify the market.

For all the internal variables, it is actually a very coherent group – with much in common – including high income levels.

Then again, is this any different from any other target market? Does this mean African Americans, Gays & Lesbians, High Net Worth Investors, Teenage Heavy-user Candy Consumers, or *any* other target markets don't also have their own complexity? Of course they do.

Part of the mission of this book is to wade through the clutter that gets in the way of understanding the APA target. For many companies, the market opportunity is big enough and the data clear enough to allow those companies to develop a firm and accurate understanding of their APA opportunity.

Challenge #2: APA Marketing Evolution

Many APA marketing "experts" would tell you differently. Why? Because many APA "marketing" services have yet to evolve from their beginnings as translation services for a narrow range of marketers – such as those selling phone cards to recent immigrants. Aside from that, they often see little opportunity. To them, and to most who have never explored the market, it is only common sense that the marketplace must be approached in one, and only one monolithic way. So you get advice like this:

> "When trying to reach Asian Americans, it's important to remember the audience is different. They fundamentally require a different approach. For one thing, Asian Americans are separate societies with their own languages, culture and media."[2]

— Rick Blume
General Manager
Database Management, NY

27

For a start, we ask "Who made these 'experts' experts?" Someone who can give a good soundbite? Someone who has a great public relations arm? Someone with a great title at a prestigious company? Or perhaps someone who has an APA translation service, looking to translate your current campaign.

We could probably add to the list of quotes as to why more companies don't have APA programs. And that list may have the potential to scare off even the hardiest Marketing Manager. However, as Former Vice President Al Gore stated in his award winning movie, *An Inconvenient Truth*: "There are a lot of people who go straight from denial to despair without pausing on the intermediate step of actually doing something about the problem."[3]

Better yet, let's see if we can see through a few of the blind spots.

A Quick Test

Let's take a quick test to see if getting into the APA marketplace might be right for your company.

If your target:

- is highly educated,
- has above-average income levels,
- shows a high degree of business ownership,
- tends to be an early adopter of new technology,
- has a higher-than-average propensity to both save and invest,
- invests heavily in education for their family,
- values quality over price,
- is highly conscious of brand names,
- demonstrates a strong desire to be recognized by marketers,
- is underserved by most product categories,
- is highly brand loyal,

then you may be looking at an APA marketing opportunity. It's probably time to look past those blind spots and do a deep dive into the APA marketplace immediately. (Guess you'd better keep reading this book.) In fact, you may be late within your industry/ category in entering the APA market. We'll get to a more rigorous test of APA "fit" as a potential target market later.

An Exercise
Straightline Econometrics: Getting to Equilibrium

In a world where it becomes more difficult to increase share and deliver growth, ethnic segments can provide many companies with the opportunity to gain new business and expand their customer base.

For example, what happens if we just get our APA sales on par with the general market? If your company has already been data mining your sales figures in the ethnic arena, you can take another 30 second test to see if entering the APA market may right for you. The following is a quick and dirty hybridization of using a Category Development Index and a Brand Development Index to try and ascertain the "APA headroom for growth" that may be present in your category or for your brand.

What we're looking for is a measure to the extent by which the sales of products or services to an APA target compare with a company's average sales, and what would happen to the bottom line if the APA market was brought up to parity (if it's underserved) with the general market, a "fair share" growth.

To take this exercise, you only need to know three pieces of data and their APA derivatives:

- your company sales by household (feel free to substitute people, heavy users, or whatever target measurement unit is most appropriate for you)
- your company sales by APA household
- your company average transaction size
- your company average ethnic APA transaction size
- your company average number of transactions
- your company average number of APA transactions

We'll provide you with the population information. Simply add your own database, CRM, personal experience or even anecdotal evidence to the equation, and plug and chug to the answer.

A - Total US households (72.3 million)
B - Total US APA households (3.8 million)
C - Total US Company X households
D - Total Company X APA households

E - % APA households of all U.S. households (**B/A**) (5.25%)
F - % Company X households of all U.S. households (**C/A**)
G - % of Company X households that are APA households
H - Relative % Company X is over/under covering APA HH (**E-G**)

I - Total Company X sales
J - Total Company X APA sales
K - % total Company X sales that are APA sales (**J/I**)
L - Relative % Company X is over/under selling to APAs (**E-K**)

M - Average Company X transaction size (**I/C**)
N - Average Company X APA transaction size (**J/D**)
O - Difference in average APA vs Total U.S. average transaction size (**M-N**)

P – Average number of household transactions per year
Q – Average number of APA household transactions per year
R – Difference between the number of APA and Total US average household transactions per year

S - Number of additional APA households Company X should cover to bring to parity (**H*B**)
T - Potential dollar increase over current Company X APA sales (**N*Q*S**)
U - Potential dollar total of APA market to Company X (**J+T**)

Let's do a quick example for the Whatchamacallit Corp. Here are the givens:

Total US Households: 72.3 million[4]
Total US APA Households: 3.8 Million

And here are some assumptions for this example:

Total US Whatchamacallit households: 14.5 million
Total US Whatchamacallit APA households: 650,000
Total US Whatchamacallit sales: $89 million
Total US Whatchamacallit APA sales: $3.7 million
Average number of household transactions per year: 10
Average number of APA household transactions per year: 6

Now let's get to crunching numbers.

The percent that APAs make up of all U.S. households is 5.2% (B/A). Total percent of Whatchamacallit households of all U.S. households is 20% (C/A). Total percent of Whatchamacallit households that are APA households is 4.5% (D/C). Already you know that the company is selling a less than proportionate number of APA households by almost a full percentage point (E-G).

Now let's start translating this into money. The Whatchamacallit APA sales are 4.1% of the company total ((J/I). This means in monetary terms, the company is underselling by over a full percentage point to the APA market, relative to the percentage of the population (E-K).

We're using the fact that not only is the average transaction size for APAs lower than the general market, but the number of transactions per year is also lower. How does this affect the bottom line?

If we don't change the transaction size or number of transactions per year, just bringing up the number of APAs buying Whatchamacallit products can show a significant increase in the total APA market value to the company. For example, if we add the number of APA households we're underreaching 26,600 (H*B), and multiply that number by the average transaction size and transaction times,

Whatchamacallit's sales can increase by almost a million dollars (N*Q*S).

Changing any of the variables, whether its households, transaction size, or number of transactions will increase the total. Of course, this is true for any segment of Whatchamacallit's customer base, but this example shows what can happen to total sales when marketers bring a target just up to parity with the rest of the market. This example showed APAs as under-represented and under performing. Imagine, as in the case of financial instruments, some luxury goods and other categories, what happens to the company bottom line when APAs are reached in accordance with the rest of the general market and outperform general market consumption.

Feel free to use this test on *any* of your current or future target markets.

"Ah, but," you ask "how much is this going to cost and what's my ROI?" We get to that in Chapter 15, entitled, "Media: How Do We Reach APAs?"

Implications for Marketers

One of the principal reasons there aren't more APA programs is simply that many companies have never asked themselves, "Does this make any sense for us? Should we look into the APA market further?"

Though, once you ask the question, you still may have some challenges. Blind spots aren't that easy to erase. For example…

- **Watch out for Stereotypes.**
  If you are beginning a new program to reach out to the APA market, it's *virtually guaranteed* someone will support the status quo by using one or more of the historically stereotypical (and often incorrect) responses for not addressing the target.
- **Watch out for Experts.**

Be careful who you hold up as "experts" (even us) in categories to which you are new. Even if multiple parties are giving you the same answer to your questions, they may not necessarily be right.

- **Make Sure There's Profit Potential.**

Remember, as stated in the beginning of this book, the reason to enter into any marketplace is to make money for your company.

Cultural Considerations:
You might be an APA if...

Comedian Jeff Foxworthy spins tales about being a redneck. Here's the APA version.

... you're ashamed that you got a 1500 on your SAT, because another Chinese kid in your class got a 1600

... your Southern California roots mean you speak Spanish better than you do Japanese.

... you just now realize that your kid got bumped out of Stanford because you supported quota systems for minority applicants of which you are not considered one.

... you know that Manzanar, Tule Lake and Poston are not vacation sites.

... you think you've got it easy by having to practice the piano for an hour a day ... because the Korean kid has to play it for two hours.

... you realize that your Jewish friends have nothing on you in the family guilt department.

... you buy soy sauce by the gallon bottle but still keep those little packets from the Chinese take-out.

... the only way you know how to make rice is by pushing the *ON* button of your fuzzy logic steamer.

... you hate explaining that language skills aren't genetic when you meet a Caucasian who speaks better Mandarin than you do.

... the same skills that caused you to flunk your driving test three times have now made you the best drift racer in Orange County.

... you end up being the neighborhood go-to expert on all things Asian, even though you couldn't find Cambodia on the globe to save your life.

... when you watch American Idol, you're quick to point out that William Hung is Chinese, not Japanese.

... even you think it's weird that you got better grades in English than in math.

... you call your parent's friends "Auntie" and "Uncle" even if they're not related to you.

... your family jokingly refers to themselves as "boat people" even though your parents came to the U.S. on a 747.

... you've explained to airport screeners for the umpteenth time that Mumbai is nowhere near Baghdad.

... you have no problem passing as Chinese if it means not getting beat up by gangsta rap fans of the Wu Tang Clan.

... if you're a woman and every white male you know wants you to repeat lines from the movie "Full Metal Jacket" like "Me so horny. Me love you long time."

... you know you were born in the Year of the Rat, but you have no idea what the hell that means.

... you realize that your conservative manner, strict work ethic and a law degree from Stanford won't do as much to break through the glass ceiling as belonging to the right country club, fraternity or Masonic lodge.

... you've been around Asian people so little that you begin to think "Hmm, maybe they do all look alike."

IV. History
A Quick Timeline with Some Interesting Facts

For a nation that professes "all men are created equal," APA history demonstrates that the American political and legal systems have constructed barrier after barrier to the creation of an APA community. This makes their success and their loyalty to the U.S. all the more interesting. Here are some of the highlights.

1693: First recorded settlement of Filipinos in U.S. They escape impressments aboard Spanish galleons by jumping ship in New Orleans.

Late 1700s: Initial Chinese immigrants settle in Baltimore and San Francisco

1790: First recorded arrival of Asian Indians in the U.S.

1848–52: The Gold Rush. Discovery of gold in California attracts Chinese prospectors. Chinese immigrants arrive as indentured servants during Gold Rush. Majority of almost 300,000 come later to work as cheap labor for the railroads and other industries.

Note: The Transcontinental Railroad was completed in 1869, with Chinese laborers building most of the Western section. Take a look at any of the pictures of the Presidents of the Central Pacific and Union Pacific Railroads congratulating each

other in Promontory Point, Utah. See any Chinese faces in the picture?

1869: First Japanese colony established in Gold Hill, CA

1870: Under the Naturalization Act, Chinese are not eligible for citizenship. Act also forbids entry of wives of laborers, effectively ending family growth.

1871: Some of the first anti-Chinese riots break out in Los Angeles and other West Coast cities. A mob of "nativist" whites shoot and hang 20 Chinese in one night in Los Angeles.

1882: Congress enacts law that suspends entry of Chinese laborers for 10 years. It excludes Chinese from citizenship by naturalization and halts Chinese immigration for 60 years.

1898: The Spanish American War Treaty officially makes the United States a Pacific Imperial Power by taking over Guam and the Philippines from Spain.

1905: Asian Exclusion League formed by 67 labor organizations in San Francisco.

1906: San Francisco School Board segregates "Oriental" schools *Note:* In the century since this segregation and subsequent desegregation, the top bastions of higher education have had to constantly re-examine the equality (or lack thereof) of entrance standards for incoming students given the disproportionately high numbers of APA students qualifying and wishing to enter the country's elite colleges and universities. Witness that a slang name for the University of California at Los Angeles (UCLA) is the University of Caucasians Lost Among Asians.

1907: Presidential Executive Order bars migration of Japanese in Hawaii to mainland U.S.. President Roosevelt's "Gentlemen's Agreement" opens jobs in Hawaii for Filipinos, but also includes a ban on Korean immigration to the U.S. as laborers.

1910: Angel Island, established as a detention center for those Asian non-labor classes desiring entry into the U.S., becomes the Ellis Island of the West. The Supreme Court extends the 1870 Naturalization Act to other Asians, making them aliens ineligible for citizenship. *Note:* The comparison between Ellis Island and Angel Island is terribly misleading. Angel Island was designed expressly as a holding area for Chinese immigrants whose right to enter the U.S. was under question. The average immigrant who came ashore at Ellis Island spent three to five hours being processed by immigration authorities. The Chinese who were detained at Angel Island stayed there an average of two to seven weeks; some were incarcerated for as long as two years.[1]

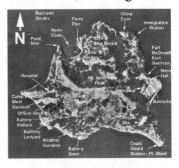

1913: Alien Land Law prevents "aliens ineligible for citizenship" from owning or leasing land for more than 3 years.

1922: In Ozawa v. U.S., the Supreme Court ruled that Japanese were not eligible for citizenship because that right was reserved for whites and blacks only.

1924: The Oriental Exclusion Act bars all immigration of laborers from Asia. The Act declares that no one ineligible for citizenship may immigrate to the U.S. excluding Filipinos, who are subjects of the U.S. The Act solidified U.S. commitment to quantify immigration numbers depending on ethnicity/nationality – based on quotas of who was here in 1890, effectively ending Asian immigration. *Note:* The total Japanese immigration to the U.S. over a 30-year span reached 275,000. While American "nativists" complained of huge waves of Asian immigrants, 283,000 Italians alone arrived in 1913–14.[2]

1934: **The Tydings-McDuffie Act** promises independence to the Philippines in 10 years from signing. It also creates an immigration quota of only 50 Filipinos per year.

1942: **Executive Order 9066** signed by President Roosevelt, authorizing the internment of 120,000 persons of Japanese ancestry, mostly U.S. citizens, into concentration camps. *Note:* The 100th Infantry Battalion/442nd Regimental Combat Team, consisting solely of Japanese Americans, becomes the most decorated military unit in American history. Each member becomes an honorary citizen of Texas, for rescuing the "Lost Battalion" of Texas where casualties outnumbered those rescued.

1946: **The Immigration and Naturalization Bill** reopens immigration, particularly for Filipinos, but with severe limits. "We are utterly justified in controlling and keeping low Oriental immigration in terms of numbers," explained Congress-woman Clare Booth Luce, "because of the fact that they in too great numbers may undermine our way of life, our living standards." *Note:* At this time, Japan and Korea were still not permitted to send any immigrants. The Philippines and India were each given a quota of 100; China, a quota of 105. By contrast, Poland alone had a quota of 6,524.[3]

1943: **The Magnuson Act** repeals the Chinese Exclusion Act of 1882. Quota of 105 immigrants per year set for Chinese immigration. Chinese granted right of naturalization

1952: **The Walter-McCarran Immigration and Naturalization Act** repeals the Oriental Exclusion Act of 1924.

1959: **Daniel Inouye elected to Congress.** As Hawaii's first representative, he is the first APA in Congress. In 1962 he wins the Senate seat, which he still holds today, also Chairing the powerful Appropriations Committee.

Note: Upon his return from the European theater, wearing the U.S. Army's Distinguished Service Cross, the Bronze Star and the Purple Heart, but absent the right arm he lost in Italy, Captain Inouye was greeted in a San Francisco barbershop with "We don't serve Japs here."

1965: The Immigration and Nationality Act, also called the Hart-Cellar Act, abolished the quota system established by the National Origins Act and designated family reunification as the guiding principle for immigration. *Note:* Former Attorney General Robert Kennedy told House Immigration Subcommittee members, "I would say for the Asia-Pacific Triangle, it (immigration) would be approximately 5,000, Mr. Chairman, after which immigration from that source would virtually disappear; 5,000 immigrants would come the first year, but we do not expect that there would be any great influx after that."[4] From 1965 through 1993, immigration from Asia as a whole totaled 5.6 million. *Note:* While this Act eliminated race as matter of principle, in actual operation the new immigration pattern was designed not to stray from the old one. The great bulk of immigrants would be relatives of then present citizens, and thus, would come from European countries.

Late 1960s through 1970s: Second wave of Korean immigrants gives birth to the so-called "1.5 generation," those born in Korea, but moving to the U.S. at a very young age, adopting both the Korean and American cultures as their own *Note:* In 1965, Secretary of State Dean Rusk, addressing the Senate Subcommittee on Immigration and Naturalization of the Committee of the Judiciary, predicted "I don't think we have a particular picture of a world situation where everybody is just straining to move to the United States."[5]

1975: The fall of Saigon signals a huge number of refugees from Vietnam. Over the next decade, other Southeast Asians (mainly from Laos and Cambodia) immigrate to the U.S. *Note:* While the vast majority of modern immigrants come to the U.S. on an airplane, for some inexplicable reason, Southeast Asian immigrants, particularly those who came to the U.S. under refugee status, are the only ones pejoratively called "boat people" no matter what their means of arrival.

1982: Ronald Ebens, a disgruntled white Detroit auto worker, and Michael Nitz, struck and killed Vincent Chin using a baseball bat. Ebens, who blamed layoffs in the auto industry on the Japanese, took out his rage on Chin, a student of Chinese ancestry. Judge Charles Kaufmann accepted Ebens'  and Nitz' pleas of manslaughter, and let the pair off with three years probation and a fine of $3,720 each. In 1984, Ebens was found guilty in civil court of violating Chin's civil rights and sentenced to 25 years in prison. An appeal saw the jury acquit Ebens of those charges and he never spent a day in jail.[6]

1987: **The Amerasian Homecoming Act** facilitated the transfer of children born to Vietnamese mothers and American servicemen. This wave of immigrants also included detainees and former prisoners of re-education camps. *Note:* Amerasian is a political term, not strictly a description of ethnic background, and refers almost exclusively to those of mixed American and Southeast Asian background. If you insist, a term such as Eurasian is a more accurate demographic description, Amerasian a more precise geopolitical description, and both are subsets of APA.

1988: **U.S. House passes HR442**, the Civil Liberties Act of 1988, calling for a public apology for U.S. internment of Japanese Americans during WWII.

1990: President George Bush proclaims May as Asian Pacific American Heritage Month. The Immigration Act of 1990 caps total immigration to 700,000, with each nation allowed 25,000 immigrants to the U.S.

Note: Employment-related exceptions were added to the Act, allowing those willing to invest $1 million in capital to a U.S. concern, thus "creating employment" to enter. Give me your tired, your *poor*?

1990: Dr. Wen Ho Lee, a government scientist at Los Alamos, was charged with allegedly violating security laws by taking classified computer files home and keeping them in an unsecured location. News accounts alleged that he was a "Chinese spy," although Lee was not charged with spying, but with mishandling classified information. Held without bail for several months, the files at the heart of the case were not given "secret" or "confidential" security classifications until after he was charged.[7]

Note: Former CIA head John Deutch was similarly charged with violating security laws by removing computer files. Deutch was not incarcerated nor racially profiled because of his ancestral nationality.

1992: Sa-i-gu. Looting and fires destroy over 2,000 Korean-owned businesses during the Los Angeles riots. Korean Americans name this event Sa-i-gu, literally April 29th. This date is remembered by Korean Americans as vividly as December 7th or September 11th.

1997: Campaign finance scandal involving APAs prompts the Democratic National Committee to target donors with Asian names.

Note: Due to the high number of Filipinos with Spanish surnames, it is virtually impossible to capture a complete Filipino American database unless you are only interested in "phone book Filipinos," e.g. those with Tagalog or other native-Filipino names.

1997: **Gary Locke** becomes the first Chinese American Governor  in U.S. history in his birthplace of Washington. He serves two terms before choosing not to seek re-election, citing threats against him and his family following his rebuttal to President George Bush's State of the Union address.

2000: President Clinton appoints Norman Mineta as U.S. Secretary of Commerce, the first APA appointed to a Cabinet level position.

2002: President Bush appoints Norman Mineta as Secretary of Transportation and Elaine Chao as Secretary of Labor.

2007:  **Piyush "Bobby" Jindal** elected as Governor of Louisiana, following two terms in the U.S. House of Representatives. At 36, Jindal is the youngest current governor in the U.S. and the first Indian American elected to that position.

2009: President Barack Obama appoints a record number of APAs to Cabinet-level positions: Secretary of Commerce Gary Locke, Secretary of Labor Hilda Solis, Secretary of Energy Steven Chu and Secretary of Veterans Affairs Eric Shinseki.

Implications for Marketers

What is a history lesson doing in the middle of a book on marketing? Plenty. Remember, as we discussed in Chapter 2, just as the perceptions of geography, culture, language, religion and colonialism are used as historical reference points in understanding the APA population, so too are the historical events that shaped those variables.

- Although APAs have been in the U.S. as long as any other ethnic group, efforts to market to this group, as a group, are less than 20 yeas old. Some would say less than 10 years old.

- The "perpetual foreigner" status of APAs as perceived by most of the U.S. has shaped marketing towards APAs quite differently compared to other ethnic groups, particularly Hispanic Americans, as we'll see in detail in Chapter 6.

- Civil rights activities have not shaped and driven marketing efforts towards APAs as they have with African Americans and Hispanic Americans.

- Unlike African and Hispanic Americans, whose immigration plan, legal or illegal, was clearly intended to serve an economic function i.e. cheap (or in the case of slaves, free) labor, to the benefit of U.S. businesses, the business model as based on APA immigration was an exclusionary plan to keep Asians out. The U.S. government and businesses viewed APAs as an unintended mass to ignore or move out.

Cultural Considerations - Borrowed Words

Among social scientists, there exists the concept of anthropophagia, a state in which one culture "eats up" the other. Spaghetti and egg rolls become as common and as accepted as a ham and cheese sandwich (which some will tell you is very French i.e. croque monsieur). If the following words feel like a normal part of the American English lexicon, the Melting Pot is working. It's *really* working if you had no idea that these words weren't English in origin.

pajamas	gung ho	tycoon	indigo
honcho	khaki	cashmere	batik
bandana	s'kosh	calico	gingham
amok	madras	chintz	boondocks
avatar	tattoo	yo-yo	taboo
parcheesi	pariah	bungalow	chow (food)
bangle	pundit	pidgin	mantra
guru	serendipity	yen (desire)	karma
crimson	shampoo	punch (the drink)	seersucker
ketchup	thug	paisley	dungarees

V. Cultural Snapshots:
Some Analogies to Help You Understand APAs

For good or for bad, Americans, and perhaps humans in general, love to simplify, list, categorize, and even stereotype. It gives structure, order, perhaps even some safety and security to our lives. That's why we buy books like "Gardening for Dummies," "1,001 Places to See Before You Die," and "The Secret." They help break the code of a complex world and simplify difficult concepts for those readers not interested in delving into the unabridged version of life. Marketers are just as guilty. In marketing research, we often ask the question, "When you think of brand/product/category, what are the first three words or ideas that come to mind?"

Frank Wu, a Professor of Law at Howard University, notes that "Stereotypes have a self-fulfilling quality. Stereotypes give us images of other people, but they also give us scripts to follow. It is easier for Asian Americans to sound exactly like their stereotype, performing exactly like their stereotype, performing according to the script."[1] While we do not wish to promote cultural stereotypes, we think it will be helpful to present an explanation of how some of those stereotypes came into being – with the desire of furthering a collective dialogue as well as providing some useful insight.

With that in mind, we present what we call Cultural Snapshots, a short-form approach to understanding why and how APA groups have developed a group "cultural consciousness."

We'll serve up Cultural Snapshots for six of the major Asian ethnic groups in America – Japanese, Chinese, Filipino, Asian Indian, Korean and Southeast Asian, as well as a short section on Pacific Islanders. These snapshots are comprised of three areas: *the Defining Moment, the Skinny,* and *the Americanization Process.*

The Defining Moment

Each immigrant or minority group in the U.S. seems to have had a specific sociocultural event or moment in time that affected the entire group and will be forever associated with that particular group. The Jews with the Holocaust. Blacks with slavery. Gays with the Stonewall riots. Irish and the potato famine. Russians and Communism. Just as for each of these, for each APA group there is a *Defining Moment* that will forever influence America's perception of that group, that group's self-perception, and their relationship with the American experience.

The Skinny

If you gamble, particularly on horseracing, you've probably heard the term, the Skinny. *The Skinny* is the inside story, the real truth, the straight dope, as in "That jockey always goes to the stick too soon after the final turn, and the horses burn out before the final furlong." The Skinny is a mix of fact, "insider gossip" and conjecture to round out the picture and give the betting man a greater chance of beating the odds. The way we use The Skinny is similar in that it allows you to draw a parallel between an APA group and another, more widely understood target to begin to more correctly understand the group dynamic and behavior. It's reasoning by analogy, if you will. Properly used, it will give you an edge, some of the time.

The Americanization Process

These are community issues and future considerations – forces that are changing internal and external perceptions and behaviors of each ethnic group. Most Irish in America can't recall a time when store owners put up signs reading "Irish need not apply." Most Blacks alive today never lived through that time of "Whites only" drinking fountains. But those things are still very much a part of each group's relationship to this country in which we live. So do the sociological forces in the APA community, even within a relatively short time span, change the perceptions and behaviors of each group in the U.S. These forces are at work today and will impact APA generations in the future.

The Japanese
The Defining Moment: World War II Internment Camps

It is impossible to overstate the impact that the internment camps had on the Japanese American community. Even today, if you overhear conversations among Nisei, the second generation of Japanese Americans living in the U.S. (at least those few that are still alive), you will eventually hear questions like "What camp were you in?"

In February 1942, shortly after Japan bombed Pearl Harbor, President Franklin Roosevelt signed Executive Order 9066. This authorized and ordered the relocation and internment of nearly 120,000 men, women and children of Japanese ancestry – two-thirds of whom were U.S. citizens. Convinced that the mere presence of people of Japanese ancestry on American soil threatened national security, Lt. Gen. John DeWitt, the military commander appointed to carry out the evacuation, proposed a mass internment policy involving anyone of Japanese descent. Perceived wartime exigencies meant that care could not be taken to sift through the entire community to find spies.

Soon after, all Americans of Japanese descent were prohibited from living, working, or traveling on the West Coast. Families were given no more than a week to somehow dispose of all of their household goods and property, including businesses, before moving to points unknown with only what they could carry in clothing, bedding and linen, kitchen and toilet articles, and "personal effects." In effect, these people were accused and sentenced without a trial. Then sent away to interment camps.

With numbered tags tied around their necks, Japanese Americans were packed onto buses and trains with the blinds drawn down. They were first sent to makeshift assembly centers, such as the Santa Anita Racetrack, and forced to live in filthy animal stalls. They awaited more permanent incarceration at one of ten internment camps in the deserts, swamps and mountains of California, Idaho, Wyoming, Utah, Colorado, Arizona and Arkansas. About half of the incarcerated were children. At the internment camps, families were told they needed barbed wire and armed guards for their own protection – from a backlash from "patriotic Americans" – but the guns pointed inward. Families lived in prison-style blocks with communal latrines and showers.[2]

You could say that in the case of the other WWII Axis Powers, Italy and Germany, familiarity did not breed contempt. Most government officials agreed that they knew enough about those of Italian and German heritage to distinguish between the loyal and disloyal. Many insisted that it was very difficult to recognize the loyalty and disloyalty in Japanese Americans because their language and culture were so strange. Business leaders pressured politicians, sensing an effective method of clearing out unwanted competition. Simply put, it was a question of race and skin color. Of the 120,000 Japanese Americans incarcerated, the government never convicted a single one of treason, sedition or disloyalty. Interestingly enough, the ideological and monetary support of Nazi Germany provided by groups such as the *Amerika Deutscher Bund* and *Friends of the New Germany* was well documented.[3]

In 1988, the House of Representatives passed HR442, the Civil Liberties Act of 1988, calling for a public apology and reparations to all Japanese Americans interned during World War II.

The Skinny: The Vanishing Japanese American
Of all APA groups, the Japanese Americans are the most assimilated, the most "American," although not necessarily by choice.

The geopolitics of the mid-20th century and the memory of their betrayal and imprisonment by their own government forced many Japanese Americans to shed their own overt Asian ethnicity and quickly assimilate into an America dominated by white European cultural values. Because of this drive to "be American," it was rare to find any third generation Japanese Americans (Sansei) who could speak more than a few words of Japanese (mostly learned from their 19th century, Meiji-era grandparents) or who knew the real meaning behind the few cultural activities practiced by their families and friends, if they were lucky enough to live in an area that even *had* a Japanese American community.

Due to the war, Japan and Japanese Americans were effectively cut off from one another, an action that is still being felt today. Japan currently represents the lowest immigration percentages of all Asian countries with established U.S. ethnic groups and Japanese Americans have the fewest ties to their ancestral homeland of all APA communities.

A resurgence in cultural interest has taken place among the Sansei, and even more so with their fourth generation children, or Yonsei. What makes this cultural recognition so remarkable among the fourth generation is that a sizeable number are *hapas*, or mixed-race Japanese Americans. At this point, over a third of all citizens who claim some Japanese heritage are of mixed race.

The Americanization Process
Because of the length of time in the U.S. and the almost complete

assimilation into "American" society, the issues that concern most Japanese Americans are far removed from those of more recent Asian immigrants and refugees such as the Vietnamese, Koreans and others.

The term Nikkei, or people of Japanese descent, has gained broader use as the demographic make-up and community issues of the Japanese American population has changed. As the population of a Japanese-only background diminishes, along with the highest outmarriage rate among APAs (estimated between 60 and 75%), the obligation to embrace mixed race children and maintain cultural traditions is felt more strongly by Nikkei than by any other APA group.

For many fourth or fifth generation Nikkei, the connection with cultural identity has become less of one with Japan than with Asia as a whole. The environment that supports the cross-ethnic blending of culture and friends has lead to a stronger notion of APA identity.

Current U.S. Population: 1.1 million

The Chinese
The Defining Moment: Not finding Gold Mountain

With the California Gold Rush that began at Sutter's Mill in the Sierra foothills just east of San Francisco, Chinese immigrants were lured by the promise of riches, the same as the European immigrants who came to America and made their way West. For the Chinese, this was more than just a get-rich-quick scheme. This was the promise of a new life – their "Gam Saan" – Gold Mountain.

Many Chinese men left behind their wives and families to seek fortune and return home wealthy. But few accomplished that dream. Although China's Open Door Policy of the latter half of the 1800s lifted the death penalty on emigration abroad, the Confucian teachings so ingrained into the Chinese psyche – that children must devote themselves to their parents and ancestors – meant that leaving one's family and ancestral home was an offense against tradition. However, the economic morass of late 19ᵗʰ century Qing dynasty China – a country fraught with starvation, government seizures of homes and land, tax increases, abject poverty and national fatigue from the British Opium Wars and the Taiping Rebellion – made the adventure and potential payoff a once-in-a-lifetime opportunity for those wanting to better their lot in life.

Initially, the Chinese were greeted with open arms in California, with newspapers like the *Daily Alta California* printing, "Quite a large number of Celestials have arrived among us of late, enticed thither by the golden romance that has filled the world. Scarcely a ship arrives that does not bring an increase to this worthy integer of our population."[4] Governor John McDougal declared that the Chinese were, "one of the most worthy classes of our newly adopted citizens – to whom the climate and the character of these lands is peculiarly suited."[5]

Governor McDougal did not predict the political climate turning quickly against the Chinese. His gubernatorial replacement, John Bigler, commissioned a report that found, "the concentration, within our state limits, of vast numbers of the Asiatic races, and of inhabitants of the Pacific Islands, and of many others dissimilar from ourselves in customs, language and education, threatened the well-being of mining districts." Further, the report identified the Chinese as "servile contract workers, not seeking to become American citizens, they degraded the American white workers already in the state and discouraged other Americans from coming to California."[6]

The first of a long line of racially motivated government acts was instituted to halt the economic growth of the Chinese in America. The Foreign Miners' Tax of 1852 called for a monthly payment by every foreign miner not wishing to become a citizen. This played well against the 1790 federal law that prevented anyone but "white persons" to become naturalized citizens. Immigration was discouraged by the 1855 law "An Act to Discourage the Immigration to this State of Persons Who Cannot Become Citizens Thereof." It imposed a tax on ship owners of $50 for every person on board ineligible for citizenship – essentially every person coming from China.[7]

As profits from gold mining shrank, both from fewer sources and from unfair taxes, the Chinese turned to being wage earners in the industrial sector of the economy – quartz miners, ploughmen, laundrymen, wool spinners and weavers, servants, and most importantly for the time, railroad workers. Following the initial 50 workers hired by the Central Pacific Railroad in 1865, the number of Chinese workers swelled to over 12,000, or over ninety percent of the workforce. Dangerous conditions, low wages, and failed strikes did not halt the railroad from being completed in 1969.[8]

By the late 1870s, the "Yellow Peril" of the Chinese in America was rampant throughout the West Coast. Murders, lynchings, farms set on fire, and an institutionalized approach to removing Chinese from America was set in place. The Chinese Exclusion Act of 1882 eliminated any immigration from China as well as preventing any Chinese in the U.S. from becoming citizens. This legislation would have implications, both political and social, well into the middle of the next century.

The Skinny: Maintaining the Middle Kingdom

Ron Takaki, Professor of Ethnic Studies at the University of California Berkeley, gives shape to the enduring Chinese American *weltanschauung* by describing a "community of memory,"[9] a recovering of roots within this country and the homelands of their ancestors. Modern grocery stores have eliminated the need to buy ducks dispatched immediately before purchase. Pharmacies have made obsolete the apothecaries offering myriad herbs, roots and other traditional medicines. However, go to any major Chinatown around the country and you'll find adherents to both, along with a number of non-Chinese fans who have "gone Bamboo."

The Chinese in America were among the first APA groups to recognize that, in Takaki's words, they were "Strangers from a Different Shore."[10] Asians were "Strangers" in America, not just because of their migration to a foreign land, but also because of their point of origin and their profoundly different experiences from European immigrants. America was a land that represented a new hope, a new life, a new perspective. With families coming from Europe, Bernie Schwartz became Tony Curtis, Issur Danielovitch became Kirk Douglas, and Edmund Marcizewski became Ed Muskie. For them, it was easy to adopt a new identity, an "American" identity that put behind them the old country. Coming across a different ocean, with different cultures, and most importantly, with a skin tone, hair color and eye shape that did not blend into "American" society. They wore what University of Chicago sociologist Robert Park coined a "racial uniform." Unfortunately, for most of the Chinese experience in America, it has been the wrong uniform.

How is this expressed? Takaki quotes Alfred Wong relaying a story from his father. "Remember your Chinese name. Remember your village in Toishan. Remember you are Chinese. Remember all this and you will have a home."[11] Continually unsure of their status in America, it was important for the Chinese to know there was a place, a home for them somewhere. Indeed, the Chinese all over the world have carved out a home in China even if they've never stepped foot on their shores. It's not uncommon for someone from the Philippines, Malaysia, Australia or any one of a number of countries to identify themselves as "Chinese-Filipino," "Chinese-Malaysian," or "Chinese-Australian."

In her book, *The Fortune Cookie Chronicles*, Jennifer Lee writes, "But as interesting as the local food was to me, I was interesting to the locals. You could see their minds processing: She looks perfectly Chinese. She speaks Chinese perfectly. But something is amiss. Perhaps it was the way I moved, the way I laughed, the way I dressed. I wasn't, they felt, of China. Hong Kong? Taiwan? they asked. 'I'm

American,' I explained. Their reply: 'No you're Chinese. You were just born in America.'"[12]

This notion has a fairly close parallel with the state of Israel. No matter where in the world a Jew might live, no matter if he or she has never been to the Middle East, Israel can be considered a welcoming homeland. In stark contrast with the emotional distance Japan and the Japanese Americans, with the Chinese, no matter how many generations someone has been away from China, no matter how little one may know of Chinese culture, a person of Chinese heritage is and always will be Chinese in the eyes of their ancestral homeland.

The Americanization Process

The Chinese in America have the longest continual stream of immigration (with some blockage periods along the way) of any APA group. This means that the Chinese American experience is and has been continually evolving with the social, political and economic environment.

More than a simple bimodal map of "haves and have-nots" the Chinese global diaspora is completely represented in the U.S: the broad range of country of origin, education, language use, the function of Chinatowns as the place of first settlement vs. immediate suburbanization, high tech vs. unskilled labor and everything in between. This diversity of experience will force current and future generations of Chinese in America to learn to navigate and negotiate not only American diversity, but Chinese American diversity as well. So, while this group has a common emotional center, it exhibits within it the wide range of diversity that is the United States.

Current U.S. population: 2.9 million

The Filipinos
The Defining Moment: Permanent "Other" Status

Even after 300 years of European involvement, including the adoption of Christianity, the status of Filipinos in the U.S. has been one of Permanent "Other" Status based on race. Technically, since the Philippines were an American protectorate territory acquired from Spain at the conclusion of the Spanish American War, Filipinos were not "foreigners." Though not given citizenship, they could still emigrate freely to the U.S. as "American nationals."

In the 1930s, almost a quarter of Filipinos in the U.S. took jobs as laborers in the service sector as janitors, valets, cooks and dishwashers. Another 10 percent worked in the West Coast's seasonal salmon fishing industry from Washington up through Alaska. The vast majority worked in agriculture, filling a need for labor created by the exclusion of the Chinese, Japanese, Koreans and Asian Indians.[13]

As with so many other immigrant groups forced into an unfair labor situation, complaints and strikes lead to punitive action by their employers. President William McKinley's stated policy of "educating and uplifting our little brown brothers" did not apply on mainland America. Soon, claims that Filipinos were "untamed" and primitive savages on the "same level as American Indians," lead the U.S. Immigration Study Commission to find that, "These men are jungle folk, and their primitive moral code accentuates the race problem even more than the economic difficulty." As with the Chinese and Japanese in America, it was this underlying economic issue that drove the racial issue.[14]

Although the exclusionists believed that the Filipinos should not have free access to migrate to the U.S., the 1924 law did not apply to them because they came from an American territory. So how to solve this unique problem? Congress found a way.

In 1934, the Tydings-McDuffie Act was passed, establishing the Philippines as a commonwealth and granting independence in ten years. The result of the act was Filipino exclusion. As citizens of a newly independent country, Filipinos no longer had free access to the U.S., nor any of the benefits of the Depression Era Relief Appropriation Act. Sponsor of the bill, Senator Millard Tydings stated, "It is absolutely illogical to have an immigration policy to exclude Japanese and Chinese and permit Filipinos en masse to come into the country... If they continue to settle in certain areas they will come in conflict with white labor... and increase the opportunity for more racial prejudice and bad feeling of all kinds." As Carey McWilliams of the *Nation* observed, the real purpose of the law was to exclude Filipinos as cheap laborers. Their "brief but strenuous period of service to American capital" was over. They were quickly replaced by even cheaper Mexican labor. The idea of repatriation was "a trick, and not a very clever trick, to get them out of this country," said McWilliams.[15]

For most of the 20th Century, the Philippines has been closely akin to Puerto Rico in terms of status in the United States. It's a part of the U.S., and yet, not a part. The citizens are welcome to travel freely between countries and cultures, and yet not welcome. The large numbers of cheap labor are highly desired, yet feared by many.

This "Other" status is still being resolved today. For example, over 70,000 non-U.S. citizen Filipinos served as G.I.s during World War II. Organized into segregated regiments, they often took the most dangerous forward positions against Japan in the Pacific. Yet, for all their efforts, these vets, until the last ten years, were not entitled to full benefits ranging from hospital and nursing home care to pensions and life insurance. For the most part, it was too little too late. It took a march on Washington D.C. in 1997, with seventy-plus-year-old men, dressed in full military uniform, chaining themselves to the fence surrounding the White House, to get Congress to end the stall on earned benefits.[16]

The Skinny: The New Irish

With all of the discrimination the Irish faced in the 18th and 19th centuries coming to America, they were still able to carve out a very specific niche in society. All Christian (two-thirds Catholic, one third Protestant), moving from a mostly rural culture to large, rapidly industrializing cities, and speaking English as a native tongue, the Irish built their middle class status in the U.S. via dominance of skilled trade sectors that could be passed along within families and clans. Police and fire departments, textile industries, meat processing and construction were at one time all dominated by Irish workers.

Similarly, Filipinos have found a way to "melt" in to America. Predominantly Catholic and English-speaking, Filipinos did not have to face two of the largest hurdles facing other Asian immigrants – there was religious acceptance and they had command of English. Having been under Spanish colonial rule for 300 years, Filipinos had a much better understanding of Western culture than their other Asian counterparts, just as the Irish understood a Eurocentric America. Like the Irish, Filipinos came to settle in large cities, choosing the West Coast

and Chicago rather than New York and Boston, and entering into select skilled trades such as teaching and healthcare.

The Americanization Process

Fortunately for Filipinos, they've generally been able to work – but
it hasn't been great work. The professions and vocations that Filipinos in America have adopted, or to which they have been relegated,
have caused them to be chronically under-employed, positioning them, for the most part, solidly in the middle to lower middle
class. The combination of a preponderance of skilled or semi-skilled
workers and the restrictive "re-certification" rules for doctors, pharmacists and even veterinarians has created a pattern of occupational
downgrading, with those in professional or technical occupations
usually settling for clerical or wage earner positions.

Current U.S. Population: 2.4 million.

Asian Indians

The Defining Moment: Cab Drivers vs. Tech Boomers

For many of the millions of viewers of Matt Groening's series, the
Simpsons, Asian Indians in America are characterized as Apu, the
Quik-E-Mart convenience store clerk. While it is true that Asian
Indians own or operate a disproportionate number of convenience
stores (50 to 70,000 of 150,000 nationwide) and drive cabs (over
50% of all New York cabs are driven by South Asians [17]), the most
significant, and probably the most long lasting effect that they have
had on America is in high tech industries.[17]

Following the 1965 Immigration Act, an Asian "brain drain" towards the U.S. was promoted by American immigration policy. Of
the almost half million Indians who emigrated to the U.S. between
the Immigration Act in 1965 and 1990, the vast majority came from
the educated upper and middle class. These immigrants came for
primarily economic reasons – the employment prospects for highly
educated people in India were extremely limited. India's employment situation had simply pushed them out. In 1972, out of almost

300,000 unemployed Indians, almost 600 held doctorates, almost 40,000 had done post-graduate study, and over 200,000 were college graduates. The surplus of engineers alone was over 100,000 in 1974. For Asian Indians entering the U.S after the Immigration Act, over 80 percent listed "professional or technical worker" under occupational category.[18]

Narayan Keshavan, special assistant to the Congressional Caucus on India and Indian Americans, states, "If it weren't for the Indians and Chinese in Silicon Valley, the whole U.S. high tech industry would collapse." He even shares a rumor that Microsoft's Bill Gates threatened to move his operations to Asia if Congress didn't increase the special visa program for highly skilled workers.[19] In the 1990s, over 40 percent of all H1b (working, non-immigrant – high tech) visas were granted to those of Indian origin.[20] In 2001, the cap on H1b visas was raised from 65,000 to 115,000 for foreign specialists to work in the U.S. for up to six years. Forty-four percent of those visa holders are Indian.[21]

The Skinny: The New Jews

Not discounting the rampant anti-Semitism and persecution in Europe, until the latter half of the 20th century, Jews came to America to take advantage of the social and economic opportunities the country offered. Large scale immigration of Jews came in two distinct waves: pre-1880, most were Ashkenazi Jews from Germany, well-educated and primarily going into businesses. Post-1880 until the immigration restrictions of 1924, most Jews arrived from poorer, rural areas of Eastern Europe, as a result of increased persecution. By the end of the 20th century, Jews had not only successfully integrated into the larger American life, but levels of income, education and advances across gender lines had surpassed that of almost every other ethnic and religious background.[22]

Similarly, the first large waves of Indian immigration to the U.S. were begun by a well-educated, urban, middle to upper class. This was followed by a more rural, lesser educated group. The last Census shows Asian Indians as having the highest levels of median household income, family income, per capita income, and annual median income of any foreign-born group – along with the highest levels of education and professional positions.[23] Similar to the first generations of Jewish settlers, the outmarriage rate is exceptionally low, and often based on the modern day caste system of education and economic position, rather than strictly religion.

Indo-Americans represent sort of a "human free trade zone" in the U.S. in that the disproportionate number of highly desired, highly skilled workers has created a special segment within the normal immigration patterns and barriers of U.S. imported talent. There is no other immigrant group that has ever and continues to dominate a business category since the Chinese built the railroads.

The Americanization Process

The pre- and post- 1965-2000 immigration wave, supported by American business has created a bimodal class system within the Indian American community. The Indian elite has had very little to do with the Indian working class.

Saddique Imam, Executive Director of The IndUS Entrepreneurs says, "TIE is strictly for entrepreneurs and business professionals. Discrimination is not a concern of our organization. Women's issues are not a concern. It is not our role to get involved in unfair practices. We stay away from making political statements. But because we are powerful and our members are extremely educated and extremely rich, the community expects us to."[24] According to *Asian American Dreams* author, Helen Zia, "The post 1965 immigrants had no historical reference to civil rights or the way that Asian Americans were vilified in the previous decades. For them being the 'model minority' seemed to capture their aspirations and the belief that through hard work and individual merit they could achieve the American dream for themselves and their families."[25]

Asian Indian parents strongly adhere to the idea of a balance of assimilation and maintaining cultural traditions. But the children are increasingly American. So it should be no surprise that inter-generational arguments regarding attendance at Indian temples and schools, arranged marriages, and the responsibility of women to carry on cultural traditions regardless of their personal or professional status, have combined to create rifts within the Indo-American community.

Because of the adherence of some specific cultural practices, particularly the wearing of the traditional headdress ("turbans") by Sikhs, Indians as a whole have been nonsensically targeted for violence by those wishing to vent their anger after the September 11 attacks in New York and Washington DC. This confusion of Indians with members of the "Axis of Evil" has resulted in them being unintended victims of the "war on terror."

Current U.S. Population: 1.9 million.

Koreans
The Defining Moment: Sa-i-gu, Riots in Los Angeles, 1992
From the 1950s until the early 1990s, Koreans in America were relegated to the traditional APA position of the more established groups – the Chinese and Japanese Americans. That all changed on April 29, 1992. Remember the Alamo. Remember Pearl Habor. For Korean Americans, it was Remember Sa-i-gu (literally, April 29).

The toll the riots in Los Angeles took from the citizens of South Central was no greater than that experienced by Korean Americans. More than half of the 4,500 shops destroyed or damaged were Korean-run. Nearly half of Los Angeles' financial loss of $1 billion was suffered by Korean "mom & pop" storeowners. Thousands of

Korean Americans lost their livelihoods and the support for their extended families over the three-day period.

Journalist Helen Zia, author of *Asian American Dreams*, writes, "The angry fracture lines and bitter divisiveness over those three days are evident from the divergent terminology that describes the event. To some observers, sa-i-gu was an urban rebellion, an expression of protest against the economic disenfranchisement of blacks and Latinos – with Korean merchants cast as the oppressor class. Others called it a food riot, a conflagration of inner-city poor and their frenzied plundering of all shops within striking distance, many of which happened to be Korean-owned. Still others, preferring a more subdued description, referred to the riot as a civil unrest, an upheaval that marked all Angelenos."[26]

One of the godfathers of Korean American journalism and former editor-in-chief of the *Korea Times* newspaper, K.W. Lee rejects those descriptions, and goes on to describe the events as "an American pogrom. Koreatown was a war zone. For us it was like the Jewish last stand in Warsaw, or the internment of Japanese Americans. Sa-i-gu was a convenient way for mainstream America to deflect black rage."[27]

Zia goes on to explain, "After sa-i-gu Americans discovered Koreans in their midst. They found a different breed of Asian – more confrontational, less accommodating. Before sa-i-gu, Korean Americans, like most immigrants and most Americans, saw themselves as individuals on their own quests for their personal dreams, bystanders to American society. Those Asians who accepted the model minority myth found it easy to believe that hard work, long hours, and a low profile would reap their eventual rewards. Sa-i-gu exposed the myth. After sa-i-gu, Korean Americans were isolated and deeply hurt by the unspoken but widely held sentiment that they somehow deserved what they got. Starkly visible and alone on center stage, Korean Americans were forced to reevaluate their place and assert themselves in America.[28]

The Skinny: The New Yankees

The very picture of the taciturn Yankee trader of the 19th century, the very definition of the Yankee spirit is now personified in America's Korean population. You could almost entitle this "The Chopsticks Culture Meets the Protestant Ethic."

The "Yankee" character traits of independence, self-reliance, community responsibility, shrewdness and frugality have aided in the Korean success story here in America. The Protestant ethic among Korean Americans is even more apropos than you might first imagine, as the majority of those who have emigrated to the U.S. in the last 40 years are Protestant. Korean Americans are almost twice as likely to own their own business than any other APA group (already higher than the general public). Highly concentrated in retail businesses such as apparel and accessory stores, food stores, clothing factories and dry cleaning establishments, Korean businesses are largely family run and labor intensive.[29] In addition to the profit potential, the satisfaction of being one's own boss, and having a mastery of the work environment is well ingrained into the Korean American psyche. Language difficulties (the Korean accent seems to be a hard one to lose) and lack of familiarity with American culture have kept many from using their educational background, instead, pushing them towards entrepreneurship.

If there were a single European parallel with Korean immigration patterns, it would be the former Soviet Union. In both geographies, at the height of immigration movements, Korea and the Soviet Union were experiencing rampant economic and political instability. This was true for Korea in the '70s and the Soviet Union in the '90s. The uncertainty and bleak projections for both countries at their respective times prompted a large wave of emigration to the U.S.

The Americanization Process

The relationship between Koreans and African Americans has stabilized somewhat since the riots of 1992, but the politics of race still needs to be examined by both sides. While it's impossible to generalize about any ethnic group, Koreans remain as one of the most homogeneous societies in the world, claiming to have one language, one culture and one ethnicity. This notion of a mono-cultural people doing business in a multi-cultural society will continue to be problematic until both sides become educated and tolerant of each other's group.

Current U.S. population: 1.2 million.

Southeast Asians

The Defining Moment: Arrival as Refugees, not Immigrants

Unlike other APA groups in the U.S., the Vietnamese immigrants, for the most part, were not here by choice, but rather, as a part of a worldwide rescue effort. They were driven out by the powerful events surrounding them. Recognizing that the Southeast Asian geography encompasses many countries in addition to Vietnam, e.g. Laos, Cambodia, etc., we focus on Vietnam due to the fact that the Defining Moment for the Vietnamese affected the entire region and all those who emigrated to the U.S. because of it.

Following Nixon's signing of the Paris Peace Agreement in 1973, America was allowed to declare "Peace with Honor" as hostilities continued through 1975 until the fall of Saigon. Most of the first 10 to 15 thousand people to be evacuated prior to the collapse of the South Vietnamese government were military personnel and their families. During the last days of April of 1975, over 86,000 were airlifted out during the final U.S. military evacuation.[30]

The first wave of refugees that arrived in 1975 (over 130,000) were generally from educated classes, mostly English speaking, and from urban areas, and as a result, more Westernized than those to follow. These were followed by an additional half million Vietnamese who were to arrive in the U.S. by 1985. Many had escaped forced labor camps and risked life at sea. The journey often included a stay in refugee camps for months or even years in Thailand until being granted asylum in countries like Australia, Canada, France and the United States.

One American veteran of the Vietnam War noted, "Remember, these are the people who were on our side. They have the right to come to this country as refugees. They just need a home."[31] Easier said than done. The welcome for all Vietnamese immigrants has not been so warm. When there is a scarcity of jobs, they have been viewed as a threat to other cheap labor. In areas with scarce low-income housing, they have been viewed as a threat to African Americans. On the Gulf Coast of Texas, where they have excelled in the shrimp fishing industry, they have been viewed as a competitive threat to white fishermen. One white fisherman was quoted as saying, "There's too many of them and there's not enough room for them and there's going to be lots of hard feelings if they don't get some of them out of here and teach the ones that they leave how to act and how to get along. I think they ought to be put on a reservation somewhere or in a compound to teach them our laws and our ways, the way we live, our courtesy as a people."[32]

The Skinny: Destroying the Model Minority Myth

The Model Minority Myth, as originally coined in the late 1960s, identified APAs as hard working, high achieving, well-educated, English-speaking, assimilated citizens who should be held up as an example to other minorities as to how to succeed in America. In 1966 *U.S. News and World Report* ran an article called, "Success Story of One Minority Group in the United States" lauding the accomplishments of Chinese Americans while making not-too-cleverly disguised comparisons to the African American community.

They wrote, "At a time when Americans are awash in worry over the plight of racial minorities, one such minority, the nation's 300,000 Chinese Americans, is winning wealth and respect by dint of its own hard work... Still being taught in Chinatown is the old idea that people should depend on their own efforts – not a welfare check – in order to reach America's 'Promised Land.'"[33] Other minorities, are, in effect, being told "Why can't you be more like APAs? Just work hard, keep quiet, and stop asking for handouts." Compared to the discriminatory, exclusionist attitudes of the previous century and a half, shouldn't APAs welcome this perception with open arms?

What support of this Model Minority Myth does is to mask the very real problems experienced by Vietnamese Americans, largely due to their status as refugees, rather than immigrants. The post-1975 wave of immigrants tended to be much less educated, isolated due to language and cultural barriers, and separated from the more established Vietnamese community by economic and regional differences. Dependence on Public Assistance, stemming from lower education and employment levels combined with relatively larger family sizes; skills for which there is no longer a market, i.e. military service; mental health issues, unresolved from a generation of refugee status; and problems among Vietnamese youth, including substance abuse and gang violence, building on a sense of alienation from their families due to cultural gaps, all add up to refute the Minority Myth and expose the segment of the APA community that could most benefit from social services from both the government and the private sector.

The immigration patterns of the Vietnamese to America more closely reflect that of Cubans, in that rather than seeking out their fortunes, those coming to the U.S. did so because the political turmoil of their own country made it impossible for them to live there. The "Operation Pedro Pan" and Mariel Boatlifts benefiting Cuban refugees are similar in scope and strategy to the waves of immigration from Vietnam.

The Americanization Process

Even after 30 years of residence in the U.S., the Vietnamese American community still feels the effects of their refugee status, and have not become part of mainstream America, or even mainstream Asian America, for that matter. Poverty rates are significantly higher and income and education are lower than most APA communities. It's telling that gangs and crime are considered among the most serious problem facing the Vietnamese community.[34] It's equally telling that Vietnamese youth gangs have chosen to adopt the American "street gang" model as opposed to the "traditional" Chinese Tong or Japanese Yakuza "crime as a business" model.

Current U.S. Population: 1.5 million.

Pacific Islanders
The Defining Moment – Annexed or Overthrown?

The Pacific Islander group (almost 50% are Native Hawaiians) are unique among all Asian Pacific Americans in that, for the most part, the U.S. came to them before they came to the U.S. Native Hawaiians, Samoans, Guamanians, Tongans, and Micronesians (encompassing the Marshall, Carolinian, and Marianas Islands, among others) all share a similar history with regard to U.S. relations. Just as we focus on the Vietnamese in the preceding section, we focus here on Native Hawaiians as their story and geographic filter for most Pacific Islanders into the United States is relevant to all in this group.

Whether for strategic military positioning, agriculture or, in the 20th century, tourism, peoples of the Pacific Islands have been subjected to "protection" by the Spanish, Germans, Japanese and finally, the United States. Despite the fact that islands like Hawaii were sovereign states with their own governments, economies and treaties with other nations, U.S. Naval forces, allied with sugar plantation owners, merchants and missionaries overthrew the monarchy in 1893.[35] The islands were claimed under full control of the U.S. government in a treaty with the Republic of Hawaii, a government established by the above forces that removed Queen Liliuokalani from her throne and placed her under house arrest for the remainder of her life.

In return for this annexation, Native Hawaiians received Christianity, small pox, measles, influenza and venereal disease that decimated the population, decreasing the aboriginal peoples from between 400,000 and 800,000 in 1778, the year British explorer James Cook arrived to less than 40,000 in 1900.

The Skinny – American Indians Redux

More than any other APA group, contact with the West has impacted the size, language, racial make-up and socioeconomic status of Pacific Islanders, both in the U.S. and in their countries of origin.

The 2000 Census was the first to allow Native Hawaiians and other Pacific Islanders to identify themselves separately from other APAs, justified by the fact that they have experienced a far different acculturation process than other APAs and a resultantly different socioeconomic position in the American landscape. NHPIs, on average, earn lower incomes, attain lower levels of education, have the highest rate of unemployment and make up a disproportionate percentage of those receiving public aid compared to the descendants of Caucasian, Chinese and Japanese immigrants who make up the majority population in the Hawaiian islands.[36] Partly because of their lesser access to top medical care, NHPIs have higher-than-average rates of heart disease, cancer, and diabetes, and have among the lowest life expectancy averages of peoples living in Hawaii. Despite a high rate of interracial marriage, NHPIs have not been allowed to fully enjoy the benefits of their own culture.

Under the U.S. Constitution, indigenous minorities can (but do not necessarily) enjoy certain rights that other racial and ethnic minorities living in the same area do not.[37] In order to "compensate" Native Hawaiians for taking over their lands, the U.S. government created the Hawaiian Homes Commission Act of 1921. The Act was designed "to enable native Hawaiians to return to their lands in order to fully support self-sufficiency for native Hawaiians and the self-determination of native Hawaiians in the administration of this Act, and the preservation of the values, traditions and culture of native Hawaiians." Unlike laws affecting Native (Indian) Americans, the HHCA, or any law since, does not recognize Native Hawaiians as a sovereign people with rights to self-determination and government. Further, the U.S. Supreme Court has placed in jeopardy the entitlements Hawaiians have benefited from for most of the 20th century by asking,

> May Congress treat the Native Hawaiian like native American tribes? And has Congress in fact determined that their status is as such? May Congress delegate to the State of Hawaii the authority to preserve that status? And has Congress already delegated to the State Government of Hawaii the authority to preserve that status?[38]

In 1977 the American Indian Policy Review Commission defined the relationship that should exist between tribes and with the U.S. government, and included Eskimos, Aleuts and Native Alaskans, but not Native Hawaiians.

Unfortunately for Native Hawaiians, included in the HHCA is the provision that "Native Hawaiians" are defined as those having at least 50% Hawaiian blood. Given that part-Native Hawaiians now outnumber 100% Native Hawaiians by two to one, it seems that this is a convenient loophole for the U.S. government to avoid its legal obligations. The lack of appreciation for historic rights of descendents of native peoples parallels the fact that only half of those residing in Hawaii were born there, and many who weren't see no obligation to bear any burden of injustices suffered decades ago.[39]

The Americanization Process

Unlike any other APA group, Native Hawaiians are outnumbered by other ethnic groups in their own land of origin. It would be inconceivable to have more non-Puerto Ricans than native-born people in Puerto Rico, determining the status of those born there. The Hawaiian Sovereignty movement is destined to continue until the U.S. government can clarify the trust relationship between Native Hawaiians and the Federal government.

Because of this state of ambiguity and the socioeconomic reality of the Hawaiian people, a "mini-Welfare State" has been created that could prevent Native Hawaiians from ever completely preserving their cultural heritage, which, ironically, is a major contributor to the State's number one industry, tourism.

For many, the self-identification as Hawaiian, even by those who are part-Hawaiian or married into a Hawaiian family, indicates that a "geographic" culture may outweigh an "ethnic" culture. As with Native Americans, this tie to the land is stronger than virtually any other ethnic group living in the U.S. For those celebrating a blending of all Pacific islands cultures, particularly on the mainland, the "Aloha Spirit" is not just based on ancestry, but also on a connection with a land, its people and its culture.

Current U.S. Population: 1.1 million

Implications for Marketers

This chapter serves as a mini-ethnography on each of the featured subgroups. It is meant to be both reflective and predictive by getting into the mindset of the major APA ethnic nationalities in America.

This background will help you begin to understand three key areas:

- What each group thinks about the U.S. and their place in it
- Why they think this way
- How they might react to marketing efforts targeted towards them based on the above two issues.

Cultural Considerations:
The Most Enduring APA Stereotype Images

We have hundreds of years of Western culture-generated literature, movies and TV to erase before any of these go away. And they may not go away. *Sopranos*, anyone?

Here are some of those stereotypes as they appeared in film and television and the APA (and non-APA) actors and actresses who portrayed them.

Wise Old Oriental – *Charlie Chan* (Warner Oland, Sidney Toler, Oscar Werner, Roland Winters, Carroll Nash, Ross Martin, Peter Ustinov), *Kung Fu* TV series

Dragon Lady – *Daughter of the Dragon*

Cruel Tyrant – *The Killing Fields, Bitter Tea of General Yen* (Nils Asther), *Mysterious Mr. Wong* (Bela Lugosi)

Self-sacrificing Wife – *Madame Butterfly, Teahouse of the August Moon, Heaven and Earth, The Good Earth* (Luise Rainer), *Love is a Many Splendored Thing* (Jennifer Jones)

Sneaky Traitor – *Teahouse of the August Moon* (Marlon Brando)

Houseboy/girl – *The Houseboy* (Jerry Lewis), TVs *Bachelor Father, The Courtship of Eddie's Father, Bonanza, Have Gun Will Travel*

Oriental Prostitute – *World of Suzie Wong*

Martial Arts Death Dealer – *Enter the Dragon, Kung Fu* (David Carradine)

Dry cleaner/Restaurant owner/Shopkeeper – *Falling Down, Menace II Society*

Triad/Tong/Yakuza Killer – *Year of the Dragon*

Corporate Automaton – *Gung Ho*

Business is War Predator – *Rising Sun*

Asian over American Loyalties by Asian Americans – *The Corruptor*

Jungle Savages – *Apocalypse Now, Deer Hunter*

Third World Refugees in need of saving from Communism – *Full Metal Jacket, Green Berets, Casualties of War*

Sidekick – *Goldfinger*, TVs *Green Hornet, Hawaii Five-O*

Nerd, smart or otherwise – *Breakfast at Tiffany's* (Mickey Rooney), *16 Candles*

Why take on a racially insensitive role? Actors need to eat too. Bonus Data: None of the "Asian" actors starring as "Asian" characters indicated in parentheses above were ethnically, culturally or genetically Asian at all.

Two of the preeminent APA playwrights, David Henry Hwang, author of the Tony Award winning *M. Butterfly*,[40] and Philip Kan Gotanda, author of *Yankee Dawg You Die*,[41] look at the phenomenon of Asians and APAs in entertainment from two different viewpoints that address the same issue – Western interpretations of Asian and APA culture.

From *M. Butterfly*, Act 1, Scene 6

Gallimard: No! I was about to say, it's the first time I've seen the beauty of the story.

Song: Really?

Galllimard: Of her death. It's a... pure sacrifice. He's unworthy, but then what can she do? She loves him... so much. It's a very beautiful story.

Song: Well, yes, to a Westerner.

Gallimard: Excuse me?

Song: It's one of your favorite fantasies, isn't it? The submissive Oriental woman and the cruel white man.

Gallimard: Well, I didn't quite mean...

Song: Consider it this way: what would you say if a blonde homecoming queen fell in love with a short Japanese businessman? He treats her cruelly, then goes home for three years, during which time she prays to his picture and turns down marriage from a young Kennedy. Then, when she learns he has remarried, she kills herself. Now, I believe you would consider this girl to be a deranged idiot, correct? But because it's an Oriental who kills herself for a Westerner – ah! – you find it beautiful.

Silence

From *Yankee Dawg You Die*, Act 1, Scene 3

Bradley (mutters): You are so jive, Mr. Chang...

Vincent: You think you're better than I, don't you? Somehow special, above it all. The new generation. With all you fancy politics about this Asian American new-way-of-thinking and seven long years of paying your dues at Asian Project Theater or whatever it is. You don't know shit, my friend. You don't know the meaning of paying your dues in this business.

Bradley: The business. You keep talking about the business. The industry. Hollywood. What's Hollywood? Cutting up your face to look more white? So my nose is a little flat. Fine! Flat is beautiful. So I don't have a double fold in my eyelid. Great! No one in my entire racial family has had it in the last ten thousand years. My old girlfriend used to put Scotch tape on her eyelids to get the double fold so she could look more "Cau-ca-sian." My new girlfriend – she doesn't mess around, she got surgery. Where does it begin? Vincent? All that self-hate, where does it begin? You and your Charley

Chop Suey roles...

Vincent: You want to know the truth? I'm glad I did it. Yes, you heard me right. I'm glad I did it and I'm not ashamed. I wanted to do it. And no one is ever going to get an apology out of me. And in some small way it is a victory. Yes, a victory. At least an oriental was on screen acting, being seen. We existed.

Bradley: But that's not existing – wearing some goddamn monkey suit and kissing up to some white man, that's not existing.

Vincent: That's all there was, Bradley. That's all there was! But you don't think I wouldn't have wanted to play a better role than that bucktoothed, groveling waiter? I would have killed for a better role where I could have played an honest-to-god human being with real emotions. I would have killed for it. You seem to assume "Asian Americans" always existed. That there were always roles for you. You didn't exist back then, Buster. Back then there was no Asian American consciousness, no Asian American actor, and no Asian American theaters. Just a handful of "orientals" who for some godforsaken reason wanted to perform. Act. And we did. At church bazaars, community talent night, and on the Chop Suey circuit playing Chinatowns and Little Tokyos around the country as hoofers, jugglers, acrobats, strippers – anything we could do for anyone who would watch. You, with that holier-than-thou attitude, trying to make me feel ashamed. You wouldn't be here if it weren't for all the crap we had to put up with. We built something. We built the mountain, as small as it may be, that you stand on so proudly looking down at me.

VI. Getting Started
Overcoming Barriers to an APA Marketing Program

Make no mistake. There are some very real barriers to putting together an effective APA marketing program. You have to overcome them. If you let them stop you, you'll never try to reach APA's again.

Here's a quick review of the most common reasons why more APA marketing programs don't exist:

"the absolute size of the market is too small"

"they're too hard to reach by mass media"

"there are too many languages to deal with"

"there are too many subgroups with too much bad history to get in a culture war"

"they don't need any help – they're the model minority"

"we already reach them – they're already assimilated"

"Asian Americans don't live here"

"we have no expertise in the marketplace"

"African American and Hispanic markets are more important to us"

"we can make more money on other targets"

"they don't want our products"

"we don't have any products targeted towards APAs"

"we're going to offend some APA subgroup if we leave them out"

"APAs already buy our products – why market to them?"

"we can't measure the results of marketing to APAs"

"we can't measure the media targeted to APAs"

"we can't reach them with a single message"

"we have no minority set-aside program for them"

"there's no such thing as an APA market – I know there are African American and Hispanic markets"

"what stereotypes?"

"if anyone wanted our attention, they'd be screaming for it by now"

"aren't they all immigrants"

"the African American and Hispanic markets are much easier to understand"

"even our Asian ad agency says that the market is too complex"

"they already know us – they grew up with us overseas"

Divers have to swim for pearls, and pigs have to dig for truffles. Given the layers and layers of information a marketer has to digest before entering into the APA arena, marketers may have to do a bit of work to uncover the road that's right for them.

Then again, is any market segment (e.g. Hispanics, Tweens, Macintosh users, or even the ubiquitous Men 25 to 54) so obvious or simple to address that it does not take research, planning and strategizing to reach?

But, for the right marketers, there is a reward at the end of the journey – a rich and responsive market.

As stated in the Introduction of this volume, the only *business* reason for a company to target a specific market segment is to increase that business' profits. If a target market cannot increase revenues for a business, it makes no sense for a business to direct efforts against that target, no matter how politically correct. Conversely, any target with a better than average ROI needs to be examined, even if it takes a little homework.

What's the Same & What's Different

Gilbert Davila, Vice President of Multicultural Marketing for the Walt Disney Co., and former client when he held a similar post at Sears Roebuck had this to offer:

> Traditionally, multicultural marketing was seen almost as a subset of general marketing. But multicultural marketing takes exactly the same skill set of the marketing discipline and applies it to a very specific audience that needs to be addressed in culturally relevant and targeted ways.[1]

To many, this may seem obvious. We can hope that this would be the rational and obvious approach that all marketers would take, recognizing ethnic markets as merely another target audience, which needs to be researched, planned for, and executed against in a deliberate and calculating manner.

Mr. Davila is absolutely correct in asserting that you cannot be a good *multicultural marketer* without being a good *marketer* to begin with. Mr. Davila states, "I know of a couple of instances where the multicultural or ethnic departments have rolled into the general marketing department. And on principle or in theory, isn't that a wonderful concept?"[2]

But it's not a rational world – particularly when it come to race. The emotional history that accompanies race relations in the U.S. has crossed over to influence ethnic marketing beyond recognition of cultural relevance to allow social causes and limited knowledge of specific market sectors to override good marketing principles. As more companies enter into the multicultural arena, with limited experience, problems seem to grow right along with opportunities.

Here's an example of what we mean:

Many companies begin on the incorrect premise that all multicultural marketing is done from the same model – identify a social problem, throw money against it, and reap the benefits of "supporting the community" – or suffer the consequences of not supporting it. Others are more successful. "From our perspective, I think we've been able to move along from a nice thing to do, to really, a strategic imperative," says Mr. Davila.[3] The Walt Disney Company's efforts, under Mr. Davila's direction, may be in the minority here.

Getting Ready for a Deep Dive

In support of Mr. Davila's stance on basic marketing skill sets, any marketer entering the ethnic arena *must* do a "deep dive" on the target, just as with any target, and not get sucked into the "conventional wisdom" of so-called experts. Witness the following:

> It makes little sense to lump all these people into one group. After all, Koreans and Pakistanis have little more in common than do Italians and Swedes, who are also part of our national fabric. Similarly, Americans who can trace their roots to immigrants who arrived here from China in the 1800s have comparatively little in common with immigrants who arrive from China today.
>
> — Alfred L Schreiber
> *Multicultural Marketing – Selling to a New America*[4]

We don't have the luxury of communicating in one language, like the Hispanic market. It's really daunting to look at it from a linguistic standpoint. To target the Asian-American market, you need language specific messages and campaigns.
> — Julia Huang, CEO of InterTrend[5]

Although there are underlying similarities among Asian cultures, marketers must sub-segment the Asian-American community. In the past, some advertisers used "Suzy Wong" ads, showing a beautiful woman in a slit dress (cheong-sam) snuggling up to a dragon to depict an Asian woman. Today, savvy marketers often must come up with at least seven different ads to cover the six major groups: Filipino, Japanese, Korean, Vietnamese, Asian Indian and Chinese (who need two separate campaigns because they may speak Mandarin or Cantonese).

— Marlene Rossman
Multicultural Marketing – Selling to a Diverse America[6]

Well, maybe not. Not only are these statements based on limited insight of the APA marketplace, the internal logic of the statements simply does not hold up. Must we talk to APAs only in the language of their country of origin? To what extent must we slice and dice a market into subsegments? Does immigration status override ethnic origin?

The logical answer, and one based on good marketing principles, is a resounding *No!* It's also bu shi (Mandarin), jii nahi (Hindi), iie (Japanese), aniyo (Korean) and hindi (Tagalog). People believed they were doing APA marketing when they were really doing Chinese marketing in San Francisco or Korean marketing in Los Angeles.

Tamara Burkett, Senior Manager, Multicultural Marketing at GlaxoSmithKline offers some useful advice. She says she'd like to get beyond "conflicting messages and opinions from experts (who) can't even agree on the use of the word 'Hispanic' or 'Latino.'" She observes that dueling specialists can "be a distraction to getting the job done. Leaders in the field need to help everyone else look more at the similarities than the differences."[7]

The Safe Hispanic

There exists an eloquent corollary in the Hispanic marketplace.

When devising marketing strategies to reach Latino consumers, the primary and most important filters agencies and marketers used were language preference, level of acculturation, and country of origin. AHAA Chairman Carl Kravetz, also Chairman/Chief Strategic Officer of cruz/kravetz:IDEAS, Los Angeles, likes to refer to this approach as the "safe Hispanic": a largely immigrant, Spanish-language dominant, conservative, blue-collar, family-oriented Hispanic who is brand loyal, lives on novellas and 'Sabado Gigante' and doesn't read or use coupons."

Today, Mr. Kravetz observes, the "safe Hispanic" has been revealed as "a simplistic and not very enlightened archetype."[8]

To get a better handle on this, the Association of Hispanic Advertising Agencies commissioned its Latino Identity Project to re-examine the who, what, and most significantly, the why of Latino consumers so that Hispanic advertising agencies can help clients establish more opportune connections. (They) asked the question, "If you take language out of the equation, what makes a Latino 'Latino'?"

The Latino Identity Project analyzed nearly 40 years of academic literature on issues of identity and culture, digging deeply into anthropology, the arts, education, healthcare, linguistics, management, psychology and sociology.

Gary Bonilla, VP-strategic services at Winglatino was a leader of AHAA's Latino Identity Project. He observed, "What was fascinating is that all the academic research and the depth of expertise and insight provided by our group of (advertising agency) planners reached essentially the same set of conclusions."

Conclusion #1: Neither language nor acculturation on its own is the true marker of Latino identity. They may be the consistent measures that have been available to marketers up to now, but their simple presence is not what makes a Latino Latino.

Conclusion #2: While there are qualities of Latino cultural identity that may be familiar to marketers – things such as collectivism, *familismo*, or *simpatico* – it's the interconnectedness, not the simple presence of these attributes, that challenges the conventional view of what makes a Latino.

Finally, there were additional factors: acculturation, ethnic pride, language preference and socioeconomic level, that were previously believed to have defined Latino cultural identity. Rather, they were contextual factors in AHAA's hypothesis of Latino identity. You could be Latino without needing to "check-off" a host of factors.

"These conclusions represent a much deeper, more nuanced and more comprehensive way of understanding Latinos than any prior approach or model available to us," noted another member of the Latino Identity task force, Andrew Speyer, VP-account planning at Zubi Advertising.[9]

So What's the Same?

The road to success comes from a real understanding of the marketplace. It is deeper. It is more nuanced. But it is also simpler. As with most other marketing based on race, marketing efforts to APAs often apply only the most rudimentary planning tools, as color often comes before culture or product usage. Add in "conventional wisdom" that is neither accurate nor useful, and it's no wonder many well-intentioned APA efforts end in frustration. Here are some thoughts that will help get you started in the right direction.

●**APAs do not react to all marketing issues as a single, homogeneous mass.**
Never have, never will. But, then again, no other target market does either. The "secret," found in every Marketing 101 textbook, is to find a common denominator within the target group that allows you to communicate, develop products and services, and grow your business to the largest group possible to maximize your ROI. And here's the good news. The hard-working, family-centric APA market has lots of common denominators – many with even broader appeal than the APA market alone.

Perhaps our frustration is showing through our stoic APA exterior. Why do so many marketers think (or at least wish) that ethnic groups react as a singular mass? We feel that it's another example of oversimplification and the desire for a "one-size-fits-all" approach to marketing.

However, we think we understand the origins. The genesis of much advertising and marketing targeted towards ethnic minorities came about as a result of the identification of social injustices identified in the civil rights era. These issues were localized by community-based organizations, which, in many instances, realized that in spite of enormous diversity within their groups, it was politically advantageous to rally around a unifying activist label. Marketers could more easily manage a business and calculate ROI based on a large bloc than many separate special interest groups. They would placate the protesting groups by some sort of politically correct communication – or media buy. Thus was born a pan-ethnic marketing consciousness.

This "over-massification" is generally unacceptable in the general market. So should it be in the ethnic arena. Would anyone ever assume that all white males, 25–54, would react as one mass?

That said, all white males, 25–54, have a useful set of common denominators. So do APAs.

●Assimilation is not a zero-sum game.

We've found that both general market and ethnic market professionals assume incorrectly that assimilation means abandoning native culture while adopting "American" culture. The use of murky terms such as "bicultural," "acculturated," "mainstream," and "general culture" serve to not only cloud the issue, but to also create artificial segments within a target market that are meaningless in today's society. It's just not that clear. And, as discussed previously, the "Americanization" process still at work has very different aspects with different APA groups.

That said, the assimilation model has been the primary framework for explaining the historical experiences of APAs. At the beginning of the 1900s it was used as justification for Asian exclusion, the rationale was that Asians were too foreign to assimilate. In the 1960s, the opposite approach was taken, as APAs were held up as an example of successful integration – the "model minority." The way it was used during the rise of civil rights consciousness for African Americans was not always with the best of intentions. But it had its impact. The message was that, in effect, APAs had become so "assimilated" that they no longer were perceived as having the same issues, problems, and needs of other "minorities."

The post-1950s paradigm for immigration is that as ethnic groups come to the U.S. they become a part of American society, retain their own cultural identities, and add their distinctive flavor to the mix. The early 20th century practice of changing your name from Doris Kapplehoff to Doris Day just to be able to fit in is relatively uncommon today. Now the 21st Century brings us a wider view of everyday fare. There now are more Chinese restaurants than McDonald's, Burger Kings and KFCs combined?[10] Would pizza, tacos, grilled bratwurst or an "Oriental" chicken salad seem out of place on any "All-American" menu? Of course not.

Language is clearly a common denominator, viewed as one of the principle barometers of "successful assimilation." In her *Declarations* column in the Wall Street Journal, Peggy Noonan writes, "We speak English here. It's a great language, luckily, a rich one. It's how we do government and business. It's the official language of the official life, the outer life, in America. As for the inner life of America, the language of the family, it would be just as odd to change long-time tradition there, which has always been: anything goes. You speak what you came over speaking, and you learn the new language. Italian immigrants knew two languages, English and Italian. They enriched the first with the second – this was a great gift to all of us – and would up with greater opportunities for personal communication to boot. Talk about a win-win. And so with every group, from every place."[11]

● **Multicultural needs are in-culture, not just in-language.**
Bank of Americas's Lynn Adrian-Hsing, Asian segments marketing manager-multicultural marketing integration, states, "We tend to forget that a culture means a culture, not necessarily a different language."[12] Word-for- word translations, tokenism, or demonstrating that you may know a few cultural facts (e.g. red is an auspicious color to the Chinese) oversimplifies and diminishes the need for a sociological, anthropological, and psychological understanding of a target market.

Beyond simply reaching the customer, it should be the goal of every marketer to understand every part of their customer proposition and make sure that products and services are addressing their customers needs. (Just like the general market, huh?)

Research techniques, e.g. ethnographies, are just starting to be used in multicultural marketing. Is it any wonder that it's not uncommon for a major advertising agency to have an anthropologist on staff?

There is a brilliant ad campaign for SiTV, a cable network targeting English speaking Latino consumers, written for marketers. The headline reads, "You lost me at 'Hola.'" This network understands that their viewers are not Spanish language-dependent. While still being Latino culture-involved, the network demonstrated to marketers that there exists a whole new, untapped realm of consumers that can be reached if marketers spend as much time learning

about an "ethnic" target as they do a "mainstream" market.[13] Who knows what niches you can find – if only you dive a little deeper.

- ● **Ethnic marketing does not often get a chair at the grownup table.**

Even in these enlightened times, with the emphasis on ROI to shareholders, ethnic or multicultural marketing is still often viewed as a "set aside" line item, and not given the *strategic* imperative Mr. Davila mentions above. He states, "This person should have a seat at the table making decisions, providing strategic direction and having the authority to make it happen. And, ultimately, you have to hold that person and department accountable for delivering measurable results to the organization."[14]

Does this happen in your company?

We should also recognize that, as previously discussed, ethnic advertising came into the discussion through the "fairness" door as part of social protest.

This book argues that APA programs should be judged on their profit potential. Again, easier said than done.

In our own experience, overseeing the African American advertising for Procter & Gamble, the nation's largest advertiser and one of the most forward-thinking companies regarding supporting multicultural marketing efforts, it was recognized that the African American ad agencies were still struggling to get a "seat at the table" during the planning process. They had limited opportunities to provide upfront strategic input to Brand plans and initiatives because they were often brought into the process well after the masterplans and budgets have been set. As a result, there was insufficient funding and many of their African American marketing plans and initiatives were tactical afterthoughts versus strategically planned to win with African American consumers. It took a directive from Worldwide Chief Marketing Officer Jim Stengel to get both the P&G Brand Groups and general market agencies to realize that integration meant a win-win for all.

This directive is a reflection of what Carla Palazio, partner at executive recruiters Heidrick & Struggles, states. While multicultural marketing is perceived as very important, there is often a lack of a real company-wide strategy to address it. "The root of this is the lack of awareness at the organization. While the CMO understands it well, they almost have to evangelize (the value of multicultural marketing) to the rest of the company." Ms. Palazio lists such roadblocks as "getting buy-in and support from company leadership" and "getting senior level marketers to understand that the world is changing."[15]

Part of the reason this happens may be due to the fact that most U.S. companies simply aren't used to planning marketing efforts around the make-up of the new America by a more diverse corporate staff. Eliot Kang of Kang & Lee writes, "I think for budget purpose sometimes, not the executional purpose, but, winning the budget, sometimes being an ethnic person within the corporation, it's not a plus. 'You're just saying it of course because you're Asian, African American and so you're going to push this.' Management devalues the actual rational logic behind why should they spend this money. So it's a difficult situation. But it does happen, and we've seen it happen."[16]

However, it works the other way as well. The history-of-social-protest, self-serving nature of many minority "expert" suppliers is reflected in a statement by the president of an African American research company on the use of general market researchers rather than multicultural agencies or researchers. "That is such a big mistake. I'm still so frustrated with general market research. So much of it is disrespectful, and it's just too vanilla – and not just for African Americans but for Latinos and Asians, too."[17] Would this "Us vs. Them" mentality and pejorative use of "vanilla" fly in the general market?

Because of thinking like this, is it any wonder that Ethnic Marketing is often the purview of the "B" Team and not given the C-Suite attention it deserves?

● **Metrics on the marketplace are spotty or non-existent.**
A typical meeting between the CEO and the Head of a Multicultural Marketing unit may go something like this:

> CEO: *Last year I gave you $10 million to spend in the ethnic market. What's my return? What's been the lift for the company? How much more do our new customers like us? What's our growth for the next three years with this target? How much are we beating the competition in this market? Do they think our advertising is relevant?*
>
> HMM: *(shaking) Here are some demographics on the projected growth of the multicultural markets.*
>
> CEO: *You're fired.*

Of course this is a fictitious dialogue (most CEOs would consult HR first), but the scenario is very real.

Earlier this year, executive search firm Heidrick & Struggles, via their research supplier Brandiosity, uncovered the fact that while 84% of marketers believe that multicultural marketing is "critical to my business," almost 40% said they don't know the financial value of multicultural groups to their companies.[18]

In many cases, this does not have to be. Mike Fasulo, CMO of Sony Electronics, was "surprised that more companies didn't know the financial worth of multicultural segments, because the data are there. In electronics, for example, many product categories overindex for multicultural groups vs. the general population. And though the economy has slowed, both disposable income and growth of multicultural segments far exceed the general market."[19]

While the data on potential financial implications may exist (take the test in Chapter 3 of this book), useful research on consumer behavior and resultant ROI typically does not. Delores Kunda, Vice President at Leo Burnett's Hispanic unit notes, "I can understand why some of the big research houses have not invested in the Hispanic market. You know, unless they get pressure from their clients or they see a return for themselves, it's difficult to justify putting together the research tools that will give us volumetrics in the Hispanic market which are very clean and very statistically significant."[20]

In response to the Federal Communications Commission's call for an industry Code of Conduct, the American Advertising Federation created the Mosaic Principles for advertisers and advertising agencies. This occurred after the disclosure of alleged discrimination in ad rates paid to minority broadcasters.

The intent of some of these basic Principles & Practices, evolving over time, is that in order to take advantage of growth opportunities in multicultural markets, companies should commit to measurable steps and goals, require accountability, monitor implementation and establish performance incentives.[21] Is this any different than what companies should do with *any* market?

More from Mr. Davila: "Specific goals should be part of a strategic-planning perspective. You should be able to gauge and measure where your company is today, and relative to the resources given, what are the realistic goals you will be able to achieve to deliver a favorable ROI. That is done through rigorous research, benchmarking and understanding the upside and profit potential of the endeavour."[22] Good advice. How is your company doing in this regard?

So What's Different?

In some ways, marketing to APAs is in the stage that marketing to African Americans was in the 1960s or marketing to Hispanics was in the 1980s, in terms of the attention it gets. Unfortunately, too many use this as a signal to simply copy previous ethnic marketing models and apply it to APAs. Two factors modify this. First, the history of APA marketing is shorter than that of blacks or Hispanics, so there may be less to "un-do." However, the misconceptions are deeply entrenched.

Second, the higher income levels of most APA groups quickly move most marketers into the kind of niche marketing more associated with higher end products and services and other techniques based on crunching the numbers to get at identifying high BDI/high ROI opportunities.

● Separate but Equal doesn't necessarily apply

Budgeting is also a concern. The easiest way for marketers to allocate funds to any kind of an ethnic marketing program is via set-aside funds based on population or product usage (see the Exercise in Chapter 3). Proponents of this method would suggest that it is "fair" to all and provides for a measurable ROI. However, this base-level planning ignores the psychological and cultural components of addressing the APA market.

If you base marketing programs on existing ethnic models, it's easy to justify separatism. Most current ethnic entrepreneurial endeavors are, by design, separatist for both the targeted group and the general market. For example, in the Latino market, the Telemundo and Univision networks are exclusive to the general market based on language, as all programming and advertising is in Spanish. The popular African American clothing company FUBU (**For Us, By Us**) excludes by choice right in the name of their company. Ethnic pride, a desire for independence, and a harkening back to civil rights based marketing do as much to bolster ethnic economies as they stir up a perceived sense of grievance by the general market.

Asian philosophies, based on thousands of years of Confucian-based thinking that cross national background, are much closer to what Harvard professor of sociology, Orlando Patterson, calls "ecumenical American culture." Patterson sees a growing pattern of post-civil-rights age culture when color, though still relevant, has less impact on what one reads, listens to or watches. It was the common crucible of popular culture, he said, that forged a truly American identity, rather than the "salad bowl" analogy cherished by diversity advocates.[23] For APAs, the "melting pot" is on simmer.

Asian philosophies stress inclusion rather than exclusion. There is a sharing of culture rather than keeping it within, and a common goal of earning their *meaningful place* in the fabric of whatever society they happen to live. The widespread consumption of manga and anime, the decline of ethnic enclaves toward a pattern of suburbanization, and the desire for the elimination of university entrance quota systems are some of the phenomena that support this trend.

This will have a significant impact in subsequent chapters on how to reach APAs.

●Ethnic marketing based on Social Cause marketing

This won't go away. As we've said from the beginning, no matter how much "experts" may tell you, sound marketing principles used to attract the APA target are not based on immigration, bilingualism, social justice or other civil rights issues. They're based on marketing principles such as product usage, brand awareness, disposable income and lifestyle aspiration.

In the 1960s, ethnic marketing, growing out of pressures first felt in the civil rights era, served to help address, solve or at least take people's minds off issues like jobs, housing and education by providing instant gratification via consumer goods. Along parallel paths, marketers sought to gain favor in ethnic markets by working at the ground level, often with community-based organizations. The common plan was to identify a problem in the community, fund a solution, and reap the benefits of community goodwill.

They were strong elements of cause marketing and, to some extent, what we now call social marketing.

Marketing to APAs veers off of this path due to the fact that the stereotypical ethnic social issues of jobs, housing and education do not exist in the same form as they do in the African American or Latino communities. As will be shown in the upcoming chapter on demographics, with the exception of some Southeast Asian and Filipino communities, these problems generally do not exist in the APA marketplace. Thus it would be wrong to focus on programs that address these issues or take this approach.

The crux issue, which we will discuss in subsequent chapters, is one that goes to the heart of Asian philosophy, that of ethnic image and identity.

●No Recognition in the fabric of Race Issues

For much of America, "minority" and "black" (or African American) are interchangeable. For those who may live in areas like Southern California, Texas or most major metropolitan areas, "minority" may also include Latinos.

David Bernstein, President of the American Jewish Committee writes, "There are two cultural narratives among immigrants – the African American and the European story line. The African American narrative, growing out of slavery and discrimination, holds that America is a racist country requiring systemic change. This story line reflects the harsh reality of America's treatment of blacks.

The European immigrant narrative – which many Jews adopted – holds that America is a fundamentally good, albeit imperfect country, that offers unlimited opportunity. Indeed, Jews developed a love affair with America long before America loved them.

To be sure, the original European narrative is outmoded, inasmuch as it implicitly calls upon ethnic communities to assimilate into an American 'melting pot.' Today's multicultural discourse thankfully places a premium upon cultural uniqueness and preservation. But even a modern version (minus the emphasis on cultural assimilation) of this narrative still greatly differs from the traditional African American narrative of oppression."[24]

Despite numerous obvious examples, APAs remain relatively invisible in the nightly news reports when discussing U.S. race relations – even though there are quite a few APA anchor persons. The literature on race relations continues to have a primarily black/white focus, with a Latino addendum. This biracial thinking fails to recognize the complex, post-civil rights era reality of an increasingly complex American identity.

Compounding this issue are attempts to place Latinos and APAs in an existing black/white paradigm. Columnist Clarence Page writes, " In the business world, you have to adapt to changing market conditions or you lose market share and die. The civil rights movement world is different. You can hang on indefinitely to a 1960s paradigm of problems (racism) and solutions (marches, boycotts and lawsuits) despite changes in both, even as old problems persist and take on a new urgency."[25]

If anything, APAs are held up to society as "anti-ethnic," using the 1980s "model minority myth" whenever possible.

The "model minority myth" seeks to position APAs as the shining examples among ethnic groups for assimilation into American society. Positioned as well-off, well-educated and well-employed, they are often used as a wedge against other ethnic groups.

On the one hand, APAs are examples of why other ethnic groups do not deserve social services, affirmative action programs and other government "handouts." On the other hand, APAs become the subject of resentment by groups who feel they do too well, as evidenced by the exclusionary laws of the 19th and early 20th centuries and rumors of quotas in top universities limiting high-performing APA high-school students.

●Media Invisibility

Syndicated columnist Leonard Pitts writes, "Beg pardon, but who died and made Al Sharpton president of African Americans?" Pitts argues that "black America is served by dozens of magazines, Web sites, television networks and media figures that did not exist when (Martin Luther) King was killed, so it's about time news media – and those who will insult us in the future – get past this notion that one or two people are anointed to speak for 36 million. This is a simplistic, antiquated and faintly condescending idea. I speak for myself. Don't you?"[26]

Of course, I do. We all do. But to say that, while the notion of a charismatic personality taking it upon themselves to be the speaker for their "people" is antiquated, it is still a fact of life and of the media landscape. This will continue until personal blogs influence the nation as much as CNN and mass media. And as long as there is media, those media personalities who can use it to further a cause will continue to be powerful tools in both civil and economic arenas.

On April 4, 2007, on his MSNBC show *Imus in the Morning*, host Don Imus made a derogatory racial reference to the Rutgers University women's basketball team. Imus was fired from his position shortly thereafter.

On the December 5, 2006 airing of *The View*, Rosie O'Donnell, in her best Mandarin, relayed the story of a drunken Danny DeVito that included a series of "ching chong" epithets. Not only was O'Donnell not fired, she refused to apologize, and further, supporters rushed to the blogosphere unwilling to equate Rosie's joke with racism.

Don Imus was fired because advertisers pulled economic support of his show, not for his being a racist, sexist, instigator which he has been for years. Without the advertising income, his bosses at MSNBC had no choice but to get rid of him.

This repeal of ad support was certainly brought on by outspoken leaders such as Al Sharpton and Jesse Jackson who became involved in the issue and demonstrated not only the civil support within the African American community that they can muster, but also the economic pressure they can bring to bear on an advertiser, should they choose to continue supporting someone like Don Imus.

The Rosie O'Donnell case was different. The racist characteristics of the case were the same, but the community she chose to offend was different. Without a media-savvy, charismatic voice speaking up for the APA community, advertisers had little reason to pull support or perhaps even recognize that issues like this exist.

This is coupled with the fact that the relatively diverse APA community has historically not gathered as a critical mass to speak out against cultural prejudice or social injustices, which advertisers can interpret as having economic repercussions.

Unlike the African American and Latino communities, the APA market is not served by "dozens of magazines, Websites, television networks and media figures" as Pitts would list, at least not in the same way. We'll focus on this subject in more detail in Chapter 15 "Media: How Do We Reach APAs?"

Judy Ching-Chia Wong, writing in the *New York Times* after the L.A. riots states, "The problems and experiences of Asian Americans, African Americans, Hispanics, etc., while sometimes similar, are not the same. Unless Asian Americans learn to think and speak out as a group, we will continue to be caught in the middle, misunderstood and pummeled by both sides."[27]

●Assimilation – an Unstoppable Train
In his article "Our Town" *New York Times* reporter Alex Kotlowitz wrote the following:

When Italians came here in the late 19th century and early 20th century, nativist Americans chafed at the new arrivals' inability – or in the eyes of some, their unwillingness – to master English, language being one of the most visible and tangible measure of whether an immigrant group is becoming American.

In 1919, shortly before his death, Theodore Roosevelt wrote, "We have room for but one language here, and that is the English language, for we intend to see that the crucible turns our people out as Americans, and American nationality, and not as dwellers in a polyglot boarding house; and we have room for but one soul loyalty, and that is loyalty to the American people."

Many suggested back then that the Italians were fundamentally different from previous immigrant groups, that they would live only among their own, that they'd frequent only their own stores, that they couldn't speak English. Edward A. Ross, a prominent sociologist at the time, wrote in *The Century Magazine*, "That the Mediterranean peoples are morally below the races of Northern Europe is as certain as any social fact." But as new immigrants had children and grandchildren, the once-new arrivals became a part of the mainstream culture (influencing it, as well) and, notably, spoke English fluently.[28]

As a Sinatra fan, I guess I'd add that they sang it pretty well, too.

The current U.S. immigration and assimilation issues focus mainly on Latinos. The speed, or in some opinions, the lack of speed at which Latinos learn English is viewed by some as a clear indication of lack of desire to "become American." While one might think that the provincial racism of the last century would be gone, Samuel P. Huntington, a Harvard professor, argues in his 2004 book, *Who Are We?* that Mexicans – unlike earlier immigrants from Europe – don't subscribe to what he calls the nation's Anglo-Protestant values and so have not become Americanized. Instead, they have formed their own social and linguistic enclaves.[29] As with many other ethnic issues, this reasoning has been incorrectly translated to apply to APAs.

It's clear that the Latino assimilation model is not so black and white. While many Mexican immigrants may be ambivalent about Americanization, a survey by the *Population and Development Review* indicates that nearly all Mexican immigrants speak at least some English at home by the third generation.

Another study at UCLA finds that the high school graduation rate among Mexican immigrants nearly doubles from 42 to 83 percent between first and second generations.[30] Nonetheless, the lower level of assimilation is a major contributor to what has been holding Hispanics back in the United States. Of the high school students learning English as a second language, nearly two-thirds are second- or third-generation Americans born in the United States. Of these, the Top native language is Spanish at 76.9%. The next closest language is Vietnamese – a mere 2.4%.[31]

The difference between the APA and Latino models, and for that matter nearly all immigrant groups before them, is the *speed* at which APAs become a part of the mainstream fabric of society.

Overall, there seems to be no resistance to assimilation, or acculturation, if you prefer.

Look ahead to Chapter 7 on APA demographics and you'll notice that the indicators of "successful" integration – English language proficiency, education, suburbanization, income levels, white collar professions – all reflect indices above the general populace and well-above every other ethnic group. Not only have these indicators reached significantly high levels, but the time across generations that it has taken APAs to get there is shorter than it is for any other ethnic group.

Implications for Marketers

Asian Pacific Americans are here to stay. Moreover, they will become "American" whether they are recognized or not. The astute marketer will be able to take advantage of both the differences and similarities of marketing to other ethnic groups by recognizing the following:

- The need for the marketing function to be able to take a "deep dive" into smaller, but potentially valuable market segments – including APAs.

- The need to consolidate work with one (or at least fewer) departments, agencies and consultants with expertise in understanding APA segments. If you trust any professional to do your mainstream marketing work, the same rules, disciplines and structure apply to working within the APA market, and in fact, all of your target markets.

- Understanding that separate but equal does not necessarily apply. You can begin your marketing planning to APAs where it should begin – right at the beginning. Since you will (hopefully) base your decision making process on ROI rather than social causes, building APA marketing into your overall plan allows you to define goals, establish metrics and evaluate results right from the start.

- You have the chance to achieve one more advantage. Since APA marketing is still in its infancy, your company can be, in many cases, first to the table. And, as we all know, it's often the first to market that wins.

Cultural Considerations: APA Restaurants

Many ask, "What constitutes an 'authentic' Asian restaurant?" There is, perhaps, no bigger argument among APAs. Asian restaurants are actually a fairly important part of the APA world. Often, it was one of the initial businesses started by each immigrant community. A family's entire livelihood could be wrapped up in the success of a restaurant. Believe me, they are paying attention to their customers. They will change their recipes if they think it means more business. Still, we always like to know what we're eating, whether it is the absolute original or a recipe developed here in the US by an APA chef. As you become more familiar with Asian food – both the original and the version that has grown up in America – we predict many delicious evenings.

Here are some of the reasons for the controversy:

- American tastes. The American taste bud is expanding and "eating" what were once foreign tastes. So it goes with Teriyaki chicken at TGI Friday's and Subway's own version of the Vietnamese bahn mi.

- Abundance of Protein. Asian cuisines simply did not develop where there was a lot of meat. But here in America, we can afford to load it on. Main dishes feature meat, not vegetables, as the star.

- Availability. Some ingredients are fresh and in abundance. Other times, it can be a problem – though less so as Asian restaurants grow as a category. Broccoli became an APA ingredient because it was affordable and readily available.

- American innovation. Here's the final part of the recipe. Most good cooks are creative, so it's not surprising that it has had its impact on the APA menu.

That said, here are some tips to enjoying Asian food – both the authentic version, and whatever the latest APA item happens to be. But "Kobe beef" sliders? Don't confuse them with real "Kobe" beef. Or real Sliders.

Here are a few Signs of Americanized Asian Restaurants:

- Here are dishes that don't exist in China: General Tso's Chicken, chop suey, egg foo young, sweet & sour pork, Hong Kong steak, and pretty much the whole menu at PF Chang's. That said, you'll want to learn to enjoy the flavors at more authentic restaurants.

- All-you-can-eat sushi. Real sushi demands top grade fish and seafood, which doesn't come cheap, even in Japan. Getting an all-you-can-eat sushi experience suggests that you should be cautious. By the way, eating copious amounts of wasabi is not a test of manhood in Japanese culture – though it is entertainment for the sushi chef.

- Soy sauce made out of anything except soybeans, salt, wheat, and the culture to get it started. Skip the hydrolyzed vegetable protein and food coloring.

- Levels of "heat." Szechuan, Southern Indian, and some Southeast Asian food can be tongue numbingly hot. If you can't stand the heat, get out of the kitchen. Or don't order the dish. Making chili crabs "mild" makes it something else.

- Thai food is complex with a balance of salty, sweet, sour, spicy, and bitter flavors. Don't put chili sauce or peanut sauce on everything. Chili sauce and peanut sauce have become today's Italian red sauce of the 1950s. They won't tell you "no." We will.

- Sake. Hot or cold? Sake is to be sipped throughout the meal – not slammed like a Jaegermeister shot. Higher quality (somewhat expensive) sake should be enjoyed chilled to taste the subtle flavors. Inexpensive sake can be drunk hot or cold. *Kampai!*

Mixing cultures via cuisines is in and of itself not a bad thing. The Chinese/French fusion cooking at Ming Tsai's Blue Ginger in Wellesley, MA is absolutely fabulous. But, as with any cooking, just be mindful of who's in the kitchen.

VII. Demographics
The APA Escalator: *Going Up*

"Immigrant groups in America take one of two paths – all up (like the Jews) or some up, some down (like the Irish)"[1]

We use the term APA Escalator, rather than elevator, to illustrate a very real phenomenon. An escalator moves in one direction only. It is in constant motion, and there is virtually no way to get off once you're on it. An escalator does not let you off until you reach the top.

While they may be excluded from some private elevators, in this chapter we'll show you how APAs find their way to the up escalator – to avoid climbing the stairs their entire lives.

Let's talk about how to identify and then reach this moving target.

Asian Pacific Americans represent a ripe 21st Century American marketing opportunity, but one that's often obscured.

A Meta-Analytic Approach
Our approach to describing this opportunity can best be described as meta-analytic. It uses a variety of the freshest primary sources of information, including:

- U.S. Census data,
- the 2005-2007 *American Community Survey*,
- the Bureau of Labor Statistics' *Consumer Expenditure Survey* and *American Time Use Survey*,
- NORC's *General Social Survey*,
- the proprietary Ronin Group Online Survey of 18–49 Year Old APAs and Non-APAs.

In addition, we'll sprinkle in some secondary sources and qualitative verbatims from 10 years of Ronin Group APA marketing research. The result – a new holistic description of Asian Americans, one that highlights their most relevant differences vis a vis other Americans. We think you'll have a better understanding of how the complex welter of different Asian ethnicities are becoming fused into a uniquely American version of Asia in America.

Okay, time to get on the escalator – going up.

Quantities

Demographically, the APA opportunity is marked more by its astonishing growth than its absolute size. Between 1980 and 1990 the Asian Pacific American (alone) population doubled. It's projected to double again by 2010.

Asian Alone. Asian in Combination

The APA market is becoming diverse in more ways than one. Intermarriage is more and more common. In census terms, this group is called "Asian in Combination." We will use this term as well as "hapa" (from Hawaiian slang for "half"). It is not uncommon, within this growing group, to self-identify as being "half."

The Asian-in-combination population is projected to grow just about as fast (38%) as the Asian Pacific American (alone) population (41%) between 2000 & 2010.

	Asian Alone	Asian in Combination
1980	3,792,000	NA
1990	7,458,000	NA
2000	10,242,998	11,898,828
2010 (est)	14,415,000	16,472,000

APA birth rates are relatively low. This rapid APA population growth is, to a great degree, dependent on immigration. This is an important point in understanding the dynamics of Asian Pacific America. For example, this is why Asians Pacific Americans seem to be and, in fact, are perpetually young. Let's look a little deeper.

The total fertility rate (TFR) or average number of children per woman, given current birth rates, was 2.1 children per woman in 2005 (according to the Population Reference Bureau[2]).

Among racial and ethnic groups, the TFR was highest for Hispanics at 2.9 children per woman. It was 2.0 for non-Hispanic blacks and 1.9 for Asian and Pacific Islanders. The rate was slightly lower for non-Hispanic whites (1.8) and for American Indians and Alaska Natives (1.7).

Immigration Drives APA Population Growth

But, between 1980 and 1990, immigration accounted for 67% of APA population growth (2,446,000 APA immigrants to an APA population increase of 3,666,000 in the decade). Between 1990 and 2000, immigration actually accounted for an astounding 94% of APA population growth (2,625,000 APA immigrants vs. an APA population increase of 2,784,998 in the decade.

The "immigration factor" is not slowing down, and is projected to account for 65%, 76% and 80% of APA population growth in the 2000s, 2010s and 2020s, respectively. Immigration inflows, of course, are often difficult to predict, depending upon both relative economic conditions in Asia & the U.S. and American politics, but clearly it will remain a major contributor.

Most recently, as the table below shows, about 67% of the growth of the Asian alone population is driven by immigration – vs. only 44% of the Hispanic population's growth in the same period because, as we saw above, Hispanics in America have a relatively higher fertility rate than APAs (as do White & Black Americans).

Here's a recent five-year snapshot.

Components of Asian Pacific American Population Change

	Asian (alone)	%
Total population change 2000 to 2005	2,098,350	
Net International Migration	1,415,274	67.5
Natural Increase (Births-Deaths)	682,925	32.5

There's more to the story. Not only are APA population numbers more sensitive to immigration, the higher the immigrant/foreign born quotient in the APA population itself often determines, as we'll see, many of the very qualities of that population. If a large majority (67%) of APAs are immigrants and we profile them against a Non-APA population that's mostly native born, are we really profiling Asian Americans or immigrants who happen to be APA? This knot needs to be untangled. And remember, most of this group of immigrants is getting on the escalator as quickly as possible.

On the whole, Americans recognize that a surge in the Asian Pacific American population is occurring. According to the 2000 *General Social Survey*, 69% of non-APAs believe that the APA population has increased in the last 25 years. They're correct. This finding correlates well with the actual expansion of the APA population – from 1.4% in 1980 to 3.7% in 2000.

One curious effect has been widely overestimated perceptions of the size of both the APA and Hispanic U.S. populations.

In the year 2000, when the APA population was only 3.7%, Americans as a whole estimated that APAs accounted for 18% of U.S. population. Similarly, in the year 2000, when the Hispanic American population was only 12.5%, Americans as a whole estimated that this segment accounted for 25% of the U.S. population.

These wild overestimations may be an artifact of higher visibility of minorities brought about by well-intentioned multicultural emphasis of the American media and education establishments. The size of the African American population in the U.S. is similarly overestimated in this 2000 survey (31% perceived vs. 12.3% actual). Meanwhile, estimates of the White population were, as you might expect, underestimated (only 59% perceived vs. 75% actual).

Yet, while Americans in general tend to amplify the size of these populations, to most marketers, particularly as regards the APA segment, it remains a blip on the radar.

Qualities

According to that same 2000 survey, 58% of Non-APAs said they know at least one Asian American. Overall, as we'll see, some of the main perceptions of characteristic qualities of APAs do ring true. But that still leaves 42% (113,823,904) Non–Asian Pacific Americans who don't know even one APA. Many of them are, we suspect, marketing decision makers. So let's get on with it.

Younger, Wealthier, Better-Educated

Demographically, APAs are somewhat younger, with close to half falling into the 18-44 age group, an index of 121 vs. the non-APA population. The very old and the very young, of course, are less likely to immigrate and recent immigrants are likely to come from precisely the same 18-44 year old age groups as Asian Americans.

And that's what we find. Sixty-two percent of past 3 year immigrants to the U.S., according to the 2005-2007 *American Community Survey*, were aged 18-44 years old. So, the main reason that APAs skew younger than other Americans is that so many of them are immigrants. And, because immigrants are younger and the size of APA population is predominantly immigration driven, the Asian Pacific American target audience is a perpetually young one.

Asian Pacific American Demographics: Age

Age Group	APA	Non-APA	Index
<18	24%	27%	91
18-24	9%	9%	99
25-34	18%	13%	135
35-44	18%	15%	120
45-54	14%	15%	98
55-64	9%	11%	88
65-74	5%	6%	80
75+	3%	6%	60

APAs also have somewhat higher HH incomes with 57% of APA households earning $50,000+ , an index of 124 vs. the non-APA population, with Asian Pacific Americans being particularly more likely to have HH incomes of $100,000+.

HH Income	APA	Non-APAs	Index
<$25,000	21%	27%	80
$25 - $49,999	21%	27%	78
$50 - $74,999	18%	19%	97
$75 - $99,999	**13%**	**11%**	**117**
$100,000+	**26%**	**16%**	**160**

APAs are also much, much better educated than their non-APA counterparts. Close to half (44%) of APAs have a college degree or better, an index of 183 vs. the non-APA population.

Education	APA	Non-APAs	Index
HS or less	33%	47%	69
Some College*	23%	29%	79
College Grad	**27%**	**16%**	**174**
Advanced Degree	**17%**	**8%**	**208**

*Some college but no degree, Vo/Tech/Bus school degree, Associate degree

While these three basic demographic characteristics paint a clear picture of a desirable, upmarket target audience, they also obscure some even more pointed differences between APAs and non-APAs. These differences explain a lot about their "place" in 2010 America.

APA education levels are most differentiating. And, therein lies the first clue to the *APA Escalator*.

The simple fact is, whether because of innate abilities, cultural advantages, or the old-fashioned American virtue of hard work, *APAs speak and understand math much better than most other Americans.*

For the average APA, high school comes with a heavy dose of math and science, as the following GSS data demonstrates.

For many non-APAs, a year or two of algebra and/or a course in geometry is viewed as sufficient. Meanwhile, a much greater percentage of Asian American high schoolers go on to take trigonometry, pre-calculus, calculus and/or statistics/probability *before* they get to college.

The Hard Road in High School: The Higher Maths

Highest Level of Math Completed in H. S.	Non-APA (3065)	APA (108)	Index
No Math / Didn't Go to HS	2%	3%	170
General, Business, or Vocational Math	16%	14%	89
Pre-Algebra	4%	3%	63
One Year of Algebra	15%	8%	57
Two Years of Algebra	16%	10%	64
Geometry (Plane or Solid or Both)	18%	7%	40
Trigonometry Linear Programming Analysis	12%	**14%**	**113**
Pre-Calculus	6%	**8%**	**141**
Calculus	9%	**21%**	**240**
Statistics Probability	2%	**9%**	**591**
Other	1%	2%	236

The higher you go, the more this difference is amplified.

Given this level of preparation and the strong desire of young APAs to please their Ivy League dreaming parents, it shouldn't be surprising to find that in 1995, according to *America in Black & White*,[3] APAs (who then comprised about 3% of the population) were 13% of all students scoring 700 or more on their math SATs and a stunning 27% of those with a score of 750 and up in math. That's an index of 400 and 900 for those of you keeping score at home. But we're getting a bit ahead of ourselves. APA mathematical abilities will be the subject of much more extensive analysis below. So let's return to high school again. This time we'll visit some of the labs where we can see the same phenomenon occurring when it comes to high school science courses.

The Hard Road in High School: The Higher Sciences

Ever took in HS	Non-APA (3083)	APA (109)	Index
Biology	80%	88%	111
Chemistry	52%	75%	146
Physics	30%	65%	217

While the vast majority of both non-APAs and APAs are exposed to biology in high school, the chemistry vs. physics line, like the geometry vs. trig/calculus line, appears to clearly separate APAs and their non-APA counterparts. While barely half of non-APAs take chemistry, 3 in 4 APA high school students do. Physics is the real differentiator – about 2/3rds of APA students take the course, while less than a third of non-APAs do.

College is more of the same. A majority of APAs say they have taken a college science course. The majority of non-APAs have not.

The Hard Road in College: Science or Not

	Non-APA (3083)	APA (109)	Index
Ever took a college science course	41%	64%	158

While the science course question may be a bit skewed because more APAs are college grads, let's look at college majors, which aren't similarly skewed. Again, we see much the same story. APAs are overrepresented in the "hard" majors and non-APAs overrepresented in the "easy" ones. Then again, why wouldn't they – given their high school courses. These more difficult majors represent 29% of the choices made by APA college students.

The Hard Road in College

College Major	Non-APA	APA	Index
dentistry	0%	1%	907
industry & technology	0%	2%	726
physics	0%	2%	726
medicine	1%	3%	544
general science	2%	8%	423
computer science	3%	10%	398
economics	1%	3%	389

APAs are more likely to major in subjects like physics, medicine, general science, computer science and engineering (not shown – that's another 5%, a 191 index). Non-APAs are more likely to major in subjects like education, law, communications, speech and other liberal arts, business and vocational majors (like art, music, accounting/bookkeeping and law enforcement). These are majors that don't require advanced math or science courses.

The Easy Road in College

Major	APAs	Non-APAs	Index
education	2%	9%	378
other vocational	2%	6%	256
law	1%	3%	243
comm/speech	1%	2%	193
general studies	1%	2%	182
english	1%	2%	143
psychology	2%	3%	132
business	10%	12%	115

As the education stage of the escalator ascends past the high school and college floors (not to mention, for many APAs, the professional schools), we can begin to get a glimpse of the upper floor destinations of high occupational prestige coupled with high income. The foundation of that top floor destination is a "good job," the very American quality/trait of occupational identity that shows perhaps the most pointed difference between APAs and non-APAs.

The APA Escalator analogy is on a solid "up" trajectory when you take the "hard road/hard work" courses in math and science. In the main, once you do that, the math and science hard road will ascend to the top.

You can still get to the top in America today, of course, without math or science, but it's less certain. To push our analogy, you'll have to "take the stairs." This is a decision many young non-APAs probably don't realize they're making when they spurn the higher maths and sciences in high school.

Another cultural factor is that Americans, of whatever race, tend to identify closely with their jobs – more closely than Europeans and other visitors.

Indeed, Europeans continue to find it curious that, upon visiting the U.S., the first question many Americans will ask them is often: "What do you do?" But it's true. That's how we are.

So, let's take a look at how APAs stack-up with non-APAs on this basic element of American identity. Let's see how APAs, 67% foreign born, do in their American jobs. This exercise will also help us demonstrate how well the APA Escalator works in practice.

The broad occupational categories in *The American Community Survey* clearly show the differences between APAs and non-APAs. APAs are almost four times as likely to work in Computer Related fields, twice as likely to work in Science or Engineering and almost twice as likely to work in Finance and Medicine. The relative absence of APAs in construction and their absolute absence from the extraction category would surely be a source of pride to their railroad building and gold-mining forebears.

The Top Floor: Asian American Occupational Indices

Occupation Category	Index
CMM - Computers	393
Science	267
Engineering	229
Finance	184
Medical	174
Personal Services	135
Eating Establishments	122
Production	111
Entertainment	111
Business	103
Sales	103
Health Services	94
Education	87
Office	85
Legal	78
Military	77
CMS - Counseling/social work	68
Repair	58
Cleaning	58
Transportation	51
Protective Services	45
Farming, forestry, fishing	31
Construction	27
Extraction	3

The strong technical/professional tendencies of APA jobs is even more apparent in the occupational sub-categories. A litany of job titles helps to paint the picture:

- CMM, yes, but especially Computer Software Engineers (an index of 790), Database Administrators (400) and Computer Programmers (364)
- Science, yes, but especially Medical Scientists (930), Physical Scientists (616), Biological Technicians (437), Chemists And Materials Scientists (368) & Other Life And Social Science

Technicians including Nuclear Technicians (266)
- Engineering, yes, especially Computer Hardware Engineers (631), Electrical and Electronics Engineers(404), Materials Engineers (282) & Chemical Engineers (266)
- Finance, yes, but especially Financial Analysts (245), Budget Analysts (240), Financial Examiners (230) & Accountants And Auditors (229)
- Medical, yes, especially, Health Diagnosing and Treating Practitioners (791), Physicians and Surgeons (442), Pharmacists (308) and Clinical Laboratory Technicians (263)

This strong technical orientation also shows up in some of the average APA occupational categories. APAs are only average (index of 96 vs. Non-APAs) in terms of being managers, but they're more likely to be in Natural Sciences (256), Engineering (215), and Computer and Info Systems (199).

APAs are only average (index of 103 vs. Non-APAs) in terms of Business, but they're more likely to be Management Analysts (155), Other Business Operations Specialists (126) & Logisticians (116).

Of course, not every APA gets to the very top of the Escalator. The latest *American Community Survey* occupational data also demonstrates the existence of the many *intentional entreprenurial niches* that various APA ethnic groups have carved out for themselves in 21st Century America.

There is an intriguing chapter of retail conquest by APAs. For example, Vivek Wadhwa, research fellow for the Labor and Worklife Program at Harvard Law, points out that "An Asian-American hospitality industry advocacy group says that Indians own 50% of all economy lodging and 37% of all hotels in the U.S."[4] This is a startling assertion, as Asian Indian-Americans comprise less than 1% of the population.

So, naturally, it's no surprise to find that APAs as a whole are more than twice as likely as non-APAs to hold the occupation of lodging manager (an index of 235). Is the fact that APAs as a whole are twice as likely to be Laundry And Dry-Cleaning Workers (201) due to Korean dominance of this category in at least some markets or the fact that APAs are almost sixteen times as likely to be Miscellaneous Personal Appearance Workers (1588) due to Vietnamese dominance of the nail bar trade – even in more obscure markets. Certainly, we can link the fact that APAs are relatively more likely to be Head Cooks (360), Food Service Managers (199), and Food Servers (165) to the wide-ranging menu of all the Asian-themed restaurants in America.

There is also a statistic called the Occupational Prestige Scale. Overall, given the very impressive APA indices for the more professional job categories, we shouldn't be surprised to find that APAs have significantly higher Occupational Prestige Scores than all other Americans combined.

The Top Floor: Asian Pacific American Occupational Prestige

	Non-APA (29248)	APA (296)
Occupational Prestige Score	43.61	49.89

In fact, APAs have higher Occupational Prestige Scores than every other American racial and ethnic group, including Whites.

The Top Floor: Asian American Occupational Prestige

Ethnic Group	OCC Prestige Score
Asian Pacific American (467)	48.01
White (23,435)	44.32
Other, Mixed (1,177)	42.19
Black (3,665)	39.65
American Indian (140)	37.81

Doing the Math

So, what is the one thing that the five highest skewing APA occupational categories and sub-categories have in common? They are technical, rational, logical and especially mathematical, since knowledge of and facility with math (and science) is a likely requirement for most of these positions.

Not surprisingly, given the occupational litany above and the earlier education-related data we examined, APAs are, in fact, better at math than other American ethnic groups – at least in terms of their SAT scores.

Ethnic Group	Math SAT
Asian Pacific Americans	532
Euro Americans	491
Native Americans	442
Mexican Americans	425
Puerto Ricans	406
African Americans	385

APA math abilities are especially pronounced at the high end of the scale. As we mentioned before, even though they comprised less than 3% of the population in 1995, APAs were 13% of all students scoring 700 or more on math SATs and a stunning 27% of those with a score of 750 and up.

Where does this mathematical advantage come from? Is it some sort of natural hard-wired innate ability, a push from their parents, just another reflection of the "hard work" philosophy of the immigrant, or something else?

In *Outliers, The Story of Success,*[5] Malcolm Gladwell argues that "being good in math may also be rooted in a group's culture." First, he establishes that Asians per se have a big edge in math vs. other countries. It's even larger than APAs domestically vs. other ethnic groups:

On international comparison tests students from Japan, South Korea, Hong Kong, Singapore, and Taiwan all score roughly the same in math, around the 98th percentile. The United States, France, England, Germany, and other western industrialized nations cluster at somewhere between the 26th and 36th percentile. That's a big difference.

Second, Gladwell observes that there is a marked difference between Asian and Western counting systems.

> It turns out here is also a big difference between in how number naming systems in Western & Asian languages are constructed. In English, we say fourteen, sixteen, seventeen, eighteen, and nineteen, so one might expect that we would also say oneteen, twoteen, threeteen and fiveteen. But we don't. We use a different form: eleven, twelve, thirteen and fifteen. . . . the number system in English is highly irregular. Not so in China, Japan & Korea. They have a logical counting system. Eleven is ten-one. Twelve is ten-two. Twenty-four is two tens four and so on.

The much simpler and more logical Asian counting systems have real behavioral consequences when it comes to students ability to learn math. Asian children learn to count much faster (4-year-old Chinese children can count, on average, to 40. American children that age can count only to 15). Asian children can perform basic functions such as addition far more easily because their number system is more "transparent."

> Ask an English-speaking seven year old to add thirty seven plus twenty-two in her head and she has to convert the words to numbers (37 + 22). Only then can she do the math: 2 plus 7 is 9 and 30 and 20 is 50, which makes 59.

> Ask an Asian child to add three-tens-seven and two-tens-two and then the necessary equation is right there, embed-

ded in the sentence. No number translation is necessary: It's five-tens-nine.

While this cultural counting theory does not take into account Asian Indians (a culture that invented the zero), nor differences in math ability among other APA ethnic groups, it does seem to provide a cogent explanation of the relatively better math abilities of most APAs though, not, perhaps, all.

An alternative, but "weird" hypotheses of Erling Boe that is mentioned in Gladwell's book suggests that mathematical ability and the ability to finish completing a long test questionnaire like the ones used for the International Comparison are the same thing because overall math/verbal completion percentages correlate highly with overall math scores. So, Asian "persistence," which, in the American context, brings us back full-circle to the "hard work" theory, is measuring the same sing as math ability.

Relative Verbal Weakness?

But APAs' strong mathematical proclivities also have a flip side. APAs have *relatively* poorer verbal abilities.

Going back to the SAT data that we showed earlier, we can see that APAs as a whole have the biggest gap of any ethnic group between their math & verbal SAT scores. APAs have a 119 point math/verbal gap vs. only 49 points for whites, 47 points for Native Americans, 53 points for Mexican Americans, 40 points for Puerto Ricans and 33 points for African Americans.

Ethnic Group	Math SAT	Verbal SAT
Asian Americans	532	413
Euro Americans	491	442
Native Americans	442	395
Mexican Americans	425	372
Puerto Ricans	406	366
African Americans	385	352

Remember that the data merely shows *relatively* poorer verbal skills compared to math. Although the gap between math and verbal scores is highest among APAs, their verbal scores are still second only to Euro Americans. This is significant for the fact that the vast majority of Native Americans and African Americans are U.S. born and considered native English speakers. Does this mean that verbal abilities are weak among APAs, or that math is just *so* much stronger?

The Census has the most direct measures on APAs' ability to speak English. Overall, APAs perform pretty "well." According to the 2005 American Community Survey, 25% of APAs say they speak English only, 63% say they speak an Asian language and speak English well or very well and only 12% say they speak an Asian language, but speak English "not well or not at all." In total, then 88% of APAs speak English only or speak English well or very well.

But, according to the more updated 2005-2007 ACS figures, close to 40% of all APA individuals speak English less than "very well," but only because so many (67%) are foreign-born.

	Native-Born	Foreign-Born	Total
English Only or very well	91%	53%	64%
English less than very well	9%	47%	36%

The behavioral expression of this relative lack of English ability plays out everyday in halting conversation, miscommunications and incomprehension epitomized among American students by the figure of the brilliant Asian-born math or science professor that none of his students can understand.

Another objective measure of this relative lack of verbal English language ability comes from the General Social Survey Gallup-Thorndike test of comprehension. As the table below shows, APAs score relatively lower than non-APAs on this test, with 46% of APAs scoring 5 or less.

Gallup-Thorndike test of comprehension

# of Words Correct in Vocabulary Test	Non-APA (5144)	APA (127)	Index
0	1%	2%	176
1	2%	4%	250
2	2%	9%	383
3	4%	8%	177
4	9%	11%	116
5	17%	12%	70
6	23%	21%	94
7	17%	15%	86
8	12%	9%	79
9	8%	5%	59
10	5%	4%	87

While APAs do worse than non-APAs overall, we always need to keep in mind that about 67% of Asians alone were foreign born in 2005-2007 ACS vs. only 40% of Hispanics in same source. So, APA's 54% 6+ passing score is better than Hispanic American's 41% 6+ passing score both in absolute terms and, especially, in relative ones, considering that only 41% of Hispanics in this time period were foreign born.

We should also stress that, lest APAs be dismissed as some sort of "good field/no hit" kind of minority, APAs' overall weakness in verbal & English is only a *relative* one, relative largely to White Americans as the combined GSS data below, shows.

Gallup-Thorndike test of comprehension

Ethinic Group	Number of Words Correct
White (17565)	6.24
Asian Pacific American (283)	5.27
Other, Mixed (604)	5.21
Hispanic (485)	5.08
Black (3058)	4.85
American Indian (102)	4.24

Still another, although this time more subjective, example of APA relative verbal weakness is provided by the General Social Survey. In administering this survey, NORC asks their interviewers to judge how well respondents understand the questions they are being asked. This data will both provide another example of APAs' relative language deficit, but also an instructive look at the dynamism of the Asian Pacific American population, how, though it may be perpetually young, well educated and higher income (thanks to the APA Escalator), today's Asian Pacific American population is in other ways different from yesterday's.

If we looked at the responses to this question in the 1990s, we would find, as the table below shows, that Whites had the best understanding of the questions and Asian Americans had the worst. Their understanding was at the time significantly worse than Black and Hispanic American's understanding of the questions at the time.

Respondent's Understanding of Questions Good	1990 to 1998
White (10352)	86%
Black (1586)	73%
Hispanic (1443)	73%
Asian American (181)	63%
Total	83%

But the 1990's were a time of high Asian immigration, a time when the overall APA population contained perhaps it's highest proportion of immigrants.

Considerable Improvement

By the 2000s, though, things had changed considerably. The escalator kept going up. Now, APAs scored on par with Blacks and Hispanics in terms of their understanding of the questions.

Respondent's Understanding of Questions Good	1990 to 1998	2000 to 2008
White (10352/11516)	86%	88%
Black (1586/2012)	73%	77%
Asian American (181/293)	**63%**	**77%**
Other, Mixed (Hispanic??) (430/780)	75%	74%
Total	83%	86%

Did a different, perhaps more Asian Indian and/or English speaking heavy mix of immigrants, those who were already more highly educated coming in on H1b visas, or was the ethnic mix largely the same but 2000s immigrants were simply better prepared immigrants, better schooled in English before leaving Asia?

Or, perhaps, English language assimilation among Asian immigrants already here accelerated? Because, looking at these cross-sectional examples, it's also important to remember that the underlying trend, both overseas among potential immigrants and domestically among Asian Pacific Americans is assimilationist when to comes to the English language.

A Decline in Asian Language Facility

Over time, America's powerful assimilationist engine dramatically erodes Asian language facility, the flip side of English language facility, from one generation to the next, as the table below shows. The ability to speak an Asian language declines from 76% among immigrants to 51% among children of immigrants to a mere 13% among 2nd generation+ APAs.

	Immigrant	Child of Immigrant	2nd Generation +
Speaks an Asian language	76%	51%	13%
Does Not Speak an Asian Language	24%	49%	87%

The history of APA immigration can also be charted in the Assimilation Matrix with more recent arrivals like South Asian/Indians being the least assimilated (more speak an Asian language in addition to English) and earlier arrivals like Japanese Americans being the most assimilated (less speak an Asian language in addition to English).

Ethnic Group	Speaks English & an Asian Language	Speaks English but no Asian Language
Japanese	25%	75%
Filipino	40%	60%
Korean	42%	58%
Chinese	63%	37%
Vietnamese	64%	36%
Other Asian	73%	27%
South Asian/Indian	85%	15%

English: The Official Language

Finally, assuming Asian language speakers speak only their own Asian ethnic language, it is inescapable that, as APAs assimilate, *English becomes THE "Official Language" of APAs.*

In other words, while 88% of APAs speak English only or speak English very well or well, the many who say they can speak an Asian language don't speak the same Asian language, as the table below shows.

Languages spoken	%
English Speaker	88%
English-only speaker	25%
Chinese speakers	12%
Tagalog speakers	11%
Vietnamese speakers	9%
Korean speakers	8%
Cantonese speakers	3%
Japanese speakers	3%
Hindi speakers	3%
Punjabi speakers	2%
Gujarathi speakers	2%
Mandarin speakers	2%
Urdu speakers	2%
Other language speaker	18%

Most of these languages are far different than, say, French, Italian and Spanish. So, if Cantonese speakers can't even understand Mandarin speakers and Gujarathi speakers can't even understand Hindi speakers, what chance does an APA have of communicating with another APA *apart from English*?

Clearly, because of the heavy contribution of immigration, Asian Pacific Americans represent a constantly evolving mix. It is, as we'll see in the next chapter, a moving target, one that may take awhile for us to get our heads around.

Overall, then the hallmarks of APAs as reviewed to date include:

- Growing
- Perpetually Younger, Very Well Educated with Higher incomes
  – Hold Higher Status & Technical Occupations
- Stronger math skills
- Relatively weaker verbal skills

In the next chapter, let's take a closer look at the specific ethnic who and where.

Implications for Marketers

We intend to go beyond a mere recitation of demographics. Some things are not exactly news. *Everyone* has shown that APAs are educated, primarily white collar, younger and wealthier than the average American. However, what "experts" don't point out:

- Language skills are *not weak*, only *relatively* weaker than math skills, which are off the charts.
- APA verbal measures are second only to Euro Americans, and higher than almost exclusively native English speaking African Americans and Native Americans.
- A high percentage of APAs are new Americans. There is still a high percentage of immigrant population that is driving growth.

- Amongst APAs there is also a drive for success. Historically, this was attained via education, which APAs embrace with enthusiasm and success.
- The traditional methods and measures of success chosen by APAs may reflect a more risk-averse attitude, at least when it comes to economic planning. Because of this, more dramatic brand loyalty and brand switching behavior may come into play when APAs are faced with purchase decisions.
- Because the immigration and Americanization process often occurs with adults 18–44, many brand choices already made by non-APAs are relatively new. For example, choice of bank and financial services suppliers or something as simple as basic packaged goods.
- It is also reasonable to assume, given the demonstrated math proficiency of APAs, that numerical and price-driven appeals may have greater salience with this group.

VIII. Diversity
The Long March to John's Creek, GA

America's APA population is becoming increasingly diverse – both ethnically and geographically. Here's an example: some dialogue from the animated sitcom *King of the Hill*.

> – *Are you Chinese or Japanese?"*
> – *I lived in California for the last 20 years, but I am Laotian. I come from Laos. A small country in Asia. Population 4.8 million.*
> – *Okay, but are you Chinese or Japanese?*

The first Asian Americans arrived in North America in the 17th century. Filipinos, fleeing mistreatment aboard Spanish ships, established a small settlement in 1693 in the bayous of current-day Louisiana.

The first systematic count of APAs occurred in the 1850 Census, when a total of 758 foreign residents from China were recorded. By 1860, this number had grown to 35,565. Most of these (34,933 or 99.99%) "Asiatics" were identified as living in California.

From this point on, America's "Asiatic" population grew slowly by fits and starts, as the graph a few pages ahead will show. It expanded with the 1869 opening of the Wakamatsu Tea and Silk Colony in California, to include "pre-tested" immigrants from Japan as well as a few immigrants from other Asian countries (although the Chinese continued to dominate immigration).

Historically, American immigration policy has constructed barrier after barrier to the creation of an Asian Pacific American community. Not only that, but American courts went to ridiculous lengths denying the idea that Asians were even "naturalizable." While the full depth of this story is best covered elsewhere, suffice it to say that for a nation that professed that "all men are created equal," whose tagline was "give me your tired, your poor, your huddled masses yearning to breathe free," the Statue of Liberty was turned toward Europe, not Asia.

One quick anecdote. According to Kronholz, "In 1922, the Supreme Court decided that a Japanese man had white skin but wasn't ethnically Caucasian, and it denied him citizenship. A year later, the Court decided a South Asian was ethnically Caucasian but not white, and it denied him citizenship, too."[2]

Things changed dramatically with the passage of the landmark Hart-Cellar Immigration Bill on October 3, 1965.

The bill opened immigration to all nations by ending nationality quotas and substituting a skill-based and family reunification system in its place. The provisions became effective in July, 1968.

While it may seem like a far-sighted attempt to address the black and white racial turmoil of the 1960s by creating a truly multiracial, multicultural society, in truth, the remarks of some prominent American politicians at the time belie that notion. Again, without going into too much depth, we offer several quotations to demonstrate the sheer cluelessness of many prominent American politicians about the likely consequences of this legislation:

> "This bill we sign today is not a revolutionary bill. It does not affect the lives of millions. It will not restructure the shape of our daily lives."
>
> — President Lyndon B. Johnson

> "In the final analysis, the ethnic pattern of immigration under the proposed measure is not expected to change as sharply as the critics seem to think."
>
> — Senator Ted Kennedy

> "The present estimate, based upon the best information we can get, is that there might be, say, 8,000 immigrants from India in the next five years."
>
> — Secretary of State Dean Rusk

As noted in the Center for Immigration Studies,[3] the source for several of these priceless quotes, there were actually 27,859 Indian immigrants over the five years following passage of the bill, three times Secretary Rusk's predicted number. And that was just the beginning.

From 1965 through 1993, immigration from India totaled 558,980 and immigration from Asia as a whole totaled 5,627,576. You see that things really started to take off after the provisions became active.

In fact, as the previous quotes clearly demonstrate, this act had the *unintentional result* of creating today's vibrant and growing Asian Pacific American community. It was an ironic answer to over a century of clearly intentional attempts to prevent it.

While Asian Pacific America may have started in the mists of history in the midst of a Louisiana swamp, and while it remained a tiny ethnic community thru the 1950s, the real action takes place, as the graph below demonstrates, after Hart-Cellar opens the Asian immigration spigot in 1968.

Asian Pacific American Population, 1860–2000 (in thousands)

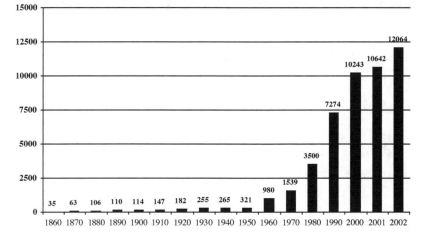

Along with this growth has come both *increasing ethnic diversity* within the APA population and a *greater geographical dispersion* of the Asian Pacific American population around the country. These trends are particularly evident since 1990.

Intra-ethnic diversity

Since 1960, the APA population has become much more diverse in terms of ethnic/national identity. In 1960, according to Collier "approximately 98% of Asian Americans were Japanese, Chinese, or Filipino Americans but today [even though these three groups have grown, they now] make up less than half of the Asian American population".[4]

Asian Ethnic Group	1960	1990	2000	2005-07 (Est)
Chinese Americans	217,000	1,645,000	2,433,000	3,016,000
Filipino Americans	180,000	407,000	2,039,000	2,345,000
Japanese Americans	360,000	848,000	996,000	823,000
Korean Americans	11,000	799,000	1,077,000	1,311,000
Vietnamese Americans	-	615,000	1,123,000	1,471,000
Asian Indian	-	815,000	1,679,000	2,449,000

There is another group – 1.5 million Asian Americans labeled "Other." As of 2005–2007, we find this diverse breakdown:

- 215,000 Cambodians
- 195,000 Hmong
- 194,000 Pakistanis
- 193,000 Laotians
- 150,000 Thai
- 93,000 Taiwanese
- 63,000 Indonesians
- 30,000 Sri Lankans
- 14,000 Malaysians

Clearly, the Asian Pacific America of 2007 looks a lot more like Asia than the Asian America of 1967.

Geographic dispersion

Immigrants have traditionally clustered in pockets of ethnic and cultural sovereignty once they've arrived in the U.S., e.g. the Irish in Butte, Montana, Basques in Boise, ID, etc. APAs were no exception to this rule. They arrived in California and clustered in Chinatowns and Japantowns for both safety and convenience.

Through the '60s, '70s and '80s, California and the Pacific region generally contained most of the APAs in the United States. But, once Hart Cellar opened the spigot, Asian Americans started to move, as the map below shows. Remember, all of this is happening while the APA population is rapidly growing across the board.

Proportion of Asian Americans Living within each Region, 1990 & 2005-7

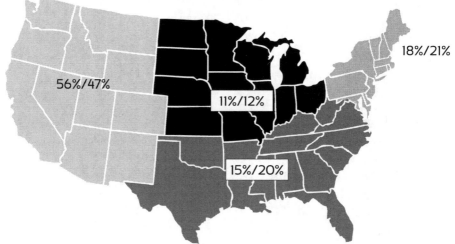

56%/47%

11%/12%

18%/21%

15%/20%

Since 1990, under the pressure of an open spigot, increased ethnic diversity among Asian immigrants and, perhaps, an opening of high tech business opportunities, the Asian American population declined significantly in its traditional West heartland region. It went from 56% in 1990 to 47% in 2007, the first time that the proportion of Asian Americans living in this region has ever been less that 50%. (Remember it was 99.99% in 1860!) But it's easy to understand as diversity grows. After all, does even the metaphorical

Chinatown have any attraction for an immigrant from Mumbai or Phnom Penh?

The APA population of the South increased significantly from 15% in 1990 to 20% in 2005-2007. APAs in the Northeast edged up a bit, while the Midwest was flat. But, again, this was flat growth in percentage only, as any Chicagoan viewing the dramatic expansion of Chinatown and the growth of the Indian/Pakistani community along Devon Avenue will attest.

Declining Proportion, Growing Population

Drilling down a bit more to the state level, we find that the most notable shifts include declines in the proportion of APAs who live in the traditional heartland states of California (from 39% in 1990 to 34% in 2007) and Hawaii (from 9.4% in 1990 to 3.4% in 2007).

At the same time, the proportion of APAs who live in non-traditional locales like Texas (from 4.4% in 1990 to 5.9% in 2005-7), New Jersey (from 3.7% in 1990 to 4.9% in 2005-7), Florida (from 2.1% in 1990 to 3.0% in 2005-7), Georgia (from 1% in 1990 to 2% in 2005-7), Nevada (from 0.5% in 1990 to 1.1% in 2005-7) and North Carolina (.7% to 1.2%) increased significantly.

The dispersion of the APA population among the states looks even more stark on an absolute basis. While the APA population almost doubled between 1990 and 2007 (an index of 177), the APA population did much more than double in New Hampshire, Delaware, Arizona, Florida, Tennessee, Texas, Arkansas, New Jersey, Minnesota, Nebraska, Virginia, Connecticut, South Carolina, Kentucky, Michigan, Colorado, Indiana, Massachusetts, Pennsylvania, Vermont, Wisconsin and Alabama. It more than tripled in North Carolina, Georgia and Nevada.

Metro area statistics tell much the same story. The proportion (but not the population) of APAs living in Los Angeles (20% in 1990, 15% in 2007), San Francisco (14% in 1990, 8% in 2007) and Honolulu (8% in 1990, 3% in 2007) all declined. Meanwhile the proportion of APAs living in New York/Northern NJ (13% to 15%), Washington, D.C (3% to 4%) and Dallas Fort Worth, Las Vegas, Atlanta and Houston (all 1% to 2%) increased.

In San Francisco itself, one of the cities with a long-established APA community, the APA population declined on an absolute basis (926,961 in 1990 to 907,431 in 2007) as it did in Honolulu (526,459 in 1990 to 404,068 in 2007). But it increased dramatically on an absolute basis in many other metro areas around the country, including the larger metropolitan areas around both these cities. The APA population:

- at least doubled in 37 metro areas,
- tripled in Austin, TX, Charlotte/Gastonia/Rock Hill, NC–SC, Worcester, MA, Orlando, FL, New Haven/Meriden, CT, Atlantic City, NJ, Nashville, TN, Phoenix, AZ and Tampa/St. Petersburg/Clearwater, FL,
- quadrupled in Las Vegas and Atlanta, and
- in Fayetteville/Springdale, Arkansas, the Asian American population actually increased from 1,043 in 1990 to 8,274 in 2007. That's a fraction under 800%.

Most Americans, of course, aren't really as cognizant about what's happening in their state or metro area as they are in their local town, city or "place" where demographic changes are much more apparent. This is where we see the real signs of the dispersal of APAs. It's also the level where we can best understand how Asian Pacific American communities are formed.

Without being exhaustive either in the research or reader senses, let's talk a look at the size and composition of APA communities in the traditional heartland state of California and three more nontraditional states in 2005-2007, using the very new and fresh American Community Survey (ACS) resource.

In the latest ACS data, a total of 45 places in California contain more than 25% APAs. Twenty places are 25% to 33% APA, 12 are 33% to 49% APA and 13 are over 50% APA. These include:

- Monterey Park (64%)
- Cerritos (60%)
- Milpitas (59%)
- Walnut (59%)
- Rosemead (58%)
- San Gabriel (57%)
- Cupertino (56%)
- Arcadia (54%)
- Daly City (53%)
- Temple City (52%)
- Alhambra (52%)
- Diamond Bar (51%)
- Rowland Heights CDP (Census Designated Place) (50.2%)

What's perhaps more interesting in an ethnographic sense is the Asian ethnic composition of these 13 places with an APA majority. First, let's take a look at how the APA population is distributed among the various Asian ethnic groups in the U.S. as well as in California.

	U.S.	U.S. %	California	California %
Total Asian Alone	12,951,215	100%	4,432,445	100%
Chinese	3,016,823	23%	1,148,800	26%
Asian Indian	2,449,173	19%	459,914	10%
Filipino	2,345,937	18%	1,111,161	25%
All Other	1,532,951	12%	460,315	10%
Vietnamese	1,471,832	11%	540,807	12%
Korean	1,311,814	10%	414,105	9%
Japanese	822,685	6%	297,343	7%

As the table above shows, Chinese, Asian Indians and Filipinos together account for about 60% of Asian Pacific Americans in the

U.S. and in California with Asian Indians being relatively more dispersed outside California and Filipinos being relatively more concentrated there.

But the question we want to address is what is the composition of APA communities in California – especially the state's 12 majority APA communities.

Chinese Majorities

Overall, even though Chinese comprise only 26% of Californians, Chinese majority composition is the rule in the 12 Asian Pacific American majority places in California we identified earlier.

- 77% of the APA population of Arcadia is Chinese, while in Alhambra, it's 76%, in San Gabriel 73%, in Temple City 72%, in Rowland Heights CDP 69%, in Monterey Park 66%, in Rosemead 61%, in Walnut 57% and in Diamond Bar 51%

Whether this Chinese American tendency "to clump" is an echo of the fortified Chinatowns of the past, the result of simple longevity, a consequence of the Hong Kong exodus, a cultural mass necessity or some other reason is hard to determine. But it's clearly apparent.

Other Asian Majorities

Only Daly City among these 12 Asian American majority places has a majority of a non-Chinese ethnic group. Two-thirds of the APAs living in Daly City are Filipino American.

Three of these places are more truly Asian Pacific American in the Pan-Asian sense, as they contain a mix of different Asian ethnicities. Cupertino, home of Apple, is more bi-ethnic than multi-ethnic. The mix is 48% Chinese, 31% Asian Indian, 9% Korean, 5% Japanese, 3% Vietnamese, 2% Filipino and 2% All Other.

Milpitas and Cerritos are more truly "melting wok," multi-ethnic Pan-Asian American communities:

- Milpitas is 30% Filipino, 26% Chinese, 20% Vietnamese, 19%

Asian Indian, 4% All Other, 2% Korean and 1% Japanese.
- Cerritos is 24% Filipino, 23% Korean, 21% Chinese, 12% Asian Indian, 8% All Other, 6% Vietnamese, and 6% Japanese.

Major Minorities
There are 45 California places that are 25% or more APA.

- Arcadia, Alhambra and San Gabriel are the most Chinese. 70% or more of their APA population is Chinese.
- Westminster (84% of its APA population is Vietnamese!), Garden Grove (71%) and Fountain Valley (57%) are the most Vietnamese.
- Daly City, Hercules and South San Francisco are the most Filipino with 50% or more of their APA population being Filipino.
- LaCanada/Flintridge (56% of its APA population is Korean), Cypress (37%) and Rancho Palos Verdes (25%) are the most Korean.
- Gardenia (44% of its APA population is Japanese), Torrance (37%) and Rancho Palos Verdes and West Carson (26% each) are the most Japanese.
- Fremont, Sunnyvale and Santa Clara are the most Asian Indian with 33% or more of their APA population being Asian Indian.

Immigration Frontiers
So much for the old established APA heartland. Now, how do trends differ on the frontiers of Asian immigration? What does the APA population look like outside of California, and more importantly, why does it exist? Particularly in the most unlikely of places – the South?

This is where we can get a real idea of community formation de novo. The common denominator appears to be opportunity, broadly defined, symbolized by growth.

The common indicators of a higher than normal APA presence seem to be white collar, particularly high tech jobs, an especially good school district for kids, and the close proximity of a university campus.

John's Creek, Georgia

First, let's take a look at the newest of these Asian Pacific American frontier communities, John's Creek, Georgia, "founded" in 2006 out of the northeast corner of unincorporated Fulton County. Overall, John's Creek is 16% APA with a total APA population of 13,349. The APA population is divided about equally among Koreans (31%), Chinese (31%) and Asian Indians (30%) with scatterings of the other main Asian ethnic groups including about 200 Filipinos and 100 Japanese.[5]

In this case, the APA escalator moved to an area of economic growth – the new South. With the balance of APA groups, one can assume there will also be a balance of APA vocations, from high-tech to mom-and-pop retail.

Spring Valley, Nevada

Spring Valley, Nevada, per *Wikipedia*, is a CDP, a Census Designated Place that began life as a giant subdivision. Pardee Homes began developing a master-planned housing community called Spring Valley, southwest of Las Vegas in the mid-1970s.

By 1981, residents grouped together to solicit the Clark County Commission to create an unincorporated town, which it did that May. The town originally encompassed just one square mile – it now occupies much of the southwest quarter of the Las Vegas Valley.

Overall, Spring Valley is 15% Asian Pacific American with a total APA population of 22,241. The APA population is more concentrated among Asian groups that have a gambling tradition – Filipinos (36%) and Chinese (28%).[6]

Cary, North Carolina

Cary is home to the SAS (Statistical Analysis System) Institute, the largest privately-held software company in the world. It has the most

PhDs per capita in the U.S. for towns larger than 75,000 people. Again, according to Wikipedia, most (60.7%) adults in Cary possess a baccalaureate degree or higher. Between January 2006 and January 2007, Cary was the 5th fastest growing city in the United States. It's also 9% Asian Pacific American with a total APA population of 10,564. Cary's APA community is a majority Asian Indian (51%) and about one-quarter Chinese (26%). It includes a scattering of other Asian ethnic groups including 145 Japanese Americans.[7]

Fayetteville/Springdale, Arkansas

Fayetteville is a city in Washington County, Arkansas. It is home to the University of Arkansas. Fayetteville was the second best educated city in Arkansas, a typical university town. While it is only 2% APA, we were struck by the fact that it seems to have one of the most ethnically diverse populations of any APA community in America. It's 24% other Asian (including 8% Hmong and 7% Laotian), 21% Asian Indian, 18% Chinese, 16% Vietnamese, 8% Korean and 8% Filipino.

This is dramatically different than the rest of Arkansas. The driving force? A major university.

An Escalator to the Ivory Towers

APA communities seem to be driven by opportunity in the guise of high-tech and growing communities and, of course, education, living more often in places that offer the most paths onto the escalator. For APAs, the door to higher education opened early. According to *America in Black & White*, as long ago as 1995, APAs were 24% of the student body at University of Chicago, 19% at Northwestern and 19% at Harvard.[8] While nobody talks about it in public, it appears that this is being managed somewhat.

More recently, according to Jennifer Rubin, "although Asians currently make up as much as 30 percent of the top college candidates as determined by SAT scores, National Merit and AP Scholar awards, and grades, the percentage of Asians admitted to Ivy League schools has held steady just below 20 percent."[9]

So it's no surprise that one can also observe the formation of Pan-Asian student communities in college towns across the country. A quick tour of the Big Ten helps to demonstrate this pattern.

- Asian Pacific Americans account for 15% of the population in Ann Arbor, MI, home of the University of Michigan vs. only 2.3% of the population of the state of Michigan,
- 9.3% in Champaign, IL, home of the University of Illinois vs. 4% of the population of Illinois,
- 7% in Madison, WI, home of the University of Wisconsin vs. 2% of the population of Wisconsin,
- 7% in Bloomington, IN, home of the University of Indiana vs. 1% of the population of Indiana,
- 6% in Iowa City, IA, home of the University of Iowa vs. 1.5% of the population of Iowa.

These communities are likely to be very Pan-Asian, as we saw with the distribution of the APA population at the University of Arkansas at Fayetteville.

To provide another example: Ann Arbor's APA community is 38% Chinese, 24% Asian Indian, 17% Korean, 11% Japanese, 5% Other Asian, 3% Filipino and 2% Vietnamese. Not only are they likely to be Pan-Asian, but the percentages of APAs represented here are for the entire metropolitan areas, not the merely campus proper, which would boost the percentages considerably.

Even though these APA student communities are only temporary, transient communities with significant turnover every year, they are one of the "futures" for Asian Pacific America writ large.

"The Melting Wok"

While we know that the future size of the APA community is highly dependent upon the spigot of immigration remaining as wide open as it has been since the 1980s and '90s, couple with the continued demand for high tech help, the future composition of the APA community is somewhat less certain. Because the next stage will ultimately depend on the *degree of interracial mixing* that takes place between APAs and the larger White, Black and Hispanic American communities as well as the *degree of interethnic mixing* that takes place within the Asian Pacific American communities. Essentially, there are three potential futures:

1. **Pan-Asian America: A solution in which Asians are both solutes and solvent**
   This scenario assumes that APAs, like the White Ethnics in *Beyond the Melting Pot* will melt into a larger Pan-Asian whole starting along predictable religious lines (e.g., Catholic Filipinos marrying Catholic Vietnamese, Protestant Koreans marrying Protestant Chinese). Eventually, this mixing may produce as many racially Asian "Americans" as it has among today's descendants of yesterday's Irish, German and Italian immigrants, who are very comfortable with their cross-cultural ancestry and increasingly describe themselves ethnically as Americans.[10]

2. **Eurasian America: A solution in which Asians are the solute and other Americans are the solvent**
   This "whitewashing" scenario assumes that APA's future trajectory will follow that of American Indians, with APAs mixing with other races to the point that the "hapa" population rivals the Asian Alone population. For example, among the current American Indian population, only 55% of what some would call Amerindians, designate themselves American Indian and Alaska Native Alone. 45% designate themselves American Indian and some other race, including 32% American Indian and White and 6% American Indian and Black.[11]

3. **Asian Ethnic America: A suspension in which the Asian ethnicities stay cohesive – at least for another generation.**
   The first two "solutions," of course, represent the two polar ex-

tremes scenarios with a perhaps more likely middle scenario resembling more of a suspension than a solution, i.e., a "flour in water" scenario, in which strong intra-ethnic bonds stay clumped together, trumping the melting pot/melting wok effect.

During the first generations of European immigration, it was much more common to marry within the community (Irish/ Irish, Italian/Italian, etc.) than in the next generation. Certainly, this scenario will hold true to some extent.

Racial Diversity and Racism

One quick note on the upcoming discussion. In this section, we will see that racism and its related behaviors and attitudes are not the exclusive domain of Caucasian America. As Asian Pacific Americans contribute to a growing diversity, they also bring their own unique perspectives. We will also see that, as the Americanization process proceeds, that APAs born in the United States evolve in the ways they add to diversity. Some trends seem to go across the board, while others are unique to individual groups. For example, Filipinos are one APA group with greater than average Hispanic intermarriage. We assume this is a result of the common Spanish language heritage. And, across the board, we see an Asian heritage that is becoming increasingly Eurasian.

Remember, the Chinese description of Europeans was "white devil." So let's not be surprised if some of America's racial attitudes aren't reflected on the other side – though not quite a mirror image. Moreover, while many Americans may still possess the "they all look alike" perspective, you will see that within the Asian community, for whatever reasons, historical or otherwise, prejudicial attitudes between groups may be both common and mutual. The numbers show some very interesting trends within this increasingly diverse group and we find that they may even have their differences in common. So let's roll up our sleeves, get out the calculators, and take a look.

Some Current Data

Since the likelihood of any of these futures is dependent upon levels of and trends in inter- and intra-marriage rates, let's turn to those numbers for some answers, particularly the Asian American numbers. But first, let's give a big tip of the cap to Dr. C.N. Le, Professor of Sociology at the University of Massachusets at Amherst for his invaluable Asian-Nation.org site, from which much of the detailed Asian Pacific American intra-marriage data was sourced.[12]

Let's also understand that, to some degree, each of these three scenarios will hold true.

Generally, according to Census figures, about 6% of American marriages are now interracial. This compares to less than 1% in 1970. Interracial marriage and dating are meeting with increasing social acceptance, with young people in the vanguard.

According to a 2005 Gallup Poll, 95% of 18- to 29-year-olds approve of blacks and whites dating. This isn't merely a stated belief. Almost 60% of 18- to 29-year-olds said they, themselves, have dated someone of a different race.

According to Lee and Edmonston as of the 2000 Census, 97.3% of Whites were married to other Whites, 90.3% of Blacks were married to other Blacks, 84% of APAs were married to other APAs. However, only 43.3% of American Indians were married to other American Indians – less than half. This last finding, which indicates that American Indians have passed the "whitewashed" tipping point (potential solution #2) at the couple level, means, inevitably, that the whitewashed tipping point at the individual level is not too far down the road.

Of course, part of the explanation for these levels, as the authors explain, is that "the intermarriage rate is inversely related to a group's size—that is intermarriage is more likely among small populations."[13]

For whatever reason, white men are more attracted to APA women as spouses than white women are to APA men, and curiously enough, vice versa. Le, at Asian-Nation.org, among others, offers a few theories including the supposed existence of some sort of Asian female fetish among White American men and on the other side of the equation, the high "income premium" that White American women, at least experimentally, demand for dating non-White men.

This data suggests that to make their Hispanic man dating likelihood the same as a White man's, the Hispanic man would have to earn $77,000 more than the White man, while a Black man would have to earn a $154,000 income premium, and an Asian man an astronomical $246,000 income premium plus. Clearly, actual human behavior is at variance with these statistics, but they do provide directional insight. Regardless of why, the tendency clearly exists as the table below shows.[14]

Asian Pacific American Inter Marriage Rates

	APA Wife	APA Husband	APA Spouse
Asian alone	77%	91%	84%
White alone	19%	8%	14%
Two or more races	2%	1%	1%
Some other race alone	1%	1%	1%
Black alone	1%	0%	1%
NHPI alone	0%	0%	0%
Asian alone	0%	0%	0%

So, 91% of APA men married women who are also Asian alone. But only 77% of APA women married men who are also Asian alone.

Mixed Marriage and Racial Identity

Looking at some of the consequences of these mixed marriages for individual's racial identity, we find, not surprisingly given age lags and the immigration factor, that in the 2005-2007 ACS, 90% of APAs chose the category Asian Alone. Only 10% chose the cat-

egory Asian and Other Race – about 6 points below the 2000 Asian Pacific American intermarriage rate among APA couples.

Overall, the APA population appears to be tending towards the "Whitewash" future but at a rather slow rate.

Given the significantly higher intermarriage rate among Japanese Americans (the vast majority of whom are third and fourth generation), this may provide insight into the future of other APA groups. Time will tell.

Here is the ACS breakdown. Remember, all the numbers below "Mixed Asian & Other Race(s)" are a further breakdown of that 10% number.

Race(s)	N	%
Asian Alone	12,951,215	90%
Mixed Asian & Other Race(s)	1,439,224	10%
White; Asian	1,011,904	7%
Black or African American; Asian	118,429	1%
Asian; Some other race	101,911	1%
Asian; Native Hawaiian/Pacific Islander	101,767	1%
American Indian/Alaska Native; Asian	27,949	0%
Population of three races	62,134	0%
Population of four races	13,807	0%
Population of five races	1,242	0%
Population of six races	81	0%

Asians in America generally intermarry within the Asian race, but to pick a probable future for them, we still need to know if and to what extent they marry within or across different Asian ethnicities. Specifically, do they marry within their "own Asian" ethnic group (Chinese-Chinese or Korean-Korean) or to an Other Asian (Chinese-Korean or Indian-Japanese) ethnic group?

Using Le's more updated 2007 figures for Asian Pacific Americans specifically from the American Community Survey, we can see that here, the picture is more mixed.

Overall, as the table below shows, all APAs have the propensity to marry within their own group. This model includes all marriages that involve at least one APA. The benefit of this approach is that you get a complete picture of all marriages involving APAs. The drawback is that since most married APAs are immigrants, many of them got married in their home countries before immigrating to the U.S. – i.e., they came to the U.S. already married. So it's certainly not surprising the data shows how much the APA marriage patterns vary, from Japanese-Americans (J) being the least likely to marry someone from their own national background (55%) to Indian Americans (I) being the most likely.[9]

Asian Pacific American Intermarriage Rates by Ethnic Group

	J	F	K	C	V	I
Own Asian	55%	70%	79%	85%	88%	93%
Other Asian	8%	3%	3%	4%	3%	1%
White	30%	19%	16%	10%	7%	5%
Other	7%	7%	2%	2%	2%	2%
Black	1%	2%	1%	0%	0%	1%
Hispanic/Latino	3%	3%	1%	1%	1%	1%
Multiracial & Others	3%	2%	1%	1%	1%	0%

Part of this, as Le points out above, has to do with the native-born/ foreign-born proportion of each group (Japanese Americans are more native-born, Indian Americans are more foreign born) and the respective size of each group (the number of Japanese Americans is smaller than the number of Indian Americans), but these caveats aside, this data has a lot to tell us about the likely futures of APAs, findings that come into sharper relief when we aggregate these six largest groups of APAs into a total.

Other factors, such as Filipinos and Hispanics often sharing the same language and the same neighborhoods, would certainly contribute.

Asian Pacific American Intermarriage Rates, All APAs

	Total*
Own Asian	81%
Other Asian	3%
White	11%
Other	3%
Black	1%
Hispanic/Latino	1%
Multiracial & All Others	1%
Total J, F, K, C, V, I Married	5056

As the table above shows, 84% of these APAs, again, married within their race, but 96% of them married within their own ethnic group while only 4% married a member of another Asian ethnic group. In fact, "out-marriage" to another Asian ethnic group is much less frequent than "out-marriage" to White Americans, although, again, this is partly due to relative population sizes. What is more surprising perhaps *and, for the moment, makes the Pan-Asian Melting Wok scenario least likely*, is that APAs are a bit more likely to marry Blacks, Hispanics/Latinos, Multi-Racial and All Other spouses (2.89%) than they are members of other Asian groups (2.82%).

Then again, does this low intermarriage rate hold up if we exclude foreign born immigrants, many of whom are already married to fellow home country Indians or Chinese or Koreans when they arrive? Again, Le's Native Born Only data is invaluable even with caveats.[10]

Asian Pacific American Intermarriage Rates, Native Born APAs

Native Born Only	Total
Own Asian	46%
Other Asian	8%
White	35%
Other (B, H/L, M & AO)	10%
Black	2%
Hispanic/Latino	5%
Multiracial & All Others	4%
N	786,500

To date, these results, overall, even with the smaller sample, are even more revealing and pretty much put the *Pan-Asian Melting Wok scenario scenario to bed*. In fact, responses to a GSS survey addressing this issue suggests that, at least ordinally, these intermarriage patterns above are grounded in solid attitudinal preferences below suggesting perhaps, some sort of equilibrium.

Asian Pacific Americans Who Favor Close Relative Marrying.

	Favor	Indiff	Oppose	+
Asian	61%	33%	6%	55%
White	41%	49%	10%	30%
Hispanic	35%	49%	16%	16%
Black	28%	47%	25%	3%

- 55% of APAs are in favor (net) of allowing a close relative to marry another APA and 54% of Native Born APAs are, in fact married to other Asians.
- 30% of APAs are in favor (net) of allowing a close relative to marry a White American and 35% of Native Born APAs are, in fact, married to White Americans.
- 16% of APAs are in favor (net) of allowing a close relative to marry a Hispanic American and 5% of Native Born APAs are, in fact, married to Hispanic Americans.

- 3% of APAs are in favor (net) of allowing a close relative to marry a Black American and 2% of Native Born APAs are, in fact, married to Black Americans.

These relative racial preferences among Asian Pacific Americans also hold up in a New American Media poll conducted among selected Asian ethnic groups in December 2006. When asked if they had ever dated someone of another race, 21% of APAs said that they had dated someone who was White, 6% said they had dated someone who was Hispanic and 3% said that they had dated someone who was Black.

Breaking down the Native Born numbers by the six main ethnic groups, again following Le's lead, we find that native born Korean and Filipino Americans are already at the same Whitewash stage as American Indians with only a minority (39% each) marrying within race and a majority (61%) marrying a spouse of another race with Korean-Americans being more relatively more likely to marry Whites and Filipino Americans being more likely to marry Whites and Hispanics. Native Born Vietnamese Americans are most resistant to marrying non-Asians, while Chinese, Indian and Japanese Americans are in the middle with about 3 in 5 marrying someone of another Asian race and about half marrying an own race Asian.

Inter- and Intra-marriage Rates among Native Born Asian Pacific Americans, by Group

Native Born Only	K	F	C	I	J	V	Total
Own Asian	29%	32%	49%	55%	52%	64%	46%
Other Asian	10%	7%	10%	2%	9%	7%	8%
White	53%	42%	35%	34%	30%	22%	35%
Other	8%	19%	6%	8%	9%	7%	10%
Black	2%	3%	1%	2%	1%	2%	2%
Hispanic/Latino	3%	10%	3%	4%	4%	3%	5%
Multiracial & Others	2%	7%	2%	2%	5%	2%	4%
N	72500	171400	185100	63500	208300	85700	786500

At this stage, the *Pan-Asian Melting Wok hypothesis* seems inoperative. Native Born Korean Americans are 6.3 times as likely to marry another race than they are to marry a non-Korean Asian American. The ratios for the other 5 ethnic groups are, respectively, , 4.1 for Vietnamese- and Chinese-Americans, 4.3 for Japanese Americans, 8.7 for Filipino Americans and a whopping, 21.0 for Indian Americans.

The source of this reluctance to marry members of other Asian ethnic groups is not hard to find, especially if we keep in mind the fact that 67% of Asian Pacific Americans are foreign born. Quite simply, as the table from Pew below shows, except for the relatively favorable reciprocity between Japanese and Indians (inspired, no doubt that they both have less than favorable views of China) only a small minority (28%) of Japanese have favorable views of China and only small minorities of Chinese have favorable views of Japan (21%) or India (33%).[15] Based on history, it seems clear that Korean attitudes toward Japan would also show negative.

Hostility Among Neighbors

Favorable Rating of	China	Japan	India
China		28%	47%
Japan	21%		60%
India	33%	65%	

These do not seem to be merely foreign policy attitudes that reflect typical big power views of competition. As Pew demonstrates, the closer one looks, the more negative the views of each other, at least for Japanese and Chinese citizens. Here are some examples.

Almost 7 in 10 Chinese (69%) think the Japanese are "arrogant." 66% of Japanese feel the same way about the Chinese. Almost 7 in 10 Chinese (68%) think the Japanese are "greedy" while 69% of Japanese feel the same way about the Chinese. Over half (57%) of the Chinese think the Japanese are 'rude' while 52% of Japanese feel the same way about the Chinese.

Not only do these two groups rate each other high on negative attributes, they also rate each other low on positive ones. Only 9% of Chinese think that the Japanese are "generous" and only 1 in 5 Japanese feel the same way about the Chinese. Only 15% of Chinese think Japanese are "honest," and 23% of Japanese feel the same way about the Chinese. Only 22% of Chinese think that the Japanese are "tolerant" and only 27% of Japanese feel the same way about the Chinese.

While we don't have similar data on what Vietnamese and Chinese or Japanese and Koreans or Japanese and Filipinos think of each other, this "imported" inter-ethnic distrust and disdain, as the figures above clearly demonstrate, presents a powerful explanation for the low level of ethnic mixing among the APA population. Unless there is a dramatic change in these attitudes, the low level of inter-ethnic mixing, whether measured among all APAs or the even narrower group of native born APAs (among whom "imported" inter-ethnic distrust and disdain should be lower) seems to pretty much rule out a Pan-Asian future.

Eurasian Growth

Although focusing on the Native Born only, may, as Le suggests, overemphasize out-marriage, it is certainly the case that the Filipino and especially Korean numbers indicate that an increasingly Eurasian future may be in the cards for at least some APA ethnicities. Then again, the relative resistance of Japanese and Chinese Americans, with a native born contingent that includes the most 3rd and 4th generation Americans is good evidence for the Steady As She Goes scenario. Add to that the fact that most of the largest Asian American places are mono-ethnic (9 Chinese, 1 Filipino, 3 Pan-Asian). And, given the low Vietnamese intermarriage rates, it's certainly no surprise that Westminister, CA is 84% Vietnamese.

While much will depend upon how wide the immigration spigot is open, other forecasters of the future of Asian Pacific America appear to lean somewhere in between.

Perez and Hirschman quoting Edmonston, Lee and Passel, observe that "assuming current trends continue to 2050, about a quarter of Asian Americans and African Americans will have mixed ancestry as will nearly half of all Hispanic Immigrants."[16]

But it seems that Asian Pacific Americans who marry outside their race don't leave their Asian heritage completely. This comes from the ancestry data in the 2005-2007 ACS survey: *a majority of Asian Americans of mixed Asian White parentage do tend to retain their Asian identity.*

As the table below shows, 62% of White-Asian Americans reported their first ancestry as Asian (including .4% who identified their first ancestry as Eurasian and 3.3% who identified as Asian (only)), while only 24%-26% reported their first ancestry as White (including 1.5% who identified their first ancestry as American/United States).

Asian Ancestry Identification among White-Asian Americans

First ancestry reported	%
Asian	62%
European	24%
Other/unc/not rept	4%
Other White (incl. "American")	2%
American Indian	1%
Middle Eastern	1%
Latin American	1%
PI	0%
Canadian	0%

Again using ancestry questions instead of race, we find that only about 1% of the estimated 2.6 million Americans who choose Chinese as their first ancestry claimed Filipino, Vietnamese or Japanese as their second ancestry, about the same number who mentioned German as their second ancestry.[13] The vast majority (92%) of those who say their first ancestry is Chinese don't claim any second ancestry.

Chinese First Ancestry

2nd ancestry	%
Not reported	92%
Filipino	1%
Vietnamese	1%
Japanese	1%
German	1%
Italian	0.5%
All Others	3.5%
Base: First Ancestry Chinese	2,660,036

Again, using ancestry questions instead of race, but this time using the estimated 2.3 million American who claim Filipino first ancestry, we see a much more dramatic difference in second ancestry. This is a more classic Melting Pot pattern – a classic White Ethnic Melting Pot pattern not a Melting Wok one. First of all, more than 1 in 4 Filipinos reported a second ancestry vs. less than 1 in 10 Chinese. But most of those second ancestries were European (especially German and Irish) rather than Asian (a scant .1% being Chinese or Japanese).

Filipino First Ancestry

2nd ancestry	%
Not reported	74.5%
German	5.0%
Irish	4.5%
English	3.1%
French	1.3%
Italian	1.3%
Chinese	0.1%
Japanese	0.1%
All Others	11.1%
Base: First Ancestry Filipino	2,313,771

Overall, these Filipino ancestry numbers more closely resemble those of a White Ethnic melting pot ethnic group like the Germans, as the table below shows, fully half of whom reported a second ancestry.

German First Ancestry

2nd Ancestry	%
Not reported	49.83%
Irish	14.29%
English	8.16%
French	3.37%
Polish	2.70%
Dutch	2.52%
Filipino	0.06%
Japanese	0.05%
All Others	19.02%
First Ancestry German	34,340,979

Implications for Marketers

Okay, lots of numbers to digest all at once. What do they mean?

This chapter is really about the American Dream as it is shaped by acculturation and assimilation, and will be explained more fully in subsequent chapters. What we can take away from the data is:

- As geographic diversity grows, the "place of first landing" has become and is becoming less and less important. No longer are immigrants siphoned off into Chinatowns, destined to stay for a generation until their children can become a part of the American fabric.
- While APA immigrants still need a connection point, there is much more choice available.
- University communities are also playing a leading role as the APA escalator makes regular stops for both students and faculty.
- A true Pan-Asian culture is emerging. Historical grievances aside, rice is rice. While another ethnic group may not be immediate

family, they are at least close cousins compared to non-APAs and share many attitudes – even when it is a negative one toward another APA group, the attitudes are surprisingly reciprocal.

- The ethnic enclaves of the 20th century are both reinforcing themselves via Pan-Asian sensibility, but also breaking out in what seems like the most unlikely of places until you connect it to expertise in specific job markets.
- Intermarriage/outmarriage amongst APAs – particularly those who are native born – may be a microcosm of where the rest of the country is headed. Less value is placed on purity of bloodline, and while not as pronounced, is reflective of mestizo/carioca philosophy (more on this in Chapter 13).
- Eurasian APAs still retain key elements of Asian cultural values.
- A prediction. With this change in biological ethnic definitions will almost certainly come attitudinal shifts to be felt and created by future generations.

Cultural Considerations: "Made in America?"

In his "Eyes on the Road" column in the *Wall Street Journal*, columnist Joseph B. White asks,

"Could there be a more American vehicle than a 'Jeep Patriot?' Nothing on four wheels says American more proudly than Jeep, the rugged brand that helped America win World War II, and that has ferried millions into our wild, Western spaces since. Yes, in fact, there could be a more American SUV than the Jeep Patriot. A Toyota Sequoia would be one of them. The Sequoia is 80% 'domestic' according to the National Highway Traffic Safety administration, while the Jeep Patriot is only 66%. 'Buy American' is back on the agenda in Washington. So what should you buy if you want to buy a truly America-made car? For the 2008 model year, the government says the Ford Crown Victoria has the highest percentage of U.S./Canada content at 90%. The only hitch: It's assembled in Canada."[17]

IX. Lifestyle
Thinking & Living Asian American

"No one who could rise before dawn 365 days a year fails to make his family rich."

— Chinese Proverb

"5 Years Business, 10 Years House."

— Korean American Cab Driver

Psychographically, Asian Pacific Americans are unique in many ways. In fact, some of the literature we'll review strongly suggests that Asians as a whole, especially East Asians, may be "wired differently" than non-Asians.

Since psychographics deals with personality, attitudes, beliefs, opinions, interests and lifestyles, perhaps the best place to start is with religion & politics, two basic foundational values.

Religion

A plurality of APAs are Christians – 43% according to 2000 to 2008 GSS data, with 23% Protestant and 17% Catholic. Generally speaking, most Filipinos and Vietnamese are Catholic, at least nominally, while most Korean Americans are Protestant.

Another large group practice Eastern religions: 13% Buddhism, 10% Hinduism. Another 7% are Islamic and 23% are secular, considerably higher than among the non-APA population.

Religious Preference	Non-APA (14531)	APA (326)	Index
Christian	82%	43%	52
Jewish	2%	1%	47
None	15%	23%	152
Eastern (B, H, Other)	1%	24%	4140
Moslem/Islam	0%	7%	2248
All Other	2%	2%	109

The large, recently released 2008 American Religious Identification Survey echoes these findings (38% Christian, 27% Secular & 21% Eastern Religions). It also shows Asian Pacific Americans to be on track with other Americans in slouching towards secularism.[1]

	2000	2008
Christian	43%	38%
Secular	22%	27%
Eastern	22%	21%

Moreover, APAs overall appear to be only nominally religious. They attend religious services less frequently than other Americans with half of APAs saying they attend only once a year or less, an index of 135 and only 23% saying they attend nearly every week or more often, an index of 68.

Frequency of Attendance of Religious Services	Non-APA (N=52,185)	APA (N=325)	Index
Never	16%	27%	173
Less Than Once A Year	8%	7%	88
Once A Year	13%	16%	125
Several Times A Year	13%	9%	72
Once A Month	7%	9%	130
2-3x A Month	9%	8%	93
Nearly Every Week	6%	3%	49
Every Week	20%	17%	85

APAs also pray less than non-APAs (23% pray several times a day, an index of 75 and 34% pray less than once a week/never, an index of 147) and express less confidence in the existence of God: 52% say they know God exists vs. 63% of non-APAs.

But part of this seemingly different, more casual attitude towards religious services and expression may simply disguise differences in types of religious practice and cloud strong differences among Asian ethnic groups.

According to the 2003–2007 ATUS Survey, while Asian Pacific Americans spend less time attending religious services than non-APAs (5.57 minutes a day vs. 6.27 minutes a day), they spend more time "participating in religious practices" than non-APAs (2.3 minutes a day vs. 1.35 minutes). When you add the two together, it's a wash. APAs spend 7.87 minutes a day either attending religious services or participating in religious practices vs. 7.62 minutes a day for non-APAs.[2]

According to a New American Media poll of selected APA ethnic groups conducted in December 2007, 62% of APAs overall said that religion or spirituality was very important in their life. This was far lower than among Blacks (88%) or Hispanics (77%). But this is because 77% of Filipino Americans, 75% of Vietnamese Americans and 67% of Korean Americans said that religion or spirituality was very important in their life vs. only 29% of Chinese-Americans (Japanese Americans were not included in the survey).[3]

Politics

Although they tilt slightly Democratic, they also appear to be only nominally political and nominally ideological. Half (51%) of APAs say they're independents, an index of 142 vs. all other Americans.

Political Party Affiliation	Non-APA (52421)	APA (325)	Index
Strong Democrat	16%	8%	50
Not Strong Democrat	21%	27%	125
Independent, Near Dem	12%	14%	117
Independent	15%	30%	204
Independent, Near Rep	9%	7%	82
Not Strong Republican	16%	8%	48
Strong Republican	10%	7%	69

While they tilt slightly liberal (20% of APAs say they're liberal or extremely liberal, an index of 133 vs. Non-APAs), 69% are, like most other Americans (68%) mostly moderates.

Think of Self As Liberal or Conservative	Non-APA (52421)	APA (325)	Index
Extremely Liberal	3%	3%	108
Liberal	12%	17%	146
Slightly Liberal	**13%**	**14%**	**104**
Moderate	**39%**	**41%**	**107**
Slightly Conservative	**16%**	**14%**	**86**
Conservative	15%	9%	64
Extremely Conservative	3%	2%	66

What is true in general is not always true in the specific. There have been numerous cases involving political fund-raising in which at least one of the principals was an APA.

More generally, APAs also have different basic value priorities than Non-APAs, values that, coming full circle, tend to propel them up the escalator toward the higher education and higher incomes noted earlier.

Family Values

When we've asked APAs in focus groups to identify basic Asian Pacific American Values, Family usually comes first (as it does with Non-APAs). This is followed by Education (*"knowledge is the power that no one can take away from you"*) and Food, neither one of which shows up among non-APAs (although Jewish-Americans will mention Education, and Jewish and Italian Americans, but not German, English or Irish Americans, will mention Food). These Top 3 pretty much play out quantitatively among Asian Pacific Americans but with some interesting twists.

Family, for instance, does appear to be the top value among Asian Pacific Americans quantitatively as well, but we have to keep in mind that *family values* may mean something very different than it does to non-APAs.

Asian Family Values involve much more than a relationship between parents and children. It encompasses patterns of rights and responsibilities involving a broad network of extended family members, a commitment to all living members of one's extended family. Often, that extension goes even further. It appears that is may include those who are no longer living and those not yet born.

— If I mess up, it makes the family mess up (or look bad).

Hard Work, as we'll see below, is also deeply connected to Family Values. The point of this Hard Work, though, is not self-promotion as might be the case among many non-Asian Americans, but, rather, the promotion of the interests of one's family.

— You work for the good of the family.

— Hard work and sacrifice to take care of the family.

Generally, the idea of parental obligation also looms larger in the minds of Asian Pacific Americans than other Americans. Almost half (45%) of 18-49 year old APAs in a 2006 Ronin Group/AZN survey said said "taking care of my parents is an important value" vs. only 38% of non-APAs, an index of 118.

Two thirds of a broader 18+ APA population sample think it's a good idea for the aged to live with their children. This is an index of 135 vs. non-APAs.

Should Aged Live with Their Children?	Non-APA (6836)	APA (148)	Index
A Good Idea	49%	66%	135
A Bad Idea	32%	18%	57
Depends	19%	16%	84

The idea of Asian Family Values also casts APAs' *drive & determination* in a different light. Perhaps the biggest difference between younger APAs and their non-APA counterparts is that 18-49 year old APAs have more of what psychographers might call an Achiever /Succeeder mentality.

- 62% of 18–49 year old APAs say that *success in their careers* is one of their Top 5 values vs. only 38% of 18-49 year old non-APAs, an index of 163.

Let's add this. They're not shy about saying that money is part of the career success equation.

- 28% of 18–49 year old APAs say that *being rich* is one of their Top 5 values vs. only 16% of 18-49 year old non-APAs, an index of 175.

But a large part of this Achiever/Succeeder mentality can be laid at the door of their stern, demanding, Ivy League dreaming parents and, to add to the pressure, their broader extended family network.

- 19% of younger APAs say meeting parent's expectations is one of their Top 5 values vs. only 11% of non-APAs, an index of 173.
- APAs 18–49 are more likely to agree with the statement they "feel great pressure from their families to succeed" (49% vs. 32% for Non-APAs, an index of 153).

We should also point out that this strong sense of family pressure for success, while peaking in the children of an immigrant generation at a level almost twice as high as among non-APA 18–49 year olds, is still significantly higher among Asian immigrants (whose parents may still be living in Asia) and among the more assimilated APAs who are second generation and beyond (Generation 2+ or G2+). While we'll show plenty of evidence that APA parents are "pushers," it's also important to keep in mind that "my family" has a broader, deeper context. It does not refer solely to the nuclear family in the Asian case.

	% "feel(ing) great pressure from family to succeed."
Immigrant (501)	45%
Child of Immigrant (334)	59%
Generation 2+ (189)	41%

Asian Pacific American parents, in the words of their children, had unquestioned authority, were extremely strict and very demanding in terms of their expectations.

APA kids show more respect for their elders in general.

> – *You respect your elders.*

> – *You don't do whatever you want to do.*

Sassing, talking back, arguing are not options.

> – *Respect and manners … no back talking.*

> – *You're not supposed to talk back, but listen.*

> – *I can't argue my way out of anything … that's disrespect.*

You have no choice but to obey:

> – *You never say no to them.*

> – *You do what you're told.*

> – *You obey your parents… whatever they say is always correct.*

The lives of APA kids are closely controlled and monitored.

> – *My dad was extremely strict … He'd have a time schedule. School lets out at 2:15. He'll have the bus schedule and he'll time it, the time it takes me to walk from the bus to get home. Then he'd call to see if I'm home.*

> – *I couldn't date until college.*

> – *I can't wear jeans with holes … I can't sit with my legs crossed.*

> – *My mom was especially controlling … I still see her over my shoulders … She'd make me feel guilty.*

> – *If you're caught smoking, you have to smoke ten packs.*

APAs also seem simultaneously mystified and disturbed by how their non-APA friends' parents behaved. They felt that non-APA parents were much more lenient than their parents.

> – *As long as you are happy. They are more worried about their kids' happiness.*

They also felt that non-APA children were much less respectful of their parents.

> – *The lack of respect for parents in America … if I said some of those things I would have got smacked.*

Most important, nowhere did parenting styles differ further than in the sky high expectations of Asian Pacific American parents – especially as presented in the AZN documentary, *Ivy Dreams.*

Here is a brief conversation between Diana Shen, a high school senior from Astoria, NY and her mother, regarding her SAT score:

Mother: *How did you score?*
Diana: *770*
Mother: *It's okay, not bad . . . not bad, but not so good.*
Diana: *I'm pretty satisfied with my score, even if she isn't.*
Mother: *Unless she get 800, then I would hug her.*

How heavy is the pressure? Here is a comment from Sophie Hu, a high school senior living in Lancaster, PA:

> – *If I don't get in to Harvard, my Dad suggested I move back to China.*

But, of course, in the Asian context, APA parents aren't acting alone with only their own desires and ambitions at stake. They, too, answer to the higher authority of the "Asian family," acting merely as the agents of their generation. It's the combination of this higher authority, cross-generational responsibilities, sky high expectations, and unquestioned obedience that defines the Asian Family Values

Contract, the ultimate source of the idea of the sub-800 "Asian fail"[4] and the outstanding performances by APA children and young adults in the American educational system. It's worth repeating.

- APAs only account for 4% of 18 & 19 year olds, but they "currently make up as much as 30% of the top college candidates as determined by SAT scores, National Merit and AP Scholar awards, and grades."[5] Nonetheless, the proportion of Asians admitted to Ivy league schools is "only" 20 percent.

It's not just demanding parents and obedient kids that make this work, it's a generational deal, a 2-way street, that really makes the Asian Family Values Contract work in practice. The dimensions of this deal are most apparent when we look at the "FOBs," using some data from Rumbaut on children of immigrants in Southern California.[6]

Most Asian immigrant parents provided their children with a safer and more stable environment to grow up in.

It is safer in the sense less than 1 in 10 (6%) children of Korean & Chinese immigrants grew up in a neighborhood with drugs and gang crime followed by Vietnamese (10%), Filipino (10%), & Cambodian/Laotian (12%) immigrants. This compares to 6%, 21% and 27% of native born Whites, Mexican & Blacks, respectively.

It is more stable in the sense that almost 9 in 10 (87%) children of Korean immigrants grew up in a family with both parents, followed by Chinese (86%), Vietnamese (82%), Filipino (81%), & Cambodian/Laotian (65%) immigrants. This compares to a two-parent factor of only 56%, 57% and 45% for native born Whites, Mexican & Blacks.

Asian Pacific American children return the favor by not getting arrested, making mostly As in high school and graduating from college.

Not getting arrested? Less than 1 in 30 (2%, 3%) children of Chinese & Korean immigrants have been incarcerated, followed by Vietnamese (7%), Filipino (7%), & Cambodian/Laotian (9%) immigrants. For native born Whites, Mexicans & Blacks, respectively, it is 18%, 27% and 27%.

Making mostly A's in high school: Half of (51%, 50%) children of Chinese & Korean immigrants made mostly As in high school followed by Vietnamese (45%), Filipino (32%), & Cambodian/Laotian (20%) immigrants. It is 31%, 17% and 13% for native born Whites, Mexican & Blacks, respectively.

College graduate: More than 3 in 4 (82%, 77%) children of Chinese & Korean immigrants earned a BA or a higher degree, followed by Vietnamese (59%), Filipino (43%), & Cambodian/Laotian (16%) immigrant. For native born Whites, Mexican & Blacks, it is 49%, 20% and 24%, respectively.

That's not an escalator, that's a rocket!

Given the zero sum nature of the value choices we offered 18–49 year olds APAs, to meet the goals of career success and being rich, young APAs have to be willing to sacrifice, at least relatively, more personal, individualist values like *peace of mind* (70% Top 5 value, an index of 84), *having new experiences* (57%, an index of 83) and, especially, *free time* (48%, an index of 77).

Many of these factors may also appear to be as much immigrant values as Asian values, as the table below demonstrates, but, two thirds of today's APAs are, in fact, immigrants. Let's take a closer look.

Value	Immigrant (501)	Child of Immigrant (334)	G2+ (189)
Success in my career	61%	67%	55%
Being rich	31%	28%	21%
Free time	45%	47%	55%
Having new experiences	48%	67%	66%

Assimilation and "Asian" Values

In addition to losing their native language (*"the first thing to go"*), the unrelenting pressure of assimilation also erodes other "Asian values" to varying degrees.

- The value of *success in my career* declines from its peak of 67% among the APA children-of-immigrants generation to 55% by the next generation. But, it still dwarfs the 38% level of non-APAs.
- The value of *being rich* declines significantly from 31% among APA immigrants generation to 21% for Generation 2+, not much higher than among non-Asian Americans (16%).
- The value of *free time* increases from 45% among Asian immigrants to 55% among Generation 2+ APAs. It is 62% among non-APAs.
- The value of *having new experiences* increases from 48% among Asian immigrants to 66% among Generation 2+ APAs. That's about the same as non-APAs (68%).

Over time, then, it appears that some, though not all, Asian values are replaced by the more distinctly American individualist values.

A related aspect of parental veneration is APAs relatively greater desire to maintain their ethnic & cultural heritage compared to non-APAs, many of whom, the Census tells us, are becoming more "American" with each passing Census.

Young APAs are relatively more likely to say that maintaining their ethnic heritage is a "Top 5" value, an index of 242 vs. non-APAs. They are also more likely to agree that *"it's important to me to maintain my family's cultural and ethnic traditions"* – an index of 133 (65% vs. 49% for Non-APAs).

Given that this is a shared value across generations, this is a sentiment that's not likely to go away soon.

	% feeling "It is important to me to maintain my family's cultural and ethnic traditions."
Immigrant (501)	64%
Child of Immigrant (334)	64%
Generation 2+ (189)	67%

Not All that Different

In many respects, APAs aren't really all that different from other Americans. According to GSS data, they're a little happier in terms of their general happiness (92% of APAs are very happy/pretty happy vs. 85% of non-APAs), a little more likely to think that life is routine (54% vs. 46%) rather than exciting or dull, and perceive other people as relatively more helpful (53% vs. 46% of non-APAs) and slightly less selfish (43% vs. 49% of non-APAs).

Perhaps because of their immigrant background and familiarity with non-American institutions, APAs do express relatively more confidence in most American institutions than other Americans. They're about average in their opinions of medicine, organized labor and the executive branch of government. And they have a below average opinion of the military and organized religion.

A Great Deal of Confidence In:	Non-APA (6650)	APA (182)	Index
Congress	11%	18%	157
Press	10%	15%	156
United States Supreme Court	32%	45%	143
Major Companies	20%	26%	132
Television	10%	12%	125
Scientific Community	42%	52%	124
Education	27%	32%	119
Banks & Financial Institutions	27%	30%	112
Organized Labor	13%	14%	107
Medicine	40%	41%	104
Exec Branch Of Fed Govt	16%	15%	97
Organized Religion	24%	21%	86
Military	48%	41%	85

Some Key Differences
One radical attitudinal difference between APAs and other Americans has to do with *individualism* (or maybe selfishness?), specifically, the relative lack of it among APAs. When asked whether *to think for oneself* was important, only a minority (43%) of APAs rated it the most important or second most important. Meanwhile, slightly over two-thirds of Non-APAs rated it the most important or second most important.

Whether this is part of the obedient/unquestioning heritage of the Asian Pacific American family writ large or a legacy of cooperative, consensual home country systems, it is a very stark difference.

Top 2 Box (Most/2nd Most Important)

Values	Non-APA (5822)	APA (154)	Index
To Think for Oneself	68%	43%	63

Here's where we are starting to see the real nature of Asian ethnicity and culture emerge – as the table below illustrates.

Top 2 Box (Most/2nd Most Important)

Values	Non-APA (5822)	APA (154)	Index
To Work Hard	54%	64%	119
To Help Others	46%	60%	130
To Think for Oneself	68%	43%	63

Asian Pacific Americans ranked Hard Work, Helping Others and To Think For Oneself 1, 2, and 3 while non-APAs rank To Think for Oneself, Hard Work, and Helping Others 1, 2, and 3.

Hard Work
Let's take Hard Work first. Another recent survey also found that 64% of Asian Americans strongly agreed with the statement "If you work hard… you will succeed in the United States." It's a gimme that an immigrant, perhaps especially, an Asian immigrant works hard.[7]

Malcolm Gladwell develops an elaborate explanation for the "hard-workingness" of Asians vs. Europeans generally based on the differences between "very hard rice cultivation" vs. "relatively easier wheat cultivation."[8] Others have suggested a religious dimension with "very hard" Confucian meritocracy (Confucious would love the very idea of chasing the Ivy League Dream) trumping the "hard" Protestant Ethic which in turn trumps "soft Catholicism."

This might explain why in the earlier data from Rumbaut, Chinese Americans just edged their mostly Protestant Korean American counterparts, while Korean Americans consistently out-performed their Catholic Filipino American counterparts. Whichever of these explanations may hold, one true proof is that non-APAs clearly recognize this as a characteristic of Asian Pacific Americans.

In 2000, about 1200 non-Asian Americans were asked to rate Asian Americans on a Likert {*Hard Working - 2 - 3 - 4 - 5 - 6 - Lazy*} scale in the General Social Survey.

A majority (57%) of non-APAs rated Asian Pacific Americans *Hard Working*, 2 or 3 on this scale vs. only 12% who rated them 5, 6 or *Lazy*. While only 21 Asian Pacific Americans rated themselves on this same scale, the results, curiously enough, were very similar: 62% *Hard Working*, 2 or 3 on this scale vs. only 14% 5, 6 or *Lazy*.[9]

So, *Hard Work* trumps *Thinking for Oneself* among Asian Pacific Americans? Check. But what about *Helping Others*?

Helping Others

Why does *Helping Others* rival *Hard Work* in importance and trump the "Non-APA" value of *Thinking for Oneself*?

Here we need a more complex explanation, a more neurological one, one that goes to the heart of Asian/Non-Asian differences. According to *Science Daily*, "Psychological research has established that American culture, which values the individual, emphasizes the independence of objects from their contexts, while East Asian societies emphasize the collective and the contextual interdependence of objects."[10] One study used brain scans to show how European Americans exhibit greater comfort with absolute judgments, while Asian comfort with relative judgment literally lit up different areas in brain scans:

> Americans, when making relative judgments that are typically harder for them, activated brain regions involved in attention-demanding mental tasks. They showed much less activation of these regions when making the more culturally familiar absolute judgments. East Asians showed the opposite tendency, engaging the brain's attention system more for absolute judgments than for relative judgments.[11]

For Asians, there is often no absolute since decisions must *always be made relative to others*. Conversely, perhaps for individualistic (European?) Americans, "thinking for yourself" means that *fewer decisions are made relative to others*.

This relates to what we see as Asian (at least East Asian) perspectives that see the forest apart from the trees, and sublimate the part to the whole, to give the background equal weight with the foreground. It is taking in the whole face, not just the mouth, and grasping the idea of a family extending in time and space.

Americans, as another study puts it, "trail Chinese in understanding another person's perspective." *Science Daily*[12] again provides the background: "People from Western cultures such as the United States are particularly challenged in their ability to understand someone else's point of view because they are part of a culture that encourages individualism. In contrast, Chinese, who live in a society that encourages a collectivist attitude among its members, are much more adept at determining another person's perspective, according to a new study.[13] Two excerpts from the original research are worth quoting.

According to the authors:

Members of these two (American & Chinese) cultures seem to have a fundamentally different focus in social situations. Members of collectivist cultures tend to be interdependent and to have self-concepts defined in terms of relationships and social obligations. In contrast, members of individualist cultures tend to strive for independence and have self-concepts defined in terms of their own aspirations and achievements.

An experimental game they set up highlighted these differences:

In the game, one person, the "director," would tell the other person, the "subject," where the objects should be moved. Over some of the squares, a piece of cardboard blocked the view of the director, so the subject could clearly tell what objects the director could not see. In some cases there were two similar objects, one blocked from the director's view and one visible to both people playing the game.

The Chinese subjects almost immediately focused on the objects the director could see and moved the correct objects. When Americans were asked to move an object and there were two similar objects on the grid, they paused and often had to work to figure out which object the director could not see before moving the correct object. Taking into account the other person's perspective was more work for the Americans, who spent on average about twice as much time completing the moves than did the Chinese.

Even more startling for the researchers, according to *Science Daily* "was the frequency with which many of the Americans ignored the fact that the director could not see all the objects. Despite the obvious simplicity of the task, the majority of American subjects (65 percent) failed to consider the director's perspective at least once during the experiment," by asking the director which object he or she meant or by moving an object the director could not see, Keysar said. In contrast, "only one Chinese subject seemed confused by the directions".[14]

Again, perhaps, "helping others" may speak to the collectivist, more team oriented nature of East Asian society & culture, a culture that is naturally more "wired" to take into account "them" rather than the strong "me" orientation of Americans who like to "think for themselves."

While neither of these studies are definitive and both raise the question of whether they could achieve the same results with, say Southeast Asians or, perhaps even more of a stretch, Asian Indians, this body of research continues to grow and is, perhaps a most important one for those who want to understand Asian Pacific America.

One last example is provided by *Science Daily*:

> Because face recognition is effortlessly achieved by people from all different cultures it was considered to be a basic mechanism universal among humans. However, by using analyses inspired by novel brain imaging technology, researchers at the University of Glasgow have discovered that cultural differences cause us to look at faces differently.

> Lead researcher Dr. Roberto Caldara said: "In a series of eye-movement studies, we showed that social experience has an impact on how people look at faces. Specifically we noticed a striking difference in eye movements in Westerners and East Asian observers. We found that Westerners tend to look at specific features on an individual's face such as the eyes and mouth whereas East Asian observers tend to focus on the nose or the centre of the face which allows a more general view of all the features."[15]

Again, it appears that Asians are better at context or as the authors conclude: Westerners appear to think and perceive focally and Easterners globally.

Now let's turn to, perhaps, the most fun part of this chapter – *The Asian Pacific American Lifestyle*. Basically, this section is grounded in two sources that measure how Americans spend their finite re-sources of time and money, supplemented by other lifestyle sources where available.

- **American Time Use Survey** (**ATUS**), 2003–2007 combined, features surveys on American's time use conducted by the Bureau of Labor Statistics (BLS).
- **Current Employment Statistics** (**CES**), 2007, is an annual survey on how American's spend their money also conducted by BLS.

We can learn a lot about Asian Pacific Americans from these sources because of the zero-sum qualities of time and money that are being measured. If APAs spend less time on Activity X, how do they spend the time they saved? If APAs spend relatively more money on Item Z, what do they spend relatively less on?

Education

As we've seen earlier, the Asian Pacific American lifestyle is all about getting on and staying on the escalator – the hard road to success in America. Hard work and education, in the main, do lead to success, and APAs practice what they preach.

It's not surprising to find that *children's education* and *continuing education* loom larger in the APA lifestyle than in that of their non-APA counterparts.

Asian Pacific Americans spend significantly more time playing with their children (but not sports), doing homework with their children and reading to their children than non-APAs.

Minutes a day	Non-APA	APA	Index
Playing with HH children (not sports)	5.32	9.89	186
Homework (HH children)	1.73	3.23	187
Reading to/with HH children	0.79	1.55	196

ATUS measures minutes a day spent on different activities and pursuits using a one-day time diary. It then averages the results across all respondents to arrive at a mean that includes zeros, e.g., in the table above, Asian Pacific Americans who read to/with their children on the day they were interviewed.

It should come as no surprise that they spend more on education (APAs account for 6.1% of American education expenditures but only 3.5% or respondents in the Consumer Expenditure Survey, an index of 174) and fees and admissions, many of which are education related (4.7% of such expenditures, an index of 134).

But what really separates Asian Pacific Americans from other Americans is their *devotion to continuing education,* a requirement of many of the high prestige occupations that employ so many of them.

- APAs, according to ATUS, spend an average of 24 minutes a day taking a class for a degree, certification, or licensure.
  - this is significantly higher than the 15 minutes a day devoted to this activity by non-APAs (an index of 160)
- APAs, according to ATUS, spend an average of 25 minutes a day on research/homework for class for degree, certification, or licensure.
  - this is significantly higher than the 7.4 minutes a day devoted to this activity by non-APAs (an index of 339)

The Central Role of Food

As we saw earlier, Asian Pacific American focus group respondents told us that food was one of the Top 3 APA Values and every bit of evidence we have supports that judgment.

There are thousands upon thousands of Asian themed restaurants in the US. The early Cantonese restaurant pioneers have now been joined by Thai, Hunan, Szechuan, Mandarin, sushi, Korean, Indian and Vietnamese counterparts. A *partial* list of restaurants available from Survey Sampling's B2B listings includes 27,735 Chinese, 1753 Indian/Pakistani, 5350 Japanese, 738 Korean, 3686 Thai and 1045 Vietnamese.[16]

Earlier, we saw that because of the ubiquity of Asian restaurants, APAs are more likely to be restaurant workers, whether managers, chefs, or servers. Certainly it communicates authenticity, but a key fact is native cuisine restaurants are a popular entrepreneurial choice for Asian immigrants. But food is also more central to Asian Pacific America's everyday lifestyle. And APA food choices are often as distinctive as many of their other characteristics.

First of all, APAs spend significantly more time on food and food related activities than other Americans. According to ATUS, they spend 78 minutes a day "eating and drinking" vs. only 66 minutes a day for other Americans (an index of 119), 30 minutes a day on "food and drink preparation" vs. only 23 minutes a day for other Americans (an index of 129), almost 8 minutes a day "grocery shopping" vs. only 6 minutes a day for other Americans (an index of 131) and even 4.4 minutes a day on "travel related to grocery shopping" vs. only 3.3 minutes a day for other Americans (an index of 135).

These findings suggest that APAs devote both more time and effort to food than other Americans – even though they don't spend any more money than other Americans on food (they account for 3.7% of food expenditures, an index of only 106).

Perhaps this is because most APA cultures view food and eating a bit differently. Anthropologist Clotaire Rapaille, in his book *The Culture Code*, describes typical American food as fuel.

> Americans say "I'm full" at the end of the meal because unconsciously they think of eating as refueling. Their mission has been to fill up their tanks; when they complete it, they announce they've finished the task.

> It is also interesting to note that on highways all across the coun-

try, you will find rest stops that combine gas stations and food courts. When you drive up to the pump and tell the attendant to fill up your tank, it wouldn't be entirely inappropriate for him to ask "Which one?"...

Interestingly, we seem far less concerned with the quality of the fuel than one might expect...

In other cultures, food isn't a tool, but rather a means of experiencing refinement. In France, the purpose of food is pleasure, and even a home-cooked meal is something diners savor for a long period. In Japan, the preparation and enjoyment of food are a means to approach perfection.[17]

Food plays a somewhat different cultural role, and, in many cases, the food itself is quite different. APAs put different items in their grocery carts than other Americans. For simplicity sake, below, we just report their food category expenditure indices vs. their share of the population, according to the 2007 CES, but even that begins to show some of the differences. For example, APAs account for 8.3% of expenditures on fish and seafood, yet they account for only 3.5% of CES households – an index of 237.

Besides the fish and seafood sub-category, one is also more likely to find meats, poultry, fish & eggs (120), fruits & vegetables (134), especially fresh fruits (137) and fresh vegetables (174) and cereal and cereal products, i.e., rice in APA grocery carts and on APA dinner tables.

These healthy skewing food choices are accentuated by the relative absence of bakery products (77), dairy products (80), sugar and other sweets (67), alcoholic beverages (56) and one of my personal favorites, miscellaneous (aka "junk") foods (77).

Their diet, their relatively young age or their exercise regimens (see below) would appear to be responsible for their relatively low expenditures in health related categories:

Category	APA Index
Health insurance	89
Health care	77
Medical supplies	71
Medical services	69
Drugs.	43

Other Expenditures
Clothing

APAs either dress for impending success as they make their way up the escalator or wear clothes that match their accomplishments in their high-prestige "have to look good" occupations. Once they arrive at the top, they spend relatively more of their budget on a wide variety of apparel (and footwear).

APA Expenditure Indices 2007 CES	Index
Apparel and services	131
Men and boys	129
Men, 16 and over	134
Boys, 2 to 15	103
Women and girls	149
Women, 16 and over	154
Girls, 2 to 15	117
Children under 2	106
Footwear	140

Investments and Insurance

APAs invest and insure. Compared to their share of the population, Asian Pacific Americans spend relatively more on Pensions and Social Security (an index of 131), Personal Insurance and Pensions (129), Life and other Personal Insurance (114) and even Vehicle Insurance (131).

Below Average Categories

What do they give up in terms of time and money? APAs show up as below average for more common American passions like *Interior Deco-*

rating, Exterior Repairs, Lawns & Gardens, and *DIY Auto Repair*.

You probably won't see them mowing the grass. Asian Pacific Americans average only 6.8 minutes a day on *Lawn, Garden and Houseplant Care* vs. 11.9 minutes for non-APAs. *Lawn, Garden and Houseplant Care* seems to be more of a White (12.6 minutes) and American Indian (12.02 minutes) "thing." Hispanics average only 8.35 minutes a day and Blacks even less (6.25 minutes).

Asian Pacific Americans average only 1.3 minutes a day on *Interior Arrangement, Decoration, & Repairs* and *Exterior Repair, Improvements, & Decoration* vs. 6.55 minutes for non-APAs.

APAs average only 2.3 minutes a day on *Pet Care* compared to 5.15 minutes for non-APAs. *Pet Ownership* also seems to be more of a White (5.62 minutes) and American Indian (5.03 minutes) activity. Hispanics average only 2.41 minutes a day and Blacks even less (1.85 minutes).

APAs average only 1.88 minutes a day on *Vehicle Repair and Maintenance (by self)* vs. 2.78 minutes for non-APAs. *Vehicle Repair and Maintenance (by self)*, seems to be more of a White (5.62 minutes), Hispanic (2.96) and American Indian (2.89 minutes) "thing." Blacks average only 1.5 minutes a day on this activity.

One also suspects that Asian Pacific Americans are significantly less voluble than other Americans. They spend only 32 minutes a day *Socializing and Communicating* vs. 40 minutes a day for other Americans, an index of 80, with American Indians (46 minutes a day), Hispanics (42), Blacks (42) & Whites (39) all spending more of their time on this activity.

APAs also spend only 4.96 minutes a day on *Telephone Calls* vs. 7 minutes for other Americans, an index of 72. *Telephone Calls* are clearly more of a Black (11.27 minutes a day) "thing" than a White (6.32 minutes), Hispanic (4.87) or American Indian "thing."

They do, however, e-mail. Asian Pacific Americans spend almost as much time e-mailing (3.67 minutes a day vs. 2.45 for other Americans, an index of 152) as they do on phone calls.

Somewhat oddly, Asian Pacific Americans are neither overly communicative nor introspective: They spend only 15 minutes a day *Relaxing & Thinking* vs. 19 minutes a day for other Americans. Black Americans, on the other hand spend more than a half hour a day on this same activity.

Socializing, Entertainment and Recreation

Asian Pacific Americans spend relatively more time *Socializing with Neighbors & Friends* than other Americans, but relatively less time *Socializing with Relatives* or *Socializing at a Bar*.

Spend Evening with More than Once a Month

	Non-APA (6832)	APA (164)	Index
Neighbor	33%	38%	114
Friends	43%	48%	113
Relatives	56%	51%	90
At Bar	15%	10%	65

They spend less time on *Tobacco & Drug Use* (.16 minutes a day) than other Americans (.54 minutes a day), much less on *Tobacco Products & Smoking Supplies* (an index of 43) and, as we saw earlier, lower *Consumption of Alcoholic Beverages* (an index of 57).

They also spend significantly less time:

- *Reading for Personal Interest* – 17 minutes a day vs. 22 minutes a day for other Americans, an index of 78.
- *Playing Games* – an average of about 7 minutes a day vs. 11 minutes a day for other Americans, an index of 67

But they spend significantly more time at the keyboard:

- *Computer Use for Leisure (excluding Games)* – about 14 minutes a day vs. 8 minutes for other Americans, an index of 170.

They also spend a little more time *Participating in Sports* than other Americans (but they are younger) – 55 minutes a day vs. 48 minutes a day for other Americans, an index of 113. They are significantly more likely to participate in Asian-themed favorites like

- *Playing Racquet Sports* – (507)
- *Doing Yoga* (350)
- *Participating in Martial Arts* (229)
- *Walking* (136)
- *Using Cardiovascular Equipment* (119)

Media

Perhaps the real secret of the Asian Pacific American Lifestyle, the behavior that makes them the most "un-American," but also one that maybe explains their success and the success of their children best is their "boob tube" behavior. Quite simply, APAs watch a lot less television than other Americans. About 40 minutes less per day.

According to the ATUS survey, APAs as a whole, spend less time watching TV – about 118 minutes a day vs. 157 minutes a day for other Americans. That's almost enough time for their class AND their class homework.

This is confirmed by the 2006 Ronin Group AZN survey: 18–49 year old APAs watch less TV than other Americans. Younger APAs say they watch 1.8 hours of TV a day vs. 3.02 hours a day for other Americans. Only 30% of APAs watch 3 or more hours a day vs. almost half of other Americans.

Hrs Per Day Watching TV	Non-APA (N)	APA (N)	Total
0	5%	7%	129
1	21%	32%	150
2	27%	32%	115
3	17%	10%	57
4	12%	9%	73
5+	17%	11%	66

One reason for this behavior is that Asian Pacific Americans appear to be ahead of the curve when it comes it comes to using internet connected computers *as a replacement for TV.*

First of all, more APAs have and use a computer and more APAs have internet access. Four in five APAs say they use a computer vs. only 64% of other Americans and four in five APAs say they have internet access in their homes vs. only 2 in 3 other Americans.

Use Computer	Non-APA (5991)	APA (88)	Index
Yes	64%	82%	127
No	36%	18%	51
Internet Access in Home	**Non-APA (3243)**	**APA (111)**	**Index**
Yes	66%	79%	121
No	34%	21%	60

Asian Pacific Americans are ahead of the curve when it comes to the Internet being their main source of information about events in the news, while half of non-APAs still rely on TV as their main source of events in the news.

Main Source of Information about Events in the News	Non-APA (3243)	APA (111)	Index
The Internet	16%	37%	232
TV	50%	29%	58
Newspapers	22%	28%	131
Radio	7%	4%	54
Friends Colleagues	2%	1%	57
Other	1%	1%	174
Magazines	1%	0%	0
Books Other printed material	1%	0%	0
Government agencies	0%	0%	0
Family	2%	0%	0

It seems no surprise that Asian Pacific Americans are ahead of the curve when it comes to using the Internet as their primary source of information about science and technology, with 43% saying that the Internet is more of a main source than either TV or newspapers, while a plurality (42%)of non-APAs still rely on TV as their main source of information about science & technology.

Main Source of Information about Science and Technology	Non-APA (3243)	APA (111)	Index
The Internet	24%	43%	179
TV	42%	25%	60
Magazines	11%	15%	138
Newspapers	11%	10%	92
Books Other printed material	6%	3%	48
Family	2%	2%	98
Radio	2%	1%	48
Friends Colleagues	2%	1%	59
Other	2%	1%	60
Government agencies	0%	0%	0

The relative absence of TV in the APA Lifestyle kills two birds with one stone. To the extent that TV watching is a barrier to getting ahead, less TV watching is good, especially, perhaps for those hard-working students dreaming of the Ivy League who still haven't memorized every episode of the *Simpsons*.

With Asian Pacific Americans, we saw, the difference between the amount of TV they watch and the amount that other Americans watch not only gives them time to "take a class for a degree, certification, or licensure," but also to do the homework for that class! To the extent that facility and familiarity with computers and the internet helps us get ahead, APAs are having fun in a more useful way. Today, even "playing on the internet" is probably good.

Implications for Marketers

What insights can we glean from all this? Clearly, there is a tight set of habits and core values that make this a very rich target for certain categories. Here are a few thoughts.

- **APA values appear to be very overt.** Respect for parents, education, drives towards success, etc., are all worn on the sleeve. This can be good news for certain types of research methods.
- **The immigrant mentality** looks as though it is amplified through cultural upbringing.
- **Commonalities.** We start to see common cohorts of sacrifice for the group, lack of self-orientation, family respect and fealty. Are you starting to see why we titled the book *Many Cultures, One Market*?
- **Family.** In Asian Pacific America it has a larger meaning. Not only reputation and immediate family members, but a larger extended family, and how the actions of each individual reflect on the family as a whole.
- **Helping Others** is a value with an Asian flavor. There is clearly greater cultural sensitivity to the other person's perspective and this may have some useful aspects in messaging.
- **A Cultural Disconnect.** We begin to see why many Americans have had such difficulty doing business overseas in Asia, where a "Yes" is not always a "Yes" and the process may be just as important as the outcome. The socialization process whereby absolutes are not preferred to perspectives relative to others/other things may help explain why comparative advertising is viewed at with such disdain in many parts of Asia.
- **TV is not as important in APA households** – and, clearly, the computer and Internet have greater importance.
- **Success. Education. Technology. Being Rich. Family.** These are values that are valued across the board in Asian Pacific American culture.

The closer we look at this group, the more we see the commonalities that define a market. This is all the more interesting when one considers the wide geographic and cultural range this group represents. Now let's examine some other factors that are turning these many cultures into one market.

X. The APA Opportunity
Products and People

Just a short while ago, Sun Wah was just one more small restaurant tucked away on Argyle Street in Chicago's predominantly Vietnamese neighborhood, where it competed neck and neck with another Chinese BBQ outlet. Today, a shiny new restaurant four times larger is open for business around the corner on Broadway. Daughters Laura, a culinary school graduate and Kelly, who has an MBA in international marketing along with brother Mike, a military vet who knows what it takes to get the job done, are running the business. It's not typical for a Chinese restaurant to spend three-quarters of a million dollars on a new space to serve high-quality but traditional Chinese dishes. But this is a new generation. The children of restaurant founder Eric Cheng have taken over.

Their signature dishes, like the Peking duck dinner, keep lines long. Where their father had prepared two Peking ducks in 35 years, his offspring prepared 12 the first day they offered it. It would hardly be a surprise if some big restaurant marketing company doesn't become very interested in their recipe for success. The second generation, the Children of Immigrants, is coming of age, and they both have sets of cultural software working: the American Spirit and APA Values.

Just because they might not put in as long a day as their parents had, doesn't mean they won't work extra hard. They just might want to raise their sights. Laura and Kelly work just as hard as Mom and Dad at the restaurant's new location, but the size of the business and the improved margins are clearly part of the next generation.

It's also good business for restaurant equipment manufacturers, contractors and a whole range of suppliers who saw their business increase. By the way, don't worry about Mom and Dad. They're still pretty busy running their Sun Hing tofu factory.[1]

The APA Escalator is having its impact. As families grow – along with their net worth – an increasing range of products and opportunities become part of the APA market.

Products – Propensity and Needs

To paraphrase a quote from an earlier chapter, we're surprised that more companies don't know about the value of the APA market, because the data are there, if not on market performance, then certainly on propensity to buy. Using any one of a number of readily available sources, such as Mediamark Research & Intelligence (MRI), Mintel's Lifestyle Reports, Packaged Facts or a host of other syndicated sources, companies can easily get a fix on the APA over and under in terms of product or service usage. Using this data, you can begin to measure whether or not a foray into the APA market makes sense for your company based on the likelihood of purchase vs. the cost of entry and the inherent efficiencies of the available media opportunities (to be discussed in the following chapters).

You know your product or service category much better than we do. But we thought it would be interesting to see the various ways the APA market might add to your business.

Here are just a few randomly selected categories with a few general examples of what you may be missing by not addressing the APA market.

- **Financial Instruments** – Because of the general APA demographic make-up, it's not surprising that the index for purchase of most financial instruments is off the charts. Check with the syndicated sources on lines of credit, mortgages, home improvement loans, savings certificates, trust agreements, cash management accounts, stock ownership bonds, Treasury bills and other government bonds, mutual funds and credit cards. For example,

APAs are more likely than any other ethnic group to use credit cards. They use them more often and for larger amounts, and pay off charges monthly rather than carrying a balance. Could this be why 75% of APAs feel confident that they will be ready for retirement vs. 50% of blacks and Hispanics?[2]

- **Health & Medicine** – Besides superficial appearance differences, APAs generally share some very real physical differences and concerns from the rest of the population. Over 50% of APAs have allergy problems vs. 37% for Anglos, 40% for Hispanics and 36% for blacks.[3] Diabetes is another problem. APAs should be tested for diabetes by age 30, as they experience a mortality rate from this disease that is 2 to 3 times higher than for whites.[4]

- **Home & Family** – Family structure offers us several clues to product categories and services that would most benefit APAs. Care-giving is often across generations – it may even be across oceans.[5] A greater percentage of APAS than any other group is caring for both children and parents (and the group most likely to say they feel guilty about not doing it). Eighty percent of APA homes are headed by married couples.[6] They are the least likely to be lead by a single mother. Given this structure and the central role of food discussed earlier, it's no surprise that APA families are more likely than any other to eat three meals together and more likely to have a variety of foods at one meal.[7] Remember, seafood indexes at about 200 with most APA groups.

- **Automotive** – APAs are twice as likely to own an Asian-origin vehicle (Toyota, Honda, Nissan et al) than an U.S. origin vehicle (Ford, Chrysler or GM).[8] However, favorite automotive marques cross nations, particularly in the luxury category, with BMW (31%), Mercedes Benz (17%) Lexus (15%) and Acura (12%) leading the way.[9] APAs are more likely than any other group to own (and insure and maintain) three cars in the same family.[10]

- **Technology** – APAs are more likely to have internet service. They are more likely to use it for functions like bill paying, e-mail, news, shopping and file sharing than any other group. APAs are most likely to use a cell phone, while not negatively impacting landlines, and the most likely to use domestic and international long distance calling plans. APAs are more likely to own the latest high tech devices such as Blu-Ray players, desktop and laptop computers, MP3 players, and LCD and plasma TVs.[11] This is also a category where APA cultural cues may have the potential to enhance the overall brand image.

- **Geography** – While it's true that APAs live in every state of the Union, even the most unlikely of places (remember Cary, NC?) and are in the process of de-enclaving from the traditional places of first landing such as Chinatowns, APAs are still geographically concentrated in California, New York, Hawaii, Texas, Washington, New Jersey and Illinois. Add the major metros in these seven states plus the locations of the top colleges and universities around the country, and you've got a "controllable" geography to reach APAs.

- **Seasonality** – Just as marketers have taken advantage of Black History Month, Cinco de Mayo, and St. Patrick's Day, APA offers some seasonal opportunities. These can be great times to promote products, ingratiate your company with a community, or just to have fun. So too can they use Asian Heritage Month (May) and the Asian Lunar New Year (Chinese New Year, Tet) to reach the APA community as well as the huge cross-over population. By the way, depending on the year (it's a lunar calendar), it will start sometime between January 21st and February 20th. It's a two-week holiday. So if you're looking to spark up sales in the first quarter, it's a holiday to consider.

- **Consumer Packaged Goods** – It's highly likely that for most Consumer Packaged Goods, the APA usage is probably not outrageously over or under the norm (it's not, but you'll have to buy the syndicated data or commission a study yourself to confirm). Then again, we've all seen case after case where a brand has made a special connection and generated a much higher share because of it. Still, in many, many categories, APAs index dramatically over the general population. You just need to know where to look. And apply the principles learned in this book to figure out why.

- **Business Opportunities** – Let's say you're part of an operation that offers franchise opportunities. Or maybe you're in commercial real estate with a brand new strip mall. Who are you going to call? You know that entrepreneurial, tech-savvy APAs will be a high percentage of your target.

So now let's look at the APA market through a slightly different lens – not as customers, but as business partners.

People – Skills and Desire
Speaking e and E
Speaking "e" and "E" are two new languages we have to speak in the 21st century. They are the two languages successful businesses must become fluent in. APAs are already fluent in both. Here's what we mean.

"e" equals the language of the electronic network.
It now connects us all. It's been said we live in a global village united by an electronic thread. e is the growing part of the way we will all do business (e-commerce), the way we communicate in general (e-mail, texting, social networking) and the specific skills we'll need. And as we've shown, with their over-representation in the sciences, engineering, finance and medicine, APAs got an A in that class.

In his book, *Saving American Manufacturing: Growth Planning for the Small and Mid-sized Manufacturer*, Mike Collins outlines some of current problems with the state of American manufacturing. Collins is quite clear that succeeding in manufacturing today is much more challenging than it once was, primarily due to the dearth of people making the factories hum.

Pressures from globalization and advances in technology are putting a high premium on the skills needed to be competitive in manufacturing. A study published by the National Association of Manufacturers and the Manufacturing Institute titled "Keeping America Competitive' states that 'today's manufacturing jobs are technology jobs, and employees at all levels must have the wider range of skills required to respond to the demands of an increasingly complex environment."

The report goes on to say "The Baby Boom generation of skilled workers will be retired within the next 15-20 years. Currently, the only source of new skilled workers is from immigration. There is a projected need for 10 million new skilled workers by 2020."

"The potential exists that manufacturers will increasingly move their production operations overseas to get the technological talent that is being strategically and purposefully prepared in places like the European union and the Pacific Rim, including China and India, if they cannot find this talent here."

First, manufacturers want "first job" applicants who are much better at math, science and writing than are currently being graduated from high school. Mr. Craig Barrett, CEO of Intel, says, "Where Americans once viewed the diploma as a common national currency, its value has been so inflated that employers and post secondary institutions all but ignore it in their hiring and admissions decisions today." In the "American Diploma Project," more than 60% of the employers rated high school graduates as poor to fair in English and math.

To get ahead in the New Economy, the degree, education, or training must be job or career specific. Degrees in engineering, nursing, accounting, teaching and other professional programs train the person to get a job. In the main, these people get the jobs they were trained for.[12]

Sound like he's describing anyone you've been reading about? He might be suggesting that some Asian manufacturers could use some Asian American competition.

"E" equals the Entrepreneurial Spirit.

Walk around any Chinatown, Little Tokyo, Koreatown or Little Saigon and you'll see hundreds of small shops and businesses. But break out into any major metro and if you look carefully, you'll see even more APA-owned businesses. APAs are more likely than any other ethnic minority to be self-employed, over 11%, compared to just over 8% of Hispanics and 5% of African Americans.[13] And not just dry cleaners and nail salons. Fifty percent of all U.S. minority-owned businesses with over a $1 million in sales are owned by APAs.[14] The biggest growth areas are high-skilled occupations and professional services like law, medicine, financial services, real estate, insurance and computer consulting. So why are so many APAs opening up their own businesses?

Four Theories

C.N Le of *Asian-Nation* posits a series of theories.

His first theory describes Labor Market Discrimination. He argues that perhaps, as APAs try to find "regular" jobs as employees working for someone else, they are met with discrimination, especially in the case of first generation immigrants.

The second theory emphasizes Cultural Traits. Many APAs go into business for themselves as it is the best way to apply their cultural traditions of working hard, delaying material gratification and sacrificing for the next generation.

Le's third theory focuses on Class Resources. APAs plan from the beginning to open their own businesses using specific education and job skills gained just for that purpose, already have financial resources lined up, and their "American-ness" allows them to relate to norms and behaviors of both APA and non-APA customers.

Le's final theory is one of Structural Opportunities, which consists of three separate models. The "Middleman" model argues that middle and upper-class white business owners don't want to deal with predominantly Black or Latino working-class customers because they fear losing money, status, or for their personal safety. They "use" APA "buffers" while still controlling the wholesale distribution as APA retailers face the hostility that is ultimately directed at whites.

The second model is one of an "Ethnic Enclave." It argues that it is in the best interest of the owner to open a business in an ethnic community because the most- well developed enclaves tend to produce more profits and at the same time shield the owner from racial issues faced in the mainstream labor market.

The last model focuses on "Economic Openings." As white business owners give up their real estate in less desirable areas e.g. Jews and Italians in 1980s New York, APAs, especially recent immigrants take over these areas. This is coupled with the general increase in service-oriented businesses, which tend to offer easy entry, but also involve high risk of losses or failures.[15]

Whether any or all of these theories are correct, the fact of APA as entrepreneurs is here to stay.

It is our best guess that all of Le's theories and observations have some validity. With all the small business activity in the APA community, examples abound for every variation and combination.

Today, every company, big and small, needs some "Big E" – a bit of entrepreneurial spirit to rev up the engine. The Cheng family is fairly good at it. They grew up with it. And now they're ready to make the next generation go.

Remember, in general, APAs are coming from a pretty good place as far as work habits and work ethics go. They want to do right by the family. They understand cooperation to get something done. They understand shared sacrifice to accomplish a goal. They express great optimism about lives in America, concluding that hard work is rewarded in this society. Who wouldn't want someone like that working for them? Or with them as suppliers. Or even as their boss?

Implications for Marketers

- Do you have your share of APA customers? It might be 4%, it might be 8%, or it might be 20–50%.
- APAs make good customers – and they also make good business partners.
- How well does your company speak "e?" Is your e-commerce program ready for the challenges of the 21st century? Does your staff have the skill set to handle those challenges?
- How well does your company speak "E?" Could your company use more entrepreneurial spirit?
- Do you really know who represents the best opportunity for your business? Who is really the low-hanging fruit? Take a wider view – you may be pleasantly surprised at the new opportunities you see.

XI. One Market
A New Paradigm to Make It Simple

So now we get to the crux of this book. How do we make all of this information simpler to understand? More importantly, how do we take the insights presented and use them to build our business? What is the New Paradigm as it relates to marketing to Asian Pacific Americans?

For some, the potential APA market is only 4%. For some, it's 8% – or more. And, for a few, it's a high-performing 20%. Moreover, if you decide that this is a market that deserves your attention, how do you reach them?

We feel there are three basic ideas that can help you define, both quantitatively and qualitatively, and then reach the APA marketplace:

- **There is an identity to which all APA groups can relate. It transcends language, country of origin, and even the number of generations in the U.S.**
- **Derived from this identity, there are commonalities that exist amongst almost all APAs –commonalities that don't necessarily exist among non-APAs .**
- **There is a market that can be aggregated under this identity.**

To help you identify and then connect with the marketing opportunity, we identify three major drivers – one is culturally based, one is physically based, and one is language-based.

Simply put, you have to understand:

The Americanization Dynamic – the cultural driver
The Own-Race Effect – the physical driver
English as a Common Denominator – the language driver

A. The Americanization Dynamic
Generational Imprints

Just as we identified a *Defining Moment* for Asian ethnic groups in Chapter 5, here we identify APA *Generational Imprints,* a set of common lifestage factors that form an indelible mark on each group of Asians coming to and living in America.

Here's a useful way of looking at it. The Market Segment Group uses an organizing principle based on food buying habits that relates to APA levels of assimilation into American culture.

These are:

> **The Ethnic Islander State:** Usually the higher proportion of recent immigrants, clustered in or near ethnic enclaves. Homeland is their primary cultural influence.
>
> **The Blender State:** Relatively new to the US. They are more regionally dispersed and work hard to maintain two cultures.
>
> **The Adopter State:** Associate mainly with others outside their own ethnicity. They prefer not to be singled out as a separate ethnic group. However, some may become "root seekers," embracing a stronger connection with their ethnic group.[1]

While these descriptors may be fairly accurate as far as they go, we feel they do not offer a holistic view of the Generational Imprint, nor do they provide the beginnings of a rationale for explaining the APA mindset. For our purposes, we will use a simple scheme to identify and categorize successive generations of APAs. This is a close corollary to generational descriptors in common use among marketers.

> **Immigrants:** The first generation in the U.S. Hard working within the system. No expectations for themselves. High achievement. They knew they weren't American – yet. Still have close ties to Asia.

Children of Immigrants: The second generation. Became educated. Grew into the opportunities their parents gave them. High expectations. High achievement. Wanted to be American. Paralleled Baby Boomer ideals and activities. Act as American cultural influencers to their parents.

Generation 2+ (G2+): The first generation of APAs to self-actualize. High expectations, but less real/tangible achievement than their parents. Expected opportunities to be given to them. They assumed they *were* American until faced with realities of racism. Paralleled by post-Boomer Generation X issues. Considered acculturated/assimilated but perhaps not completely "American" due to racial stereotypes.

The Drive Towards Assimilation

Currently, two of three APAs are foreign born, versus "only" 40% of Hispanic Americans.[2] Further, almost two thirds of the growth of the APA population is driven by immigration versus 44% of the Hispanic population's in the time period covering the years 2000 to 2005.[3] So how is it that we can claim that APAs are part of some transcendent identity that can be identified by marketers as a mass audience large enough to address as one?

Simply put, APAs are caught up in the Dynamics of Americanization like no other immigrant group. Generally among APAs, there is no resistance to the Americanization process. This rush towards Americanization is the reason they came here in the first place.

This is somewhat in contrast to Hispanic Americans, who maintain more of that identity. Research points out that while 22% of Hispanic Americans think of themselves as Hispanic, not American, only 13% of APAs feel this way. Of those accepting a hyphenated view of who they are, 25% of Hispanics think of themselves as Hispanic first and American second compared to 16% of APAs.[4]

Here is a way of thinking about this graphically as we begin to understand the APA opportunity. Let's put it in the context of the Generational Imprints listed above:

Immigrants = *Asian* Americans

Children of Immigrants = Asian Americans

Generation 2+ = Asian *Americans*

Perhaps the real test of assimilation, beyond the demographic indicators (e.g. high levels of education, suburban home ownership, preponderance of white collar jobs etc.), is the erosion, or at least generational change of "Asian" values and attitudes. In our research with AZN-TV, we uncovered a pattern of "Americanized" value systems that cross Asian ethnic groups in a predictable manner across generations.

For example, the values of "success in my career" and "being rich" become less important by the second generation, and the value of "being cultured" declines after the Immigrant generation. These were replaced by the more distinctly American individual values of "free time" and "having new experiences."

Value	Immigrant	Child of Immigrant	G2+
Success in my career	61%	67%	55%
Being rich	31	28	21
Being cultured	50	38	37
Having free time	45%	47%	55%
Having new experiences	48	67	66

Supporting the descriptors of each of the Generational Imprints above, we also found that changes in "Asian" values did not "Americanize" in a one-way stream, but rather, followed the lifestyle experiences of each generation.

Attitude	Immigrant	Child of Immigrant	G2+
"I feel great pressure from my family to succeed"	45%	59%	41%
"It is important to me to maintain my family's cultural traditions"	64%	64%	67%

So, for example, "Feeling great pressure…" is more a hallmark of the Child of Immigrants generation. The Immigrant generation's parents are likely still overseas, while the G2+'s parents are, after all, Americans. We find that maintaining an allegiance to Asian values is important, but as part of becoming American, APAs recognize the pull from both directions.

Asian Values	American Values
Group, family, clan Hierarchy	Individualistic & Independent
Formal	Casual, Relaxed
Quiet, Reserved	Loud, Opinionated
Delayed Gratification	Instant Gratification
Strict, Respected Parents	Lenient, Disrespected Parents
Want Kids to Succeed	Want Kids to be Happy
EDUCATION	Education

This drive to become American has a practical aspect. It was common in our research to be told, "As an Asian American, you have to assimilate or you get stepped on." So, Americanization is, in many ways, one more success strategy on the escalator.

Cultural Connectivity

It is exceptionally difficult to describe a single "culture" for any group, whether based on language, national background, religion, music, food or any one of a number of categories into which marketers try to slot consumers. Even though you may describe African American or Latino "culture" into a short, neat set of phrases to fit on a Creative Strategy document, the fact is that the variations within any group make these phrases an oversimplification of a rich cultural tapestry. For that reason, we will not try to define APA culture.

Rather, we will take an approach used by such global marketers as Procter & Gamble and Clinique. They allow consumers to self-select their "tribes" as they define them individually. Then, they cater to particular subcultures of customers who share very similar outlooks, styles and aspirations despite their different nationalities and languages. We find this "tribal" approach more useful. It is still relatively simple and direct, yet it does not oversimplify unnecessarily.

The *Wall Street Journal* reports:

> "We're seeing more and more global tribes forming around the world that are more and more interconnected through technology" says Melanie Healey, president, Global Health and Feminine Care at Procter & Gamble, Cincinnati. "If you focus on the similarities instead of the differences (in these tribes) key business opportunities emerge," says Ms. Healey.

> "Historically, we used to be focused on discovering the common hopes and dreams within a country, but now we're seeing that the real commonalities are in generations across geographical borders," adds James Haskett, brand franchise leader of P&G's Global Always/Whisper brands.[5]

Even as "culture" is difficult to define for a group, consumers are one hundred percent certain it exists for them, if only by their own definition. Just as some marketers using certain criteria may claim that there is no such thing as an APA market, one exists for the simple reason that *APAs say it does*. The "tribe" defines itself.

The core issues are identifying the opportunity and then finding a way to aggregate this market into a viable candidate for marketing support.

In our work with AZN-TV, we found a strong need for cultural connectivity as part of the Americanization Dynamic. Over 61% of those surveyed agree with one or more of the following statements:

– *"I want to stay connected to my culture"*

– *"I want to learn about other Asian cultures"*

– *"I want to expose my children to our family's culture"*

– *"I want to learn about my family's culture"*

– *"It helps me to better understand my parents and grandparents"*

As APAs become more assimilated, their need to be connected to Asia and Asian culture fades a bit, but it is still powerful. It is a driver that, in an important way, includes about half of Generation 2+ APAs and APAs who speak only English. To some degree, it includes virtually every Asian Pacific American. This is a powerful – and useful – tribal connection.

Group	% Feel Need to Connect to Asian Culture
Immigrants	66%
Children of Immigrants	59
Generation 2+	51
Speak English & an Asian Language	71
Speak English Only	49

In our AZN research, respondents revealed, not surprisingly, that the main reason they watched Asian and APA television programming was because they liked the programs. However, apart from program hedonics, the other main driver seemed to be a need for cultural connectivity and learning.

Reason for Watching	%Response
I like the programs	48%
I want to stay connected to my culture	42
I want to learn about other Asian cultures	36
Want to expose children to our family's culture	27
I want to learn about my family's culture	25
Helps me to better understand parents/grandparents	19
It is programming my family can watch together	19
My spouse likes it	16
Other	5

The reasons APAs watch Asian/APA TV vary among age groups. This closely follows our Generational Imprint issues. The two cross-generational constants appear to be a desire to learn about their own and other Asian cultures.

Media Attitudes: Why Watch	Immigrant	Children of Immigrants	G2+
Peaks among Children of Immigrants			
It helps me understand parents/grandparents	16%	25%	16%
Constant			
Learn about other Asian cultures	36	36	35
Learn about my family culture	22	29	26
Declines with Assimilation			
Like the programs	50	48	41
Stay connected w/ culture	50	40	28
Expose children to family culture	31	23	23
Programming family can watch together	24	16	11

Once thought of as the place of first landing for immigrants, Chinatowns across the country have experienced residential and business booms over the past decade. Not only is it the neighborhood of choice for new arrivals, Chinatowns are becoming hot spots for Americans of Chinese and other Asian descent for food, fun and a healthy dose of ethnic pride.

The increasing affluence of young APAs and the freedom that goes with it means that many now have the time and money to spend on leisure activities, previously spent on education. Having attained the familial education obligations, parents are actively encouraging their children to get out, especially if it means going to Chinatown, as a tangible measure of ethnic pride. Noreen Ahmed-Ullah of the *Chicago Tribune* reports:

> "I tell people that Chinatown is not your grandpa or grandma's Chinatown anymore," said Z.J. Tong, president of the Chicago Chinese Cultural Institute. "There's many new establishments that are catering to the young and hip population."

> "Chinese businesses started to change because they realized there was a market out there," noted Kensen Lam, pastoral assistant at Chinese Christian Union Church. "Young professionals wanted something different, something cutting edge. They also wanted something true to their own culture. As American culture began seeing something special about Asian culture, the ABCs [American Born Chinese] picked up on that and said 'We're Asian too,'" Lam said. "They realized it's cool to be here in Chinatown."

> Living on the campus at the University of Illinois at Chicago, Christine Leung, 22, began coming here with friends from college because of cheap food. Her sister Kelly, 16, began driving down with other Asian friends from Niles North High School in Skokie. Their mom, Linda, who immigrated

from Malaysia 33 years ago, was pleasantly surprised. Their father Chi is from Hong Kong. "We're happy they're finding out who they are," their mother said.

That attraction of an authentic Asian experience pulls in young people from far beyond the Chicago area. Visal Kith, 23, made the three-hour drive from Indiana University with a group of friends. "There's very few Asian people in Indianapolis," said Kith who is from Cambodia. "One of the reasons we come here is because you will see all these Asian people and it feels like you're in an Asian country."

Underlying these hopes and dreams is a desire by young Chinese Americans to hang out together, immersed in a culture that combines ancient traditions and cutting edge fun.[6]

B. The Own-Race Effect
A Distinctively Homogeneous Look
Whether you think about race in terms of being defined as people of a common descent, a biological taxonomy to categorize human groups, a way of dividing groups by culture as well as physical appearance, or merely an idea that exists only as a social construct, in America the concept of race, while being difficult to define, exists as an issue not only for sociologists, but for marketers as well.

There would be no African American, Hispanic American or Asian Pacific American marketing programs if the concepts of black, white, brown and yellow did not exist.

The issue at hand for marketers is not only one of how to reach, address, and sell to "races" as a target, but more fundamentally, how to set parameters for who is in the group and who is not, in order to build a sufficiently large base to which to advertise.

We clarify the definition of the APA market via two opposing views – looking alike and looking different.

Take a look at the pictures below.

Most of you can assume that each person is of Asian descent, but can you really tell who comes from a Chinese, Japanese, Korean, Thai or Filipino background? Can you tell how many generations each has been in the U.S.? Can you tell who has a good command of English? Unless you're a mind reader, the answer to all of these should be a clear, "No."

With the exception of those of South Asian background, e.g. Indian, Pakistani, Bangladeshi et al, APAs share *a generally homogeneous look*. Just as most whose ancestors immigrated from Europe share their own characteristics, so do those from Asia. We will not be so politically incorrect to suggest that "all Asians look alike" but APAs, from a biological perspective, share many physical features.

We get uncomfortable when these things manifest themselves into social issues (e.g. hate crimes, stereotyping, ethnocentricity). But the fact remains – marketers, for good or bad (we think bad) continue to ignore, or at least lessen the value of a variety of demographic and psychographic measures and insights in order to create monolithic marketplaces based on race. If an African American or Hispanic market exists, primarily based on the interpretation of "race," then logically, so does an APA market.

So is *looking alike* (aggregation) enough to qualify for being thought of as a separate group or market? No! APAs face the additional issue, along with Blacks and Latinos, of *looking different* from the "general market." Nobel Prize winner John Steinbeck, recognized this fact back in 1952 in his book *East of Eden*. The following is a conversation between Sam Hamilton, an Irish immigrant settling in the Salinas Valley of California shortly before World War I, and Lee, his Cantonese cook and major domo.

> *Lee: I understand you were not born here.*
>
> *Hamilton: No, in Ireland.*
>
> *Lee. And in a few years, you can almost disappear, while I, who was born in Grass Valley, went to school and several years to the University of California, have no chance of mixing in.*
>
> *Hamilton: If you cut your queue, dressed and talked like other people?*
>
> *Lee: No, I've tried it. To the so-called whites, I was still Chinese, but an untrustworthy one. And, at the same time, my Chinese friends steered clear of me. I had to give it up.*[7]

Even the act of getting dressed can pose dilemmas of choice and identity for Americans with distinct ethnic identity. The dynamics of generations, immigration, history, economics and politics impact attire and appearance. The experiences of one of the authors when growing up is profoundly different from those of his children.

> They are just coming into a time whereby they can express a cultural identity visually. Up until now, it seems as if APAs have borrowed liberally from other cultures e.g. preppy, hip hop etc., because they had neither the outward symbols e.g. clothing jewelry that said who they were, or they were embarrassed/discouraged from displaying an ethnic identity.

> With culture/fashion adopting Asian (if fake) icons and symbology, it's becoming okay to wear visual identifiers because it's been adopted by the mainstream. I think that this is combined with a more global outlook by younger kids, at least more than when we were growing up.

> I've noticed among younger kids that the ethnic identity is more a natural part of who they are than it was when I was growing up. They feel very much at ease mixing and matching and being able to pick whatever cultural identifier they feel good about that day.

While we do not look at "race" as a nominal measure, we do look at it as an identifier and differentiator.

Clinique, a unit of Estee Lauder, sells skin care products and make-up in 130 countries, but the differentiator is skin tone. They market products that sell to particular skin tones regardless of the consumer's nationalities.

CEO Lynne Greene observes that, because women all around the world buy about the same fashions and cosmetics on the Internet, beauty regimens, in general, are becoming more universal.[8] This issue does not seem to connect with more specifically ethnic communication. When one of the authors was working for Procter & Gamble's Olay skin care products, he brought up the idea of a "Brazilian palette" of colors, when referring to the skin tones of African

American women. African American women range in skin tone from very dark to very light and everything in between, but are still considered black by the general populace, just as the women of Brazil range in skin tone but are still considered Brazilian. The idea was not understood and, subsequently, dismissed.

It would seem that, for women, they have already worked their way to a beauty regimen that works for them, and this is either old news or no news at all.

The Own-Race Effect

Lest you think that this notion is a matter of simple racial profiling, the concept of the Own-Race Effect has been well documented by psychologists and sociologists. It has been recognized as a determinative point in developing legal statutes on jury selection, and is even a factor in Major League Baseball.

Xiaoguang Lu and Anil Jain of Michigan State University observe, "The human face is a highly rich stimulus that provides diverse information for adaptive social interaction with people. Humans are better at recognizing faces of their own ethnicity/race than faces of other races. Golby et al show that same-race faces elicit more activity in brain areas linked to face recognition. O'Toole et al investigate the differences in the way people perceive own- versus other-race faces. They found that the perceived typicality of own-race faces was based both on global shape information and on small distinctive feature markers, whereas the typicality of other-race faces related more to the presence/absence of local distinctive features."[9]

Sangrioli, Pallier et al of the University of Paris go a step further to explain, "It is a common experience that faces from 'other races' look more similar than faces from 'one's own race.' Feingold (1914) remarked 'to the uninitiated American, all Asiatics look alike, while to the Asiatic, all white men look alike.' The reality of this so-called 'other race effect' has been confirmed in several experimental studies."

Own Race – Other Race

The Other-Race Effect is thought to reflect the differential amount of experience that an individual has had with other individuals from various race groups. Studies with children and adolescents support the "experience hypothesis." There is a larger Other-Race Effect in children and adolescents living in segregated neighborhoods than in those living in integrated neighborhoods in the USA. The advantage of for "same race" faces was stable across the age range, suggesting that the other-race effect is already present at age three.

The effect of early visual experience may be erased as a result of immersion in a totally novel face environment. There is an analogy between the sensitive periods for the development of the face processing systems and the speech processing systems. In the face processing domain, as in language, environmental inputs can influence normal behavior over several years in childhood, until the age of nine at least.

The early existence of the Other-Race Effect together with the protracted development of face processing shows that the face processing system is built through interaction with the environment and is specified by this interaction."[10]

Academic research supports both a Nature and Nurture position. To some degree humans are hardwired to be able to identify members of their own ethnic group. But childhood and adolescent environment can reinforce the strength of this ability.

Legal Considerations

The legal world has used this fact to its advantage, so much so that legal statutes have been put in place to prevent abusing the Own-Race Effect. This is a book about marketing, not legal issues, but we think the following will demonstrate the strength of the Own-Race Effect.

In jury trials, the jury selection process allows for a condition called the peremptory challenge. Simply put, during jury selection, it's an opportunity for a party to a lawsuit to dismiss or excuse a potential juror without having to give a valid reason, as would be the case when a juror is challenged for cause. Depending on the court rules, each party typically gets to make from five to fifteen peremptory challenges. Although parties may generally use their peremptory challenges as they see fit, the U.S. Constitution has been interpreted to prohibit their use to eliminate all jurors of a particular race or gender from a jury.[11]

Picking a jury in a multi-defendant case requires considerable negotiation and compromise between defense counsel. It also demands that with regard to "reverse Batson" challenges, the defense speaks with one voice, as illustrated in *United States v. Rodriguez*. ("Reverse Batson" is where the government accuses defense counsel of engaging in discriminatory exercise of its peremptory challenges during voir dire.) In *Rodriguez*, the district court granted the government's reverse-Batson challenge as to one juror, noting that the defense exercised 85% of their challenges against white jurors where the panel was 65% white, and that the proffered race-neutral reasons for dismissing the re-seated juror were suspect where the defense had not challenged similarly-situated minority jurors.[12]

Relying on gut or statistical evidence that mixed juries are less likely to convict than predominantly white ones, defense lawyers often try to redress these disparities in their use of peremptory challenges – not necessarily to discriminate against individual whites, but rather to engage in some ad hoc affirmative action in favor of minorities, especially those of the defendants race. Like colleges seeking diversity on campus, defense lawyers are seeking diversity in the jury room, in hope that some jurors may identify with the defendant or with arguments raised by the defense, and in so doing, subject the government's case to a greater degree of scrutiny.

Dirk Olin, national editor of *American Lawyer* magazine blogs:

> Who are your peers? People of a different background? But

that's not the test. Both sides are entitled to affair opportunity to have seated a cross-section of the community, and group discrimination is a no-no. Yet it recurs, human nature being what it is. Each side wants justice, but each side wants to win, believing justice to be on its side, not the other. And so it goes...

One irony of this is that "peers" are among the first to be bounced from panels, because we can't of course, trust Latinos to weigh evidence against Latinos, or dentists to do the same with doctors. But the costs are broader. Rich defendants buy high-priced consultants to sift would-be jurors through a sieve of identity politics (a reality that's either profoundly unfair or profoundly wasteful, depending on your view of their effectiveness). And those with the weakest cases can game the system by dumbing down the 12 through peremptory legerdemain.[13]

Even that most All-American of pastimes, baseball, is not immune to the Own-Race Effect. A research study carried out by the University of Texas at Austin examined every pitch in Major League Baseball from 2004 through 2006, some 2.1 million pitches.

Controlling for umpire, pitcher and batter fixed effects, the study found that strikes are more likely to be called against a batter if the pitcher and the umpire are of the same ethnicity.

The study says "the highest percentage of called strikes occurs when both umpire and pitcher are white, while the lowest percentage is when a white umpire is judging a Black pitcher. What is intriguing is that Black umpires judge Hispanic pitchers harshly, relative to how they are judged by white and Hispanic umpires; but Hispanic umpires treat Black pitchers nearly identically to the way Black umpires treat them. Minority umpires treat Asian pitchers far worse than they treat white pitchers."

Daniel Hamermesh, professor of economics at the University and author of this paper states, "One pitch called the other way affects things a lot. Baseball is a very closely played game. Baseball is a game of strategy. If a pitcher knows he's more likely to get questionable pitches called as strikes, he'll start picking off at the corners. But if he knows he's at a disadvantage, he might feel forced to throw more directly over the plate, possibly giving up hits."

Interestingly, the study found that the bias can be erased where the game's attendance is high, when the call is made on a full count, or when QuesTec is used in the park. QuesTec is the electronic system that evaluates balls/strikes called and is used in 11 parks. It is the system MLB uses to help evaluate home plate umpires.

"Pitches are more likely to be called strikes when the umpire shares the race/ethnicity of the starting pitcher, an effect that becomes significantly stronger when umpire behavior is less well-monitored." Hamermesh says, "When you're going to be watched and have to pay more attention, you don't subconsciously favor people like yourself. When discrimination has a price, you don't observe it as much."[14]

These factors add up to identify a distinctly separate group who can't hide who they are or look like or how they are treated as a group.

The Look-Like-Me Need

We see this as a growing trend. The dramatic rise in Bollywood and Hong Kong cinema in the U.S., Asian pop culture becoming more accessible, and the freedom and means to enjoy them, combined with the increased desire for Cultural Connectivity add up to an indication that APAs not only want their ancestry to be a part of their lives, but that they are driven by a strong *Look-Like-Me* need as well.

Simply put, APAs want to see other people who look like them. We wanted to take a look at just how strongly directional a phenomenon this is and how it could impact marketers.

In our work with AZN-TV we uncovered the fact that the need to "see people who look like me" on TV and in commercials is strong among APAs. In fact, it is second only to African Americans. Over 60% of APAs agree with at least one of the statements below:

"I notice and pay more attention to commercials that have Asian actors in them"

"I wish there were more television programs that featured actors and characters who look like me"

"I'd like to see more people who look like me in TV commercials"

Group	% Agree with One or More Statements
White	5%
Hispanic	46%
APA	61%
African American	79%

This is a real issue. *Jet* magazine, one of the most widely circulated periodicals directed towards the African American community, has continuously run a listing of television shows for the upcoming week featuring African American actors. This listing, located on a premium position on the last page of the magazine, was designed to alert Jet's audience to TV programming that would feature those actors. This feature was initiated at a time when African American actors on Prime Time TV were few and far between. It allowed Jet's readers to tune in not only to support actors and actresses from their community, but also to *see people who looked like them*. Today, given the strides African American actors have made entering mainstream entertainment, perhaps this feature in Jet is no longer necessary. But that's not the point.

Our point is simply this – the *Look-Like-Me Need* is real.

As seen on the following chart, our AZN APA respondents have a stronger need to see *people who look like me* on TV than non-APA respondents. This can be traced to dissatisfaction with the job that

American TV does in portraying APAs. Almost half of APAs agree with each of the key *people who look like me* statements. About a third take pro-active measures to see more Asian faces. Finally, as a preview of things to come, over a fourth of APAs currently say they reward advertisers who show them more *people who look like me.*

	APAs	Non-APAs	
	%Somewhat/ Strongly Agree	% Somewhat/ Strongly Agree	Index
I notice and pay more attention to commercials that have Asian actors in them/I notice and pay more attention to commercials that have actors from my racial/ ethnic group in them	42%	18%	233
I wish there were more TV programs that featured actors and characters who look like me	46	21	219
I'd like to see more people who look like me in television commercials	46	24	192
I purposely tune into TV shows that feature characters from my racial/ethnic group at least once to give them a try	36	19	189
I am more inclined to buy products from companies that advertise to my racial/ethnic group	26	17	153
American television does a good job of portraying people in my racial/ethnic group	13	38	34

The data is quite clear. APAs have a strong need to see *people who look like me* on TV and in advertising. Here is a comparison. As you will see, this is a need that while not quite reaching the very high levels of African Americans, does exceed the comparative need to see *people who look like me* on TV among Hispanics.

Please note that "African American," "Hispanic" and "White" were substituted for "Asian" with the respective groups.

	Whites	Hispanics	APAs	Blacks
I notice and pay more attention to commercials that have Asian actors in them/I notice and pay more attention to commercials that have actors from my racial/ethnic group in them	12%	25%	42%	50%
I wish there were more TV programs that featured actors and characters who look like me	13	31	46	64
I'd like to see more people who look like me in TV commercials	16	36	46	66
I purposely tune into TV shows that feature characters from my racial/ethnic group at least once to give them a try	11	29	36	56
I am more inclined to buy products from companies that advertise to my racial/ethnic group	13	19	26	39
American television does a good job of portraying people in my racial/ethnic group	45	14	13	15

Unlike the need to feel connected to Asian culture which does fade somewhat with successive generations, the *Look-Like-Me Need* appears to be less immune to assimilation. The *Look-Like-Me Need* is, on the whole, cross-generational, and, perhaps, as the *Own Race Effect* would suggest, inherent.

	Immigrants	Children of Immigrants	G2+
I notice and pay more attention to commercials that have Asian actors in them/I notice and pay more attention to commercials that have actors from my racial/ethnic group in them	42%	52%	42%
I wish there were more television programs that featured actors and characters who look like me	43	54	41
I'd like to see more people who look like me in television commercials	42	47	35
I purposely tune into TV shows that feature characters from my racial/ethnic group at least once to give them a try	40	34	32
I am more inclined to buy products from companies that advertise to my racial/ethnic group	28	24	22
American television does a good job of portraying people in my racial/ethnic group	19	10	15

The Look-Like-Me Need is observed in our AZN respondents in very specific ways as it relates to both TV programming and advertising. Respondents noticed a wide array of APA characters on some of network TV's most popular Prime time shows including *Grey's Anatomy, Lost, Heroes, Desperate Housewives, Law & Order* and others. While recognizing that APA roles on TV were changing for the better, particularly the complexity of some of the characters e.g. Sandra Oh on *Grey's Anatomy*, respondents overall still had problems with the quantity and quality of TV portrayals of APAs. The primary objection was seeing the same old stereotypes for Asian characters and the fact that APA actors were generally relegated to secondary or minor roles. They told us:

> *"I'm sick of the stereotypical Chinese. There's more color and character out there."*

> *"Why can't you have normal Asians?"*

> *"They don't show reality. They show very old stuff… nothing current."*

> *"They're always a geek."*

> *"They show Indians as hotel owners, or they own a 7-11 or they're taxi drivers. They don't show the doctors or engineers."*

> *"They're usually just backup roles."*

> *"It's extras and little parts, not big parts."*

> *"How can you have a show about doctors or one set in LA or San Francisco and not show a whole bunch of Asians? It's almost as bad as those old shows, Hawaii Five-O and the Streets of San Francisco, where they hardly showed any Asians living there at all."*

In the case of advertising, the Look-Like-Me Need in APAs became clear for the opposite reason of television programming.

Instead of the presence of APA characters in TV shows, respondents noticed the *absence* of people who look like them in commercials. When asked if they could recall any Asian faces in advertising, none came immediately to mind.

> *"What commercials?"*

"There aren't any!"

"Seeing an ad without an Asian face is normal. We're forced to accept it."

"It's bothersome… especially because this is a highly concentrated Asian area (San Francisco)."

Aligning with the precepts set forth in Chapter 6: Getting Started, while APAs want more people in advertising who look like them, they were realistic. They did not expect, or even desire, a predominant place, only to be in the mix.

"If you see someone who looks like you, you are more likely to watch."

"When I see a diaper ad with a white, black and Hispanic baby, I really notice the absence of an Asian baby."

Attentiveness

Now that we had a general understanding of what APAs wanted out of TV programming and advertising from a qualitative perspective, we tried to get a feel for the impact of featuring APAs in terms of attentiveness and feelings towards advertisers. We set up a matrix of choices of "No Asians," "Some Asians," and "All Asians" in TV programming and advertising, and asked respondents to rank order their preferences.

The total absence of Asians in either programming or advertising yielded the lowest attentiveness scores. The "No Asians" in Ads/"No Asians" in TV Program cell had far and away the lowest score. The effect of having an Asian in an advertisement trumps the effect of having "Some Asians" or "All Asians" in TV programming. Overall, the "rainbow cell" ("Some Asians" in Ad/"Some Asians" in TV Programming) scores the highest.

	No Asians in TV Program	Some Asians in TV Program	All Asian TV Programs	Average
No Asians in Ads	1.97	3.00	2.81	2.59
Asians in Ads	4.06	5.03	4.47	4.52
Average	3.02	4.02	3.64	

The total absence of Asians in either programming or advertising, predictably, yields the least positive feelings towards the advertiser by the respondents. Again, the effect of having an Asian in an ad trumps the effect of having "Some Asians" or "All Asians" in TV programming. Again, the "rainbow cell" ("Some Asians" in Ad/"Some Asians" in TV Programming) scores the highest.

	No Asians in TV Program	Some Asians in TV Program	All Asian TV Programs	Average
No Asians in Ads	2.03	3.03	2.83	2.63
Asians in Ads	4.21	4.87	4.77	4.61
Average	3.12	3.95	3.80	

This is very interesting news for advertisers that want to reach this market. Now it's time for one more bit of good news.

C. English as a Common Denominator

By now you understand the **Americanization Dynamic** and the **Own-Race Effect**. Now we'd like to provide some hard, quantifiable evidence that demonstrates the viability of a mass audience with the use of **English as Common Denominator.** *The key fact* that the earliest APA "marketing experts" communicated ad nauseum was that marketers must use their services – particularly due to the welter of Asia-originated languages used by APAs.

Not surprisingly, the result is market complexity that no one else can navigate. The simple argument that the majority of APAs are foreign-born seems to meld well with the idea that they can only be addressed in their native language. After all, isn't that how they handle the growing Hispanic market?

The argument grows in complexity at the same time it seems to limit opportunity. The president of an Asian American advertising agency has stated, "We don't have the luxury of communicating in one language, like the Hispanic market. It's really daunting to look at from a linguistic standpoint. To target the Asian American market, you need language specific messages and campaigns."[15]

Well, perhaps you can make an argument for translating materials that help sell recent immigrants long-distance services and that first bank account – but the expense of running a complex translation service quickly makes many straightforward marketing approaches too costly and complicated. Moreover, it's not necessary.

Let's look at the facts.

Like Hispanics, the majority of APAs are foreign born – 67%.[16] Like Hispanics, about one in four speak English *only*.[17] This is the argument used to support marketing efforts to the APA community in a Asian-based language. The assumption is that the remaining 75% speak, predominantly or exclusively, a language other than English. However, most "experts" stop at this level of data. Because, after all, their business model depends on selling translation services. Let's look deeper.

The U.S. Census reports that while 77% of APAs spoke a language other than English, it also reports that 63% of APAs aged 5 and older spoke English only or well/very well.[18] The American Community Survey reports an even higher percentage – 88% of APAs spoke English only or well/very well, even as 75% speak another language.[19]

	Hispanic/Latino	APA
Speak English only	22%	25%
Speak English Well/Very Well +Foreign Language	54	63
Speak Foreign Language Well & English Not Very Well	24	12

The Americanization Dynamic is powerful. 88% of the market is operating in English, and that remaining 12% is a moving number, being replenished by new immigrants as others develop and improve their English skills. First, because the escalator runs on English. Second, because the APA commitment to come to America is deep and strong – learning English is part of it.

We think many APA marketers have done themselves no favors. The usual chain of logic used by marketers with the APA market goes something like this:

1. Most APAs are foreign born
2. Most APAs speak a foreign language (with or without a command of English)
3. We should speak to APAs in a foreign language as we've done with Hispanics
4. Unlike Hispanics there are a slew of foreign languages we must deal with
5. It's too expensive to try to reach APAs in all of their Asian-based languages, so we won't bother with an APA based marketing program.

If this is the chain of logic companies use, we agree wholeheartedly with points 1, 2 and 4. However, take a look at the chart below and see if points 3 and 5 still make sense.[20]

Language Spoken	Percent APA Speakers
English	88%
English Only	25
Other Language	18
Chinese (unspecified)	12
Tagalog	11
Vietnamese	9
Korean	8
Hindi	3
Japanese	3
Cantonese	3
Urdu	2
Mandarin	2
Gujarathi	2
Punjabi	2

"Language Is the First to Go"

In the research we did for AZN-TV, APAs told us that "language was the first thing to go" (food is the last). Asian language status is strongly related to generation, as America's assimilationist engine dramatically erodes Asian language facility, a vital element of culture, from one generation to the next.

	Immigrant	Child of Immigrant	G2+
Speaks an Asian Language	76%	51%	13%
Doesn't Speak Asian Language	24	49	87
Total	100%	100%	100%

But even Asian group membership is entwined in the Assimilation Matrix. With more recent arrivals like South Asians/Indians being the least assimilated (more immigrants, higher Asian language facility) and earlier arrivals like Japanese Americans being the most assimilated (less immigrants, lower Asian language facility) the interplay of immigration status and generational imprint become clear.

	SA/I	Other	V	C	K	F	J
Speaks English & Asian Language	85%	73%	64%	63%	42%	40%	25%
Speaks English & No Asian Language	15	27	36	37	37	60	75
Immigrant	78	55	42	45	45	47	17
Child of Immigrant	18	33	54	39	39	42	25
Generation 2+	4	11	4	17	17	12	58
Total	100%	100%	100%	100%	100%	100%	100%

Clearly, foreign language *preference* has little or nothing to do with English language *performance*. According to some research, there may not even be a *preference* for using a language other than English. The Market Segment Group reports, "while Hispanics and African Americans support bilingualism in various aspects of American life, Asians (despite their reliance in many cases on a language other than English) are more likely to mirror the attitudes of Anglos on this question. While 80% of Hispanics and 65% of African Americans believe that the U.S. should have a bilingual education system, only 46% of Asians and 38% of Anglos agree. In addition, while 78% of Hispanics and 59% of African Americans believe that there should be bilingual signs in public areas, only 30% of Asians and Anglos agree."[21]

Speaking of performance, it would not surprise many, parents and educators alike, that APA Scholastic Aptitude Test (SAT) average test scores for math reflect the highest percentages in the country across all ethnic groups. But reading and writing are actually in pretty good shape. Take a look at the Critical Reading and Writing scores. Not only are they significantly higher than "native" English speakers (Native Americans and Blacks) and "Immigrant groups" (Mexicans, Puerto Ricans and Other Hispanics) but the scores are also near or on par with White test takers.[22]

Group	Critical Reading	Math	Writing
American Indian	485	491	470
Asian American	513	581	516
Black	430	426	424
Mexican American	454	463	447
Puerto Rican	456	453	445
Other Hispanic	455	461	448
White	528	537	518

In addition to SAT scores, the California Department of Education's Standardized Testing and Reporting (STAR) Program, which tests all California students from second grade through junior year in high school on a variety of subjects, shows that APA students score higher than in English language proficiency than all other students – including Whites. The following scores reflect an additive rating of Advanced or Proficient on the STAR test.[23]

Group	2nd Grade	6th Grade	9th Grade	11th Grade
All APA	74%	71%	73%	58%
Black	38	33	34	22
Hispanic	35	33	34	22
White	64	66	68	53

While these results can feed into the Model Minority stereotype, they also point out something quite different. *AsianWeek* reports:

> The use of English among Asian Americans reflects a bicultural nature that combines traditional Asian characteristics with modern Western practices. And it's not just happening in America.

> English is the official language of India and the Philippines. A 2006 British study found 450 million native English speakers around the world. But as many as a billion people, mostly from China and India, were learning English as their

second language.

"Asia, especially India and China, probably holds the key to the long-term future of English as a global language" the report called *English Net* reported. Asians in America are learning English for the same reason. It's not a matter of becoming "honorary whites." It's a matter of adopting the most effective means of communications to add to our up-bringing in Asian heritage and culture.[24]

Desire for Cultural Connectivity aside, this should come as no surprise. The rush towards globalization, particularly in Asia, is driving English as a lingua franca by the sheer numbers of users in countries around the world. *Wired Magazine* estimates that by 2020, only 15% of the 2 billion people using English will be native speakers.[25] An estimated 300 million Chinese, roughly the equivalent of the total U.S. population, already read and write English. In his brilliant book *The Post-American World*, *Newsweek* editor Fareed Zakaria puts it most eloquently:

Americans talk about the appeal of our own culture and ideas, but "soft power" really began with Britain in the nineteenth century. Thanks to the Empire, English spread as a global language, spoken from the Caribbean to Cairo, and from Cape Town to Calcutta. English literature became familiar everywhere – Shakespeare, Sherlock Holmes, Alice in Wonderland, Tom Brown's School Days. Britain's stories and characters become more securely a part of international culture than any other nation's.

What sounds young and modern today is English. No language has ever spread so broadly and deeply across the world. The closest comparison is Latin during the Middle Ages, and it is a poor one. Latin was used by a narrow elite in a time of widespread illiteracy, and most non-Western countries were not even part of the Christian world.

Today, almost one-fourth of the planet's population, 1.5 billion people, can speak some English. And the rate of English's spread is increasing almost everywhere, from Europe to Asia to Latin America.

Globalization, which brings ever more contact and commerce, creates an incentive for an easy means of communication. The larger the number of players, the greater need for a common standard. Some 80 percent of the electronically stored information in the world is in English. When diplomats from the twenty-five governments of the European Union gather to discuss business in Brussels, they have hundreds of interpreters. But mostly, they all speak English.

Does a common language make people think in similar ways? We will never know for sure. However, over the last century, English has become the language of modernity. The word for tank in Russian is "tank." When Indians speaking in Hindi want to say nuclear, they usually say "nuclear." In French, weekend is "le weekend." In Spanish, Internet is "Internet." Increasingly, the English that people speak is Americanized, with certain distinctive features. It is colloquial, irreverent, and casual. Perhaps that irreverence will spill over into other realms.[26]

Perhaps cultural connectivity *is* the driving force behind English usage by APAs, but it's not just their desire to connect with their Asian heritage. The fact that the vast majority of APAs came to America in search of something better, something bigger, a brighter future, the Americanization Dynamic has taught APAs to believe in connecting with their American heritage as well.

An editorial in *AsianWeek* reads:

For most living in the United States, English is essential. Even within our own community, where a plethora of languages is spoken, English is the linguistic currency that enables us to communicate amongst each other – Korean Americans can speak to Chinese Americans, Japanese Americans to Filipino Americans. But at a time when language is a proxy for culture, we emphasize that learning English does not come at the expense of our identity or heritage. We consider ourselves 100 percent American in our English proficiency and still consider ourselves 100 percent Asian American as we celebrate and draw upon our heritage. We are one of the communities most adept at retaining our culture while at the same time being proficient in English.[27]

Implications for Marketers

This chapter makes some important points.

- First, the conventional "wisdom" of "translation service" marketing to APAs is basically wrong. While there may be some niche opportunities, primarily for recent immigrants, it misses the point of the whole APA experience.

- Three drivers define this dynamic market:
  - The Americanization Dynamic – a culturally-based driver
  - The Own-Race Effect – a physically-based driver
  - English – a language-based driver

These commonalities allow a marketer to reasonably approach the APA market as a true market. They also generate these additional implications.

- The Americanization Dynamic overrides nation of origin boundaries. You can see it at the high-school level, where it is not uncommon for young APAs of different backgrounds to "hang together." As they say, "rice is rice."

- We all respond to faces that are part of our own ethnic origin. This seems true across all racial groups. In addition, each racial group appears to be better at discerning differences, while other races tend to "look alike." This provides some useful clues in developing visual communications.

- Despite the wide variety of native languages, English is a common denominator, with increasing English proficiency a characteristic of the APA market. The 12% that lacks proficiency seems to be fed by ongoing immigration with basic proficiency achieved within a few years. The next generation is English dominant, as "language is the first to go."

- Translation-based approaches to the APA market may be appropriate for certain narrow marketing opportunities (i.e. communications specifically directed at recent immigrants), but, overall, they are unnecessary for effective communication.

- Finally, some very good news for advertisers. The APA market clearly searches for "own race" faces, and specifically states that they will support advertisers who recognize them in an appropriate way.

Cultural Considerations:
APA Culture – 20th Century vs. 21st Century

What *was* vs. what *will be*.

20th Century	21st Century
Hop Sing & Mei Ling	Chow Yun Fat & Ziyi Zhang
Rickshaws	Yamaha superbikes/Prius hybrids
Abacus	Charles Wang of Computer Associates
Rubber suit monsters	Multi-billion dollar anime industry
"Made in Japan" junk	Sony Aibo Robots
opium dens	Ayurvedic/acupuncture/holistic medicine
bad dubbing	Bollywood producing more movies than Hollywood
Overstock dumping	largest consumer markets on the planet
Ping pong	Ichiro, Yao Ming, Tiger Woods, Michelle Wie

XII. Bonus
Non-APAs as a Crossover Opportunity

Which would you rather have, a base of 1 million customers, or a base of 14 million? Which is easier? Reaching 80% of a small, specific target or 4% of a larger, more general target?

Philip Kotler, the godfather of Marketing 101 textbooks, writes: "Historically, American business firms saw the key to profits in the development of a single, uniform product mass produced, mass distributed and mass communicated. The market was treated as a collection of buyers undifferentiated in their needs and desires. Uniformity of production, distribution, and communication presumably would lead to lower costs and prices, and thereby create the largest potential market for the product. Market segmentation, the most recent idea for guiding marketing strategy [this was written over 40 years ago in 1967], starts not with distinguishing product possibilities, but rather with distinguishing customer needs or interests. Market segmentation is the sub-dividing of a market into homogeneous subsets of customers, where any subset may conceivably be selected as a market target to be reached with a distinct marketing mix."[1]

Market Segmentation: Not a New Idea
For the past half century, marketers (in particular, media planners and buyers) have been using fairly standard descriptors to slice and dice a market – demographics, including age, income, education, or gender; product usage, including usage rates, brand loyalty, and price sensitivity; more recently values and lifestyles including attitudes, benefits and psychographics; and, of course, the focus of this book, ethnic subculture.

What we hope to convey is an understanding of the Crossover Opportunity – a reverse engineering of the ethnic subculture target, especially as it pertains to the APA marketplace.

Most marketers, when looking at any ethnic subculture, tend to focus so narrowly on the ethnic group itself that they often don't see the forest for the trees. The attention to a specific target, driven by media optimizers and such, generally ignores the vast non-APA market that could be reached via messages directed towards the APA market. Efficient reach against an APA target becomes a hindrance to true corporate metrics, because, in an effort to maximize "*ethnic* Costs Per Thousand" (CPM) and "*target* ROI" the *overall return* on any specific marketing effort is not taken into account. Should non-APA sales not be included in the success of a promotion just because the promotion was aimed at APAs?

Marketing academics, Rajeev Batra, John Myers and David Aaker, propose two ways of reaching a target audience: controlled coverage and customer self-selection. In the controlled coverage approach, the objective is to reach the desired target segments and to avoid reaching those who are not in the target segments, an exclusionary principle. In the alternative scenario, customer self-selection, programs are directed to a mass audience of which the target segment may only be a small part – an inclusionary system. Those in the target segment are attracted to the marketing effort since it is tailored to them. Those not in the target group will probably avoid exposure, not because the program is unavailable to them, but because they either consciously or unconsciously choose to avoid it.[2]

The point that most marketers miss, is that both and neither of these concepts are currently used successfully in targeting APAs. Controlling coverage by ethnicity alone, as is done in most ethnic marketing programs, ignores the large percentage of non-APA potential customers who may be interested in goods or services targeted at APAs. By avoiding mass media vehicles based on an "efficiency to target" rationale, many marketers assume that too much will be wasted on an APA program using other than APA-exclusive vehicles. More on this in Chapter 15, "Media: How Do We Reach APAs?"

For a start, you need to wrap your mind around this interesting fact. At present, the vast majority of Americans involved in APA or Asian culture are not of Asian descent. The APA population is simply not large enough to drive the volume of all U.S. Asian-culture related phenomenon. On a percentage basis, this is dramatically different from Black or Latino, due partly to the relatively small numbers of the APA population compared to whites, Blacks and Latinos, and the "Inclusion/Exclusion" principle discussed in previous chapters. How do we know there's an interest for "Asian" culture outside of the APA market? Let's look at some examples.

- Kikkoman Soy Sauce, the nation's number one brand (brewed in All-American Walworth, Wisconsin) sold over 31 million gallons in the U.S. in 2006 with worldwide sales of nearly $2 billion. This compares pretty favorably with America's favorite condiment, Heinz Ketchup (ketchup being an Asian invention) whose worldwide sales are only around $1 billion.[3]

- The U.S. market for anime and manga, or Japanese animation, is worth approximately $4.35 billion, according to the Japan External Trade Relations Organization (JETRO).[4] Now only about 5% of the worldwide market, the U.S. is predicted to grow to double the size of anime's home market of Japan.

- The number of participants in martial arts training is around 6 million. It's influence is even greater. The famous (infamous?) rap group, the *Wu-Tang Clan* takes their name straight from a type of Shaolin kung  fu. Spearheaded by the "RZA" the self-proclaimed "abbot" of the Clan, the Wu-Tang persona is an intricate web of alter egos, warrior codes, numerological systems, and Eastern spiritual ethics. RZA writes, "The last movie that formed the Wu-Tang Clan brotherhood is called the Eight Diagram Pole Fighter. That was a movie I saw on tape for the first time with my brothers and sisters. It was a movie about eight brothers who get betrayed, go to war, and many get killed. And the family has eight brothers, I have three sisters and there are three sisters in the movie ... everyone at the projects was fiended out on kung fu ... this story is real. It's a kung fu movie, but it's a real story. These eight brothers who go out and they get betrayed and they fight to the death for each other – it hit us. And niggas was saying 'I'm the Fifth Brother!' 'I'm the Sixth Brother!' They were relating to us on that level. So we started calling each other by the names of those brothers."[5]

- Brooklyn-based duo *dead prez* also weaves elements of martial arts, philosophy and war strategy into their music and image. The dead prez's use of references to the I Ching, the 3,000 year-old book of divination, is explained as "a system used by wise men and women of China as a means of analyzing reality and perfecting the art of foresight. That process of change is symbolized in dead prez's music and they believe there is a common link between all historically oppressed people."[6]

- Instant ramen noodles, the quintessential cheap, filling meal for college students (and others pinching pennies), full of fat, salt and MSG, sell in excess of 4 billion packages per year in the U.S. alone (it's over 85 billion worldwide). Campbell's Soup, on the other hand, one of the most ubiquitous items on grocery store shelves and consumer pantries, reportedly produces *only* 2.5 billion cans per year.[7]

- Acupuncture, one of the oldest healing practices in the world aims to restore and maintain health through the stimulation of specific points on the body, usually via the insertion of thin, metallic needles. It's estimated that over 8 million Americans have taken advantage of this alternative form of medicine.[8]

- Does your local YMCA or Corporate Fitness Center offer a

yoga class? Growing from the fringe to mainstream America, yoga is now a $30 billion business with almost 18 million participants spending an average of $1,500 a year on instruction and supplies. According to the *Yoga Journal*, this ranks "Yoga Inc." larger than Dow Chemical and slightly smaller than Microsoft.[9] And then there's Tai Chi...

- Everyone has a go-to Chinese restaurant. You may also have a favorite Thai restaurant, curry restaurant, and sushi bar. As previously cited, with over 40,000 restaurants in the U.S., Chinese food is available in virtually every corner of the country. *Fortune Cookie Chronicles* author, Jennifer 8. Lee writes, "Our benchmark for Americanness is apple pie. But ask yourself: How often do you eat apple pie? How often do you eat Chinese food?"[10]

- In terms of number of movies made and worldwide viewership, Bollywood, India's Mumbai-based, Hindi-language film industry, is the world's largest cinema producer. With an average of 1,000 films made per year, and an audience of 3 billion, Bollywood surpassed Hollywood in 2004. Though the entire U.S. market is only the size of the typical Hollywood blockbuster, it is still substantial. Bollywood films in the U.S. earn around $100 million a year through theater screenings, video sales and movie soundtracks. At present, films from India do more business in the U.S. than films from any other country, a remarkable feat, given that only around 80 theaters around the country show first-run Indian movies.[11]

- Asian culture is entering the U.S. in one more small, but significant way. The large numbers of couples in the U.S. who are unable or unwilling to conceive children themselves combined with a drop in the number of American babies available for adoption has led to an increased demand for overseas adoptees.

The growing level of adoption of children born in Asia far outweighs adoption from any other geographic area. In 2004, the number of adoptees from China alone (7,044) was over 20% higher than that of the highest non-Asian country, Russia (5,865).[12] Each child enters an extended family – and that family is changed forever in terms of their awareness of APA-style values and culture.

Each of these behavioral data points seem to be part of a cumulative effect. Michael Huh, VP Marketing and Strategic Development for ImaginAsian TV notes, "We found that in our e-mails, about half our feedback is from non-Asians interested in Asian culture."[13] These statistics should surprise no one. Just as an Asian-themed restaurant or two is part of your menu collection, these cultural touch points open the door to a deeper connection.

Discovery Gateways

We call these means of entry discovery *gateways*. Our research has found that these gateways are portals to introducing non-APAs to Asian and Asian American culture, and from this initial awareness to an eventual affinity to a culture not their own. As an individual develops an affinity for one gateway, that seems to open another. And so we find that he or she tends to accept and include more and more APA practices within their lifestyle. From our focus groups with non-APA audiences, the most common gateways appear to be:

- Martial arts
  - "the whole Bruce Lee thing."
  - "I study classic style martial arts."
  - "My brother teaches kung fu."
- Anime and Manga
  - "A friend got me into anime."
  - "All of the best video games come out of Japan."

- Other Asian culture-based entertainment
  - "Korean soap operas are addictive, and I can't even understand what they're saying."
  - "Our Japanese friends got us into karaoke, and now we go out all the time, even without them."
- Food
  - "We've eaten Chinese food all our lives. Now we've branched out to Thai, Korean, and Vietnamese."
  - "My kids bought me a home sushi-making kit for Father's Day."
- Visited/live in Asian country
  - "I've been to China twice… it's fun to see how fast the country is growing."
  - "I got my first experience traveling for the military."
- Culture pervasive in geography
  - "There's a lot of Asian influence here in San Francisco."

Our work with AZN-TV, as outlined in the last chapter, fully supports the notion of a huge Crossover Opportunity, and one with a *non-ethnically derived* base of viewers. Let's look at a comparison between the Non-APA current viewers and Non-APA non-viewers (*general market*) of AZN-TV.

Members of the crossover target audience for AZN are a pretty even mix of men & women, have a somewhat younger skew (18-39) and have a mix of employment status.

	AZN Viewer	Not AZN Viewer	Index
Gender			
Male	51%	50%	101
Female	49	50	99
Age			
18-29	34%	32%	106
30-39	33	38	87
40-49	33	47	71

Employment Status

Employed full time	55%	69%	81
Student	17	16	104
Employed part time	13	15	89
Self-employed	11	12	96
Not employed, but looking for work	10	8	130
Homemaker	7	10	75
Retired	3	2	161
Not employed and not looking for work	1	3	47

Members of the Non-APA target audience for AZN are relatively more likely to be married with children.

	AZN Viewer	Not AZN Viewer	Index
Marital Status			
Single, never married	41%	34%	119
Married	45	62	73
Divorced	6	9	65
Separated	2	1	148
Widowed	0	1	44
Living with partner	6	10	55
HH size			
1	15%	13%	109
2	26	28	93
3	21	21	99
4	23	22	103
5+	15	15	101
Presence of Children			
Yes	47%	56%	84
No	53	44	120

While the majority of current Non-APA viewers are white, members of the Non-APA audience are relatively more likely to be black or Hispanic than the make-up of the U.S. population.

Race	AZN Viewer	Not ANZ Viewer	Index
White	61%	92%	66
African American	23	14	162
Hispanic/Latino	19	14	132

In this example, the behavior of watching Asian genres on TV, which is a reflection of an affinity for Asian culture and entertainment, trumps demographics. Given the huge potential of a cross-over audience, the marketer's total APA program target and goals should be defined, not by *APA ethnic makeup alone*, but rather, by the size of the *potential audience measured psychographically* for the product or service.

Implications for Marketers

Clearly, the APA opportunity is bigger than the APA market alone. So many products, services and relationships have crossed over into the mainstream that much of the "foreign-ness" has been removed.

- Getting the APA agenda to the planning table early is crucial to be able to see the big-picture content of how an APA program will help your entire marketing efforts. By identifying the drivers for your consumers (e.g. type and amount of product usage, relevance outside of ethnic content, gateways to entry) marketers can evaluate the best ways to reach far beyond the APA market with little or no incremental funds. The cross-over audience is a plus. So, if you start to look at a market through an APA lens, don't be surprised if you see more people than you expected.

Cultural Considerations:
APA Influences on American Culture

They did that? An incomplete, mostly trivial list of contributions to American culture that, at the outset, seem to be incongruous with Americans of Asian descent.

First grew nectarines and Bing cherries
Directed *Sense and Sensibility,* the *Sixth Sense, and Brokeback Mountain*
Was the *Last Comic Standing*
Won 9 Nobel Prizes
Created *Scooby Doo*
Invented surfing
Was Chief of Staff of the U.S. Army
Designed the World Trade Center in New York
Was *Time* magazine's Man of the Year for AIDS research
Were lead band members for the *Smashing Pumpkins,* the *Pixies* and *Linkin Park*
Won *Survivor: Cook Islands*
Designed JFK library, Jacob Javits Center, Rock & Roll Hall of Fame
Won the French Open Tennis Championship
Conducted the New York Philharmonic and the Boston Symphony
Opened more restaurants than McDonalds, Burger King and Wendy's combined
Founded YouTube, Yahoo, Bose and NVIDIA
Invented fortune cookies (yes, APA, not Asian)

XIII: "Hapas"
Half or Double? A Special Group

Today, Tiger Woods is a controversial figure. However, he is still one of the most well-known individuals who is "half Asian" or "Hapa." That said, here's the example that started the chapter prior to all the controversy.

Pearl Fuyo Gaskins, author of *What Are You?* writes:

> It was April 24, 1997. Golfing phenom Tiger Woods and his father, Earl, were guest on the ever-popular Oprah Winfrey show. Just a week earlier, Tiger, then only twenty-one, made sports history by becoming the youngest golfer and the first "African American" to win the prestigious Masters golf tournament. His victory by an incredible twelve strokes broke course records and left many of the world's best golfers in the dust.

> Within hours Tiger became the biggest and most sought-after celebrity on the planet, and a role model to millions of kids. Golf, viewed by many as a stuffy sport played by rich white men, was suddenly cool. Tiger could do no wrong – except for one thing. He refused to label himself as simply African American. He was more than black, he told Oprah Winfrey, and proudly claimed his multiple heritages. "Growing up, I came up with this name – I'm a Cablinasian," said Tiger, whose father is African American, American Indian and Chinese, and whose mother is Thai, Chinese and white. Cablinasian, he explained, was shorthand for Caucasian, black, Indian and Asian.

> Asked by Winfrey if it bothered him to be labeled only African American, Tiger said it did. When he had to identify his

racial background by checking off one box on school forms, he usually picked "African American and Asian, because those are the two households I was raised under."

Tiger's racial identity immediately became national news. Some journalists and sportscasters were obviously amused and reported it as some strange eccentricity of the boy genius of golf. "Cablin – what?" they cracked. But many African Americans were not amused. They quickly denounced him: "He's black. He's denying his blackness." "He doesn't know who he is." "He's confused." For a while, the controversy over Tiger's racial identity threatened to eclipse his amazing achievement.[1]

Was he confused? Or did he know himself better than anyone else?

When referring to someone of mixed race heritage, Spanish speaking countries use the term *mestizo* for a mix of European and Amerindian ancestry. Throughout the Caribbean and parts of the South, the term *Creole* is often used, usually referring to someone of mixed French or Spanish, African and Native American background from before the time of the Louisiana Purchase. It also refers to a type of cooking that mixes culinary traditions. Among Asian Pacific Americans, the term *Hapa* is used.

No, it's not an acronym for "Half Asian Pacific American" – though it might as well be. Hapa is a Hawaiian word literally meaning *half* or *part* with no racial or ethnic reference. It was first used to describe *hapa haoles* or half-white descendants of Native Hawaiians and white immigrants to the islands. Hapa covered a whole range of mixed ethnicity (e.g. Japanese/Hawaiian or Chinese/Filipino) and mixed race (e.g. Asian/White or Asian/Hispanic).

In the first half of the 20th Century, hapa was often used in a derogatory manner, to encompass the ideas of "less than pure blooded" or possessing a less desirable half.

Today, hapa is in common (and often proud) usage among mixed race/mixed ethnicity APAs, particularly among college age students. It's not an insult.

It is also part of many APAs' extended families. And it is part of the family structure of a growing number of Americans of virtually every ethnic background.

To understand the impact of hapas on the APA community we need to go back to the beginnings of the U.S.' measurement and categorization of its citizens. Just before the Civil War, in 1860, there were only three U.S. Census categories – white, black and "quadroon," or someone whose ancestry was one quarter black.

Today there are 30 designations. This includes 11 subcategories under Hispanic.[2] In earlier Chapters, we spoke of sociologists "scientifically" constructing dozens of "races" based on a wide variety of variables, none of which recognized the fact that "race" is itself not biologically determined, but is a social and cultural construct. So is the Census measuring race or ethnicity or both or neither?

In a word, *Yes*, to all of the above. As a former statistics professor once said, "The real world is messy." So is the understanding of the growing impact of hapas on the APA community and their place in society.

History can also be messy. It was not uncommon for states to have anti-miscegenation laws, prohibiting people of different races to marry (obviously, this has never been 100% effective – love will find a way). This is what sociologists call exogamy, or marriage outside the group ("outmarriage"). It can refer to racial, ethnic, class or religious groups. In the case of hapas, it encompasses all of them. By the way, this isn't exactly ancient history. It wasn't until the Supreme Court ruled in Loving v. Virginia in 1967 that the last miscegenation law was deemed un-Constitutional.[3] It's sobering to realize that in this author's lifetime, marriage to his Scotch/Irish/ English wife would not have been legal in all states of the Union.

Today, anyone can marry any one else regardless of race, ethnic group, class or religion. Now we ask, what has the government done to try to enumerate this new population?

For the first time in the 2000 Census, citizens were given the option to mark one or more races to indicate their identity. In addition to the five major racial categories of *white; black* or *African American; American Indian* and *Alaska Native; Asian;* and *Native Hawiian* or *Other Pacific Islander,* the U.S. Office of Management and Budget has added two categories of ethnicity, *Hispanic* or *Latino* and *Not Hispanic* or *Latino.* This acknowledges that Hispanics and Latinos may be of any race. Meanwhile, the *Some Other Race* category is intended to capture responses such as Mulatto, Creole and Mestizo. There are six specified Asian and three detailed Pacific Islander sub-categories along with a write-in section for Other Asian and Other Pacific Islander.[4] Whew! That statistics professor was right.

While this certainly complicates the counting (although much more clearly than was done by sociologists in the early 20th Century), it finally allows for a real representation of who hapas are. Matt Kelley, the half-Irish/half Korean founder of *Mavin,* a magazine for mixed race APAs writes the following:

> Identity is how you see yourself and how others see you. And when every form you fill out tells you that how you identify yourself is not an identity you can have, how can that not affect how you see yourself? You end up feeling, "I'm a freak."[5]

Well, as you will see, Matt is actually part of a very normal and growing segment of the APA community.

Until 1989, children continued to be classified as belonging to the race of the non-white parent.[6] In the 2000 Census, almost 7 million citizens identified themselves as having a background of two or more races. Of these, an estimated 4.5 million were under the age of 18.[7] Further, some estimates claim that 2.1 million, or almost a third of all U.S. citizens self-identifying as more than one race are APA hapas! This is an interesting statistic. For a community that is only about 4 percent of the total U.S. population, to represent one third of all mixed-race citizens indicates that something is going on.

While mixed race ethnicity is not exactly news, three factors make this a rather significant issue in the 4% of America that is APA – all or in part.

The Second Largest Asian Ethnic Group

First, if the size of the hapa population in the U.S. is truly as large as some claim at 2.1 million, it becomes the second largest APA "ethnic" group behind the Chinese at 2.4 million. There's a good chance it could top all APA sub-groups in the next Census, depending upon how strongly the need to indicate multiple races/ethnic groups hapas may feel. So why is size an issue? Simple. Everything we measure connected with voting districts, affirmative action quotas, hiring practices and college entrance standards are tied in some way to ethnic and racial measures. The *New York Times* writes:

> Ever since the framers of the Constitution reached a compromise to count black slaves as three-fifths of a person, racial numbers have been political power. In contemporary America, the apportionment of political power on the basis of population, the use of race in drawing legislative districts and racial bloc voting have prompted people to inflate their numbers. Or at least fear their dilution. That was why several civil rights groups and the Congressional Black Caucus opposed allowing people to choose more than one race in the 2000 Census.[8]

Again, you need to see this not as 2.1 million individuals, but as 2.1 million family members. Here's where America's "Melting Wok" is starting to go to work. As we have discussed, there are powerful cultural values that go across virtually all APA groups. Hapas share this identity at the same time that they branch out into the non-APA world in surprising ways.

Cultural Clashes with "Mono-racials"

As we noted before, Caucasian America does not have a monopoly on racial or ethnic prejudice. The clash can be particularly poignant when older family members with deeper roots and more insular habits are faced with other cultures and other races intruding into a previously closed family structure. But this is something America has always done, as the first-generation ethnic neighborhoods give way to a new generation. Sometimes it can be painful.

As we saw earlier, the growth of the APA population is fairly recent. This is one more way that America is "stirring the wok."

Many people become uncomfortable when they can't easily slot their fellow citizens into one of five standard racial pigeonholes. It's often a common human psychological response. If you are not white, black, yellow, brown or red, then what are you?

Besides the fact that the few APAs of the pre-World War II generation still consider the term hapa derogatory, as with other races and shown in the Tiger Woods story above, many view racial identity as a choice that denies loyalty to the "oppressed" racial group. Many "mono-racials" feel comfortable pressuring multi-ethnic/multi-racial people to choose or assimilate into a single racial group. Barack Obama, the first U.S. President with a multi-racial background, even with pictures of his white grandmother sent around the world, is still recognized as black, and denounced when claiming other than black heritage.

New Identity/New Challenges

Can you create a community based on inclusivity rather than exclusivity? Is there a hard and fast way to define who belongs to this community and who doesn't? Will the hapa "community" eventually include people with a completely non-APA background? Can a group be based on a collective effort that is often based on little more than being asked the complicated question "What are you?" Or, perhaps, the simple question one hapa often asks another, "Are you half?" Time will tell.

The American school system is already doing this to a great degree. While school children will always cluster in groups and cliques, we see that a bit of Asian heritage is often one of the differentiators. The things that might have meant a great deal to the grandparents are pretty much a non-issue for their APA grandchildren.

But this doesn't mean it won't be a complicated world.

What is guaranteed is that hapas will face different challenges maintaining their cultural heritage, not just in determining what to preserve, but also to what degree. We can predict hapas will have an obligation to accept (and promote) mixed race children as a part of whatever racial or ethnic group they are "part" of and work a little harder to pass along cultural heritage and history.

Growing Size, Cultural Clashes, New Identity

These three issues will force hapas and the APA community to continually revise what it means to be APA. San Francisco artist Claire Light writes that hapas are moving into virgin territory as they try to organize a group around a racial principle without having an actual race to unite them. "No one has done this before. Hapa is not an ethnicity. We're not immigrants from Hapaland."[9] Fellow hapa and teacher at San Francisco State University, Wei Ming Dariotis reflects optimistically on the hapa movement, "It's so inclusive, and it's morphing constantly. That's what I love about it. Ambiguity and fluidity allow us to include people in it."[10]

At a recent dinner with Kevin Maher, the Consul General of the U.S. at Okinawa at his home near Naha City, the subject of mixed race children came up. Kevin has first hand experience, as he (of Irish background) and his wife Sadako (of Japanese background), have two children of their own. The Consul General showed great insight in telling his children that they should not think of themselves as "half" anything, but rather "double." Recognition of the fact that more and more of APA hapas will self-identify, choosing the best of their multiple background and shaping it into something new and special will allow marketers to really address the New America.

Implications for Marketers

As the number of hapas increases in the U.S., less value is placed on "purity" of bloodline. Is this a microcosm of what's happening in the U.S. and the world as a whole? Are visual identifiers of race becoming so blurred that communications featuring Hapa/Mestizo/Creole faces can appeal to everyone but the most hard-core separate-race proponents?

Clearly, there is a broadening and blending perception of what it means to be APA – or hapa.

- More and more, marketers can view the APA market as a cohesive market segment.
- The impact of hapas is magnified when you realize that each is part of a larger family structure – even the first family has a hapa family member.
- The "Melting Wok" effect goes both ways. As APAs become more American with each generation, our popular culture will add an APA flavor – often in ways we barely notice. Many hapas will be on the cutting edge of this cultural blending.

Cultural Considerations:
People You Never Knew were (at least part) APA

This group is having more impact on our culture than many realize. We are now going to list prominent hapas in American media. You may be surprised to recognize more than a few names from the movies, television, or the face on the cover the fashion magazine.

They may not look like it or announce it, but they are.

Actors & Actresses
>Kate Beckinsale – Burmese
>Dean Cain – Japanese
>Phoebe Cates – Chinese
>The Rock (Dwayne Johnson) – Samoan
>Val Kilmer – Mongolian
>Ben Kingsley – Indian
>Kristin Kreuk – Chinese
>Lou Diamond Phillips – Filipino
>Lindsey Price – Korean
>Keanu Reeves – Hawaiian Chinese
>Rob Schneider – Filipino
>Jennifer Tilly & Meg Tilly – Chinese

Athletes
>Baseball player Johnny Damon – Thai
>Pitcher Ron Darling – Hawaiian Chinese
>Football great Roman Gabriel – Filipino
>Diver Greg Louganis – Samoan
>Football player Johnny Morton – Japanese
>Superbowl XL MVP Hines Ward – Korean
>Golfer Tiger Woods – Chinese Thai

Models
>Naomi Campbell – Chinese
>Brooke Lee (Miss Universe 1997) – Chinese

Vanessa Minnillo (Model/MTV VJ) – Filipino

Musicians/Vocalists
  Michelle Branch, Singer – Indonesian
  Anthony Brown, Jazz musician – Japanese
  Kirk Hammett, Metallica – Filipino
  Norah Jones, Singer – Indian
  Neal McCoy, Country singer – Filipino
  Freddy Mercury, Queen – Indian
  Eddie Van Halen – Indonesian

Newscasters
  Frank Buckley – Japanese
  Ann Curry – Japanese
  Jan Jeffcoat – Chinese

& Congressman Bobby Scott – Filipino

XIV. Messages
What Do You Say to APAs?

Every year, more and more Asian faces show up in TV spots and magazine ads. In many instances you will find that including APAs in your messaging in a normal and appropriate way will have an impact. Yes, sometimes it's that easy. Not only that, but more and more marketers are adding a bit of APA "flavor" to their messaging.

2007 through 2009 have been banner years for Asian faces showing up in ads, TV spots in particular, for products not necessarily targeted towards the APA community. You might want to take a look at the list in Cultural Considerations at the end of this Chapter for a quick refresher. Add this to the ever increasing number of TV shows that feature at least one APA actor, as well as a growing population of TV newscasters, and the public is seeing more Asian faces than ever before. Does this help satisfy the "Look-like-me Need" discussed in Chapter 11?

Is the use of an APA face in a commercial or print ad enough to communicate that a company is extending an invitation to purchase a product or service? To some extent, yes. Meanwhile, the absence of an Asian face is, to some extent, saying "We know that you're there and it's okay if you buy our product, but we're not actively seeking you out." A concern in the not-too-distant future will be how to walk the thin line between having the APA market think "I'm glad they're recognizing me" versus "They're patronizing me by singling me out."

We developed some perspective on this while working at Burrell, a unit of the Publicis Groupe and one of the oldest, largest and most successful African American ad agencies. There, the question was frequently asked," What makes this ad black?" It was almost as if some list of tangible, measurable, executional elements could be inserted and used as a diagnostic tool to differentiate a "black" ad from a "white" ad, or as we more euphemistically called them "general market." It often seemed like we needed to measure if it was "authentically black" or, worse yet, "black enough."

For the most part, the answer revolves around the thought that it includes cultural and consumer cues and symbols, both intrinsic and extrinsic, that a significant number of the target audience can identify with and relate to. If you can do that, they'll understand that this message is "for them," while not alienating anyone outside of the target audience who may not recognize the culturally relevant messaging. So, more often than not, messages relied on overt cultural stereotypes (e.g. gospel music, athletes, hip hop or rap artists) and "street culture" slang.

Often it was left up to casting to answer the "What makes it black" question, with few differences in copy compared to General Market work, and virtually none in Creative Strategy. Given this notion of the simple injection of an African American face along with a simple "ethnic icon," virtually anyone can create a black, Hispanic, APA or general market communication. It may not be done well, but anyone can do it, regardless of ethnic background. More on this later. Another quick side note – some of the most culturally stereotypical advertising is created by ethnic agencies every year. Go figure.

The logic of "cut and paste" substitution creative has been the bane of ethnic agencies everywhere. Time after time, general market agencies have successfully demonstrated, via creative testing scores, awareness levels, and significant savings on production budgets, that many advertisers simply do not need a specialist ethnic agency. If an ethnic agency cannot provide differentiating insight into the consumer and brand, creating instead a black/Latino/Asian "pool out" of a general market consumer strategy execution, there really is no *business need* for a specialist ethnic agency. Notions of political set-aside funding notwithstanding.

There's one more hidden dimension here – unintended consequences. Not all are bad. One of the most successful TV spots produced to help sell Tide detergent to a Black audience used an "anti-cultural stereotype" completely by accident.

The spot featured an African American man in a brilliant white t-shirt lying on a bed with his (presumably) son, also in a white t-shirt laying on his stomach. The spot featured the lyrics by a little known artist named Cait La Dee singing "Take me home to my family. I need to be surrounded by the ones who care for me." While the spot was beautifully shot, and graphically communicated the cleaning power of Tide detergent, consumers responded more enthusiastically to "a Black man taking care of his children."

While this interpretation was viewed as a positive in building the brand image, it was a completely unintended result. The creative brief never read, "Turn a cultural stereotype around in order to create a favorable impression that can be associated with the product." Subsequent attempts to reverse engineer the Strategy to fit the Execution have appeared rather derivative.

This issue is even more important and more apparent in the APA community. What makes an effective TV commercial, print ad or even website banner targeted to APAs is not the use of the color red or making reference to one's ancestors. If these simplistic notions were all it took to reach an ethnic market, then truly, anyone could do it. The real answer lies in digging deep to find the cultural and consumer cues that resonate with the target.

Simply put, the real test of whether or not a piece of communication is "for APAs" is if an APA will say, "This ad is for me." That's different from a marketer saying "This ad is for you." An ad for a college savings program may not feature a single Asian face or icon, but the smart media planner will place an ad for this sort of product in TV shows that are heavily viewed by an APA audience. Copy testers and market researchers, are you listening?

As with all parts of the Marketing Communications Plan, you must first start with an assessment of the situation. How is your company/brand currently positioned with the APA community? How should your company/brand be positioned amongst APAs if you want to reap an increased share of the marketplace? Finally, what message directed at the APA target will accomplish this?

We assume your Communications Strategy and whatever it is that defines your brand, whether your ad agency calls it Brand Essence, Brand DNA, Brand Personality, Brand Genetics or some other "proprietary" moniker, is under control.

What you want from us are the guidelines for creating great communications that will attract and entice APA consumers to select your brand? Fair enough. The first piece of good news is that APAs understand brands. From the beginning, they have been guide posts as they boarded the APA escalator. They are badges of success for the new generations – a reward for hard work and accomplishment.

In some categories, such as food, they may resolutely go their own way – persuasion will only come from connecting with deeply established behaviors. In other categories, such as fashion for APA teens and the latest high-tech, you will find eager clusters of "early adopters."

Most books on multi-cultural marketing are happy to give you the "rules" of developing creative tactics to reach the APA market, or at least tell you what you should not do. We usually start with classic mistakes. Here are some samples:

> Unfortunately, when companies do attempt to target Asian American segments, they make all the usual flubs and mistakes made when marketers try to save money by having cultural interpretations and language translations done by amateurs. One company placed an ad in Chinese newspa-

pers to wish the community a Happy New Year; the printers dropped the line of type and replaced it incorrectly so that they wound up wishing readers a "Year New Happy." Another advertiser used Korean models when advertising to the Vietnamese community in Los Angeles. Koreans, who have a different lineage, rarely look anything like the Vietnamese. Another US company that manufactures sporting equipment packaged golf balls for export to Japan in a special four-pack promotional deal, instead of in the usual three-pack. They didn't know that four is considered bad luck because the sound of the word for four (in both Japanese and Chinese) is close to the sound of the word for death.[1]

The author goes on to offer helpful tactical "pointers" on the use of time, formality, rank, hierarchy, tradition, religion, taste and diet, colors, numbers and symbols. Copywriters and cultural anthropologists, take note.

Actually, our two favorite mis-translation examples came from early cola advertising – discovering the difficulty of translating American English into another culture and language. Perhaps you've heard of the classic translation of Coca-Cola. Phonetically, it showed up as "bite the wax tad pole." But we still think the best example came years ago when they translated "Come alive with Pepsi." The result? "Pepsi-Cola brings your ancestors back from the dead." That's one heck of a product benefit.

When working in a language that you don't know, be careful. If and when there is a solid business case for translation-driven marketing programs, the best advice is to check and double-check. Build in a second opinion to keep your brand out of articles on classic marketing mistakes.

Same Race, Same Face
And what do you show to an APA? As we've noted before, APAs respond to seeing other APA faces.

We'd add a few additional observations – informed opinion based on some of the factors we've already covered. APAs pay attention. First, they're watching a lot less TV – when they do take time for media, it's a bit more purposeful. Second, remember that forest/trees discussion? Their antennae are tuned in. For many APAs, they don't just watch and read the media, they study it. If you have a message of genuine benefit and value, and it's in some "sweet spot" of family, finance, technology or education, this is an audience that will take note of your message.

That said, are there any real "rules" for developing messages to the APA market? Yes, inasmuch as there are "rules" for addressing any target market. Will your message be relevant? Are you communicating the Essence/Personality/DNA of your brand? And is that essence relevant? Will they understand the benefits of your product? If appropriate, does your message demonstrate that you acknowledge and respect them as a culture, as individuals, and as consumers? After you make a connection, do you have a way of building a relationship with your APA customer?

Cultural Cues and Social Signals

All Tactical considerations on cultural and social cues and signals should flow out of your Strategies. Don't pander. Just because someone knows that the color red is auspicious in the Chinese culture does not mean that they should be developing your APA marketing program.

You're already a lot more of an APA expert than you were 200 pages ago. If you have a strategy that connects with core APA values, you should do well. If it's appropriate, and APA faces are part of the message, so much the better. It's not rocket science – unless, of course, you're hiring for that particular industry.

Then again, you may have some questions about what kind of help you might need. Maybe this will help.

One from Column A

In an effort to again simplify what we are talking about, let's look at a simple matrix of options for developing your message within the context of the APA market. One column, reading left to right, will force, or at least direct, the decisions made in the subsequent columns. We'll look at helping you determine (based on your rigorous marketing research) what is the best route for your company to take in developing an APA marketing communications program.

CREATIVE STRATEGY	AD CONTENT	AD PRINCIPALS	MEDIA STRATEGY
General Market	General Market	Non-APA	General Market
General Market	General Market	Non-APA	High APA Viewer, General Market
APA Inclusion	APA Focus	APA Casting	High APA Viewer, General Market
APA Inclusion	APA Focus	APA Casting	High Viewer APA Vehicles
APA Focus	APA Focus	APA Casting	High Viewer APA Vehicles
APA Focus	APA Focus	APA Casting	Asian Language Vehicles

This matrix is not designed to give you answers, but to help you ask the right questions. We've stated previously that the essence of your brand should remain true, no matter whom you're talking to. However, positioning demands specificity. Does your research tell you that the Creative Strategy makes sense across multiple audiences or should it be adapted for specific target markets? Does the execution, both in Ad Content and Casting change with your Creative Strategy? Is it relevant to multiple audiences? Is it insightful and resonant? Do these decisions drive your Media Strategy, or does it come into play at a much earlier stage?

The first line reflects the fact that you will be using the same Creative Strategy, Ad Content, Casting and Media Strategy to reach APAs that you would use for everyone else. For ubiquitous convenience or package goods such as the above example of Tide detergent, this may be a perfectly rational and efficient way of defining your Communications Program. This is not to say that the Casting or Media Vehicles used in this scenario couldn't reflect an APA influence, but overall, the message is "We want everyone to buy our products." This is certainly the simplest and most cost effective means of reaching mass audiences, but will it be effective against a specific group like the APA market?

The last line identifies that you have chosen a Creative Strategy, Message, Casting and Media selection that is completely distinct from your overall corporate approach. This scenario is the most complex, takes the most research, manpower, and specific expertise to pull off, and calls for a budget adjunct to your General Market funds. You have to ask questions like this. Will it drive your business with a sufficient ROI to make all of this worthwhile? Will it plant your brand firmly in the hearts and minds of the APA audience enough to make it worthwhile in the long term?

As we've said consistently, all of the above options should be based on your overall Marketing Strategy. All will have widely varying outcomes in your efforts to reach the APA market, and all will certainly come with varying price tags.

It is often said, by account planners specifically, that in communications directed towards African Americans, casting African Americans in principal roles in advertisements is no longer sufficient to drive attention, interest, desire and action amongst viewers. Researchers advise that communications directed towards African Americans should also include the presence of unique cultural cues that are grounded in the "Black experience."[2]

Again, we remind you that the APA marketing model, just as with any specific target audience, cannot and should not be cloned from any other ethnic model. Unlike the African American market, which, arguably, has existed for over fifty years in various product categories, the APA market, is still so new to most marketers that some may still debate whether or not it exists at all. Remember what some of our respondents said in Chapter 11?

> *"I notice and pay more attention to commercials that have Asian actors in them."*

> *"I wish there were more television programs that featured actors and characters who look like me."*

> *"I'd like to see more people who look like me in television commercials."*

> *"How can you have a show about doctors or one set in LA or San Francisco and not show a whole bunch of Asians? It's almost as bad as those old shows,* Hawaii Five-O *and the* Streets of San Francisco, *where they hardly showed any Asians living there at all."*

> *"What commercials?"*

> *"There aren't any!"*

> *"Seeing an ad without an Asian face is normal. We're forced to accept it."*

> *"It's bothersome… especially because this is a highly concentrated Asian area (San Francisco)."*

> *"If you see someone who looks like you, you are more likely to watch."*

> *"When I see a diaper ad with a white, black and Hispanic baby, I really notice the absence of an Asian baby."*

Is injecting an Asian face into a TV spot, absent of any other APA cultural reference enough to create a strong brand loyalty among

APA consumers? Maybe not. But is it enough to begin driving attention, interest, desire and action amongst APA consumers? Our research indicates the answer is "Yes!"

By using APA actors in their TV spots and print ads, are the advertisers listed at the end of this chapter gaining ground with the APA consumer to the point whereby they're seeing an ROI in this marketplace? You'd have to ask them that question. However, looking at some of the brands using APA faces in their communications, we'd be willing to bet that some of those advertisers are becoming solidly entrenched in the considered set of the APA population in their respective product categories. To make the leap from no APA targeted efforts to customized, in-language APA programs is a leap that most marketers do not want to and should not take. We're of the position that sometimes a face *is* enough. At least to start. Baby steps are better than no steps at all.

Suppose you decide to use APA actors as principals in your TV commercial, print ad or web home page. As we've seen in the recent election of Barack Obama as the nation's 44th President, racism in this country is certainly not dead. One of the big questions throughout the campaign was "Will white voters vote for a black (or at least half black) candidate? Does this phenomenon cross over to marketing and advertising? Is there a "Bradley Effect" present in APA advertising?

The Bradley Effect

For those of you not familiar with this bit of research history, in the early 80s, the long-time mayor of Los Angeles, Tom Bradley, an African American, ran in the California gubernatorial race against Republican George Deukmejian, who is white. The polls showed Bradley with a sizeable lead in the days just before the election. However, when all votes were counted, Deukmejian won the election. The so-called "Bradley Effect" theorized that some white voters polled before the election claimed that they were undecided and did not announce their true intentions for fear of opening themselves up to claims of racial motivation in their choice of candidates. The "Bradley Effect" theorizes that some citizens will provide false polling information because of a bias towards social desirability, in this case, the notion that race did not affect their voting decision. Could a similar situation be present in marketing communications featuring APA principals, or is this merely a theory in search of data?[3]

Initial Research: Categories Where APAs May Add Brand Value

To date, little research has been focused on this topic in the APA marketplace. Extrapolations of research findings related to ethnic minorities are dangerous in the absence of data. The bulk of research on creativity has been concentrated on white, middle-class males. However, one of the few pieces of authentic research on the topic of social desirability bias was presented in the Journal of Consumer Marketing in 1992.[4]

The theory to be tested was simple – while advertisers may use minority group models in ads in an attempt to appeal to members of those groups, they may also be concerned that such advertisements will cause non-minorities to react unfavorably. The basis for the researchers theory was, that while Americans could not ignore the success story that Asians and Asian Americans may represent, these groups have experienced discrimination since first coming to the US, and thus, may extract negative feelings among non-Asians.

The researchers theorized further, that the response to different types of models used in advertising was heavily dependent on the product being advertised, that is, the "fittingness" of the model for the product. In other words, were some products more appropriate to use Asian models than others? The researchers set up three hypotheses:

H1: For products based on up-to-date engineering technology and/or products associated with Asian manufacture, white consumer reaction toward Asian models in advertisements will be more favorable than white consumer reaction towards white models. The rationale for this hypothesis was that the use of Asian models in such products would communicate that the product has the high level of quality that Asians are expected to produce and that in that sense, Asians are the "expert consumers" in certain product categories. Products used for this test cell were stereo speakers and small pick-up trucks.

H2: For products associated with social status, white consumer reaction toward Asian models will be less favorable than white consumer reaction toward white models. The rationale for this hypothesis was that since Asians have faced a history of social discrimination in the US, products associated with status or success may evoke negative reactions. The product used in this test cell was men's suits.

H3: For convenience products, white consumer reactions toward Asian models will not differ from white consumer reaction toward white models. The rationale for this hypothesis was that some products, such as convenience goods, were low-involvement purchases, and that since the ownership or use of these products implies neither expertise nor social standing, consumers will not associate these products with Asians or non-Asians. Products used in this test cell were pantyhose, children's vitamins and pain relievers.

All respondents were white, with a median age category of 46 to 60, two-thirds of whom had a white collar background, with a median education of at least some college, and slightly over half were female versus male.

Each respondent was shown a portfolio of experimental ads (using Asian models) and control ads (the same ads using white models) mixed together to avoid heightening the respondents' sensitivity towards the experiment's purpose. Respondents were asked to rank the ads on a semantic differential scale of the following statements:

"I feel this advertisement is:"
> Pleasant – Unpleasant
> Great ad – Poor ad

"Compared to products similar in price and function, this product appears to be:"
> High Prestige – Low Prestige
> Satisfactory – Disappointing
> Good – Bad

"I feel that the company which sponsored this ad is:"
> Reliable – Unreliable
> Friendly – Unfriendly
> Up-to-date – Old-fashioned

Overall results proved mixed. But not without an insight or two.

For stereo speakers, responses to Asian models were significantly higher than responses to the white models. For small pick-up trucks, there was no difference in responses to Asian versus white models. For men's suits, the response towards white models was higher than those of the Asian models. However, the mean response towards Asian models was significantly more positive than a neutral response. For pantyhose, children's vitamins and pain relievers, there were no significant differences in responses to Asian versus white models.

This is a primary consideration for marketers evaluating whether or not to use Asian models in advertising. These research results are very limited. Decisions based on any kind of empirical evidence such as this are inconclusive. However, the Strategies in your (hopefully) well-thought out and researched Marketing Plan may lead you to believe that featuring Asian actors may be a benefit to your Communications?

Then you may need to answer a few more questions. Do APA values reinforce your brand values? Can you find APA actors that can do as good a job in selling your creative concept as non-APA actors? Does it make any difference, either real or perceived to your product category? Should you just trust in your Creative Director to cast the appropriate actors for your commercial? Does common sense override personal prejudices?

Suppose you have decided that the best way to enter into the APA market is to produce targeted ads in several different Asian languages running in (by necessity) Asian language media vehicles. You've found an agency that can act as a translation service and production facility and media buyers for local Asian language media. You're set to start reaping the rewards of reaching the APA market, right? Not so fast! One of the key areas companies entering into the APA marketplace forget, particularly if they go the route of Asian language ads/Asian language media, are the "back office" operations.

Do you have an infrastructure that could support an in-language effort? Do you have a call center that can field questions in a dozen different languages (or even two languages)? How about a web site with customized language options, or at least a toll-free phone number that can do the same? Do you have sales reps, agents, or other field people who are armed with customized collateral materials? Do they have the language, social and cultural skills needed to represent your company to your potential customers? Even before you get to the field, do you have a marketing staff with both marketing experience and APA cultural sensitivity? If you answered "No" to any of these questions, perhaps you should re-think your rush to approach the APA market with a language other than English. More on this in Chapter 16.

But if you can say "yes," well you're probably ready. And we bet you'll know what to say to an APA. Now all we have to do is figure out where to say it. Next chapter.

Implications for Marketers

As we said at the beginning of this Chapter, we are not going to give you the answers in marketing to APAs. We can't give you a Creative Strategy, come up with a Media Plan or suggest who is going to execute the plan for you. However, if you can answer the questions posed in this Chapter, it's likely that you can answer them yourself.

- You don't need to use Asian faces in communications, but it sure can help. Sometimes using an Asian face is all it takes to communicate that you are serious about extending an invitation to buy to the APA market. There is rarely a downside to using an APA actor in a commercial, and it can be a benefit even if you're not trying to reach an APA audience.

- Cultural and ethnic cues, including language specificity if recent immigrants are a major part of your target, should be built into the Creative Strategy right from the start, not just a footnote in the Tactics section.

- Work to understand the buying habits of the APA market with no outward ethnic symbols used in the communications at all. Often, there will be a bit of history – or a surprising cultural cue – that helps you "get it." If you have a history of success with the market, chances are there's a leverage point.

- If your brand is not favored, study the buying habits in the category – and double-check the history of the preferred brand(s). Is it just an accident? Or is it the result of a consciously adopted APA program?

- Using a language other than English in your communications automatically dictates your Media selections and determines the course of your entire marketing program. Again, if recent immigrants are a part of it, or it's a cultural event, by all means, have translated communications. But remember, the APAs with money speak English.

Cultural Considerations: APAs in Advertising, Yesterday and Today

As with movies and TV, advertising portrayals of APAs have run the gamut from accurate, positive APA representations to blatantly racist depictions.

For the first 50 years or so of television broadcasting, APAs didn't really exist, or if they did, it was as the most basic stereotypes. Who can forget the Calgon Fabric Softener "Ancient Chinese Secret" spots? The Timex "Sumo Wrestler" torture tests? If you can remember back before Bill Cosby, how about the Jell-O gelatin "Poor Chinese Baby" animated spot, featuring a caricature in a high chair eating "glape" Jell-O with "that 'glate' Western invention, the spoon?" Then there was Charlie Chan on the late movie – and maybe *Tora Tora Tora*.

But, just as our population began to change – becoming more diverse – so did our tastes in entertainment. Pat Morita, a comedian and actor, gave us Mr. Miyagi in the *Karate Kid* and Arnold on *Happy Days*. Today, Sandra Oh is one of the people we expect to see on *Grey's Anatomy*. And APA faces are an increasing part of the casting mix across the board.

Ultimately, the true measure of success for TV commercials for their advertiser is to sell more products or services to their intended target audience – and we see clear indications that the APA audience pays attention.

Face Value

APA faces in commercials are an easy and effective way to appeal to the APA audience. Sometimes, it's just that simple. As stated at the beginning of this volume, the principles we set forth are not about social services, civil rights or politics. They are about doing good business. But understanding some of the very basic APA cultural concerns can, in our opinion, lead to a more successful marketing effort. It's a group that has worked hard to become part of America. So if you make them a part of your messaging, you may be pleasantly surprised.

We think marketers are getting the message. 2007 through 2009 were banner years for the number of APA actors appearing in television commercials, most of which were produced by "general market" ad agencies. We've never seen such a relatively large number of APA actors in such a wide range of executions as in the past year and a half. Since no formal, structured means to track APA actors in television commercials exists, a simple notepad by the TV set has had to suffice (with thanks to the many who reported "Have you seen the TV spot for …")

In the last three years, we've tracked over two hundred and thirty TV spots featuring APA actors. While this is a drop in the bucket given the thousands of commercials produced by advertising agencies each year, it is a clear indication that APAs in advertising as a target audience or as a part of color-blind casting are here to stay.

We've sorted the TV spots by advertiser, given each of the spots a title or product description, and separated them into four categories:

- APA actors chosen to fulfill an "Asian" cultural reference. In these cases, a non-APA actor could not have played the part accurately or as successfully, as the "Asian-ness" of the actor had direct bearing on concept that the advertiser was trying to communicate. The danger here is walking the thin line between stereotyping and reflecting a propensity of APAs to act/react in a certain manner. Are there a disproportionate number of APA scientists given the population in America? Yes. Is it easy to stereotype APAs as nerdy technicians? Also, yes.

- APA actors assumed to be chosen for their significance as a target audience for the featured product or service. Not being privy to an advertiser's Target Strategy Statement, we cannot know for certain if APAs were cast specifically to attract other APAs or not. However, whether intended or unintended, the advertisers in this group demonstrate an insight into the APA consumer mind.

- APA actors chosen with a non-specific role i.e. "color-blind" casting. No real demonstration, either intended or unintended of APA propensity to buy a particular good or service, or a creative need for an APA to reflect a specific cultural theme, but rather, a reflection of APAs as a normal part of American society, just as has happened with African Americans. The debate is still out on how accepted and "normal" Hispanic Americans have become in television commercials.

- The rarest of the rare, an entire cast of a TV commercial made up solely of APA actors, mixed race couples, a mixed race family, or within which An APA actor is a principal as opposed to an extra. Though you will see quite a few commercials like this in Hawaii.

Here are the spots by category.

"Asian" Cultural Reference

Advertiser	Featured Spot
Hall's Mentholyptus	Sushi Bar
Schick Quattro Razor	Test Lab
Snapple	ECGC Green Tea
Boeing	That's why we're here
Shell	Gunky Build-up
Gain	Mandarin Lime detergent
Blink Car Care Products	Test Lab
Arby's Toasted subs	Monkeydance
PineSol	Powerful Scent of Clean
Burger King Spicy Chicken	Little Kick

Toyota Corolla	Toxic Blowfish
Comcast	1,000 HD Choices
Visa	Wedding
Zetia	Interns
White Castle	Grim Reaper
Geico	Chinese Restaurant
Palm Pre	Life Flows Together

Assumed APA Target

Advertiser	Featured Spot
Ford Trucks	Lee's Landscaping
Best Buy	PC/Geek Squad
Capital One	Small Business
Intel Duo Core Processor	Dance
Ameriprise	Dennis Hopper Dreams
Microsoft	Windows Vista
Cingular	Italy Stole Your Phone
Dell	Intelligent School
Chase	Mortgage & Financing
Actonel	
AstraZeneca Nexium	Finisher
HP	Vera Wang
SoyJoy	Real is Revolutionary
Travelers Insurance	Rabbit's Foot
Nintendo DS	Pokemon
SAP	
Mirage Hotel	Beatles Cirque du Soleil
Farmers Insurance	HelpPoint
Walmart	Season's Hottest Electronics
Bank of America	Mortgages
Citibank Business Banking	Woodshop
Century 21	Computer vs. Agent

Cisco Telepresence	Staring Contest
Liberty Mutual	Pay it Forward
Cisco	Are you in?
Garmin	Give a Garmin
HP	Gwen Stefani
Visa	Life takes Visa – Rockit
American Express Plum	PinkBerry
Ebay	Stargazer401
E*Trade	Dirt Squirrel
Discover Card	Pay-down Planner
Verizon Wireless	Red Hot Deal Days
Bank of America	Risk Free CD
Mutual of Omaha	Long Term Care
Hampton Inns	With a Little Help From My Friends
Volvo X90	Something in the Way You Move Me
Range Rover	Have You Ever?
AT&T Advanced TV	4 Shows at Once
AT&T Wireless Internet	Jump Rope
Volvo C30	Lease Options
AT&T	Total Home DVR
Wii	Let Your Music Out
Geico.com	Number 1 Fan
Web MD	Better Living, Better Health
CVS Pharmacy	For All the Ways You Care
Potawatami Casino	Hit It Big
Discover Card	Spending Analyzer
Capital One	Triple Rewards-Your Choice
American Chemistry	Essential
Hyundai	It's Like Sunday

Verizon	Small Business Toolbox
Bausch & Lomb	Goodbye Readers
Intuit Quickbooks	Small Business
Geek Squad	Summer Academy
Domino's Pizza	American Classics
Garmin	Nuvifone
Merrill Lynch	Wealth Management
Potawatami Casino	Easter Island

"Color-blind" Casting

Advertiser	Featured Spot
Ziplok	Families
Nationwide Insurance	Breakdown
Nissan Sentra	
Taco Bell	Karen's Lunch
Quaker rice Cakes	Movies
Orbitz	Bad Weather
Quiznos Prime Rib	That's what real women want
Verizon Wireless	Mobster
Fiber One Cereal	Grocery Store
VW Jetta	Movie
Remax	Lighthouse
Starburst	Juicy Goodness/Whale
Volvo S-80	Fingerprint
Home Depot	We need a new fridge
Bare Essentials Make-up	Large cast
Hillshire Farms Meats	Salad
Cook's Ham	Grocery Store
AquaFresh White Trays	Better than stickers
Best Buy	Appliance Specialists
Walmart	Spiderman 3 Action Figures
UPS	Gifts

AARP	General information
TJ Maxx	Flight Attendant
VW	3 under $17,000
Kraft Miracle Whip	Scooter Chair
Lincoln MKX	Perfect Wave
Oscar Meyer	Deli Creations – Office
Toyota Rav4	Dinner
Walmart	Back to School
Pier 1	Candles
BrainAge	Nintendo
Juicy Juice	School Play
AARP	Divided we fail
Listerene	Rinse at night
La-Z-Boy	Dance
Advocate Lutheran Hospital	General information
American Airlines	Karaoke
Domino's Pizza	Crispy Melty
Honda Accord	Hold on tight
Dell	Burt Reynolds
Best Buy	Peeping tom
Buitoni	Muse
Sony PSP	Darth Vader
Tropicana Orange Juice	Made by oranges
Russell Stover Candy	Valentine's Day
Campbell's Soup	Tomato
Disney Theme Parks	Year of a Million Dreams
KidzBop	13th Edition
Dunkin' Donuts	Fritalian
Propel Fitness Water	25 Calories
Six Flags	More Flags, More fun
Quizno's	$5 Deli Favorites

McDonalds	Good Morning Chicken
Courtyard by Marriott	24 Hour Market
Planet Green TV	Naked Bank
Orbitz	Beach Finder Vacation
Lowes	Creative Ideas
Glade Plug Ins	Scented Oil Fan
Gillette	High Performance Shampoo
Nivea for Men	Smell Like a Grownup
Orbit Gum	Cheer for Orbit
Cadillac STS	Perfect Summer Accessory
Bounce	New Awakenings – Subway
Maytag	Voter Booth
Popeyes	Loaded Chicken Wraps
Bud Light Lime	Summer State of Mind
Playskool	Glide to Ride
Ikea	Stash Your chocolate
Burger King	Steakhouse 'shrooms & Swiss
Ask.com	Pregnant Questions
Trivial Pursuit	Digital Choice
Little Tykes	Get Up and Grow
Head & Shoulders	Respect the Scalp, Love the Hair
Great Clips	Walk Right In, Sit Right Down
Kashi Frozen Entrees	Made From the Best Stuff
Halls	Pep Talk in Every Drop
Pledge	Clean More, Faster
Lawry's Marinades	What's Your Flavor?
GNC	Vita-Packs
Bing.com	
Olive Garden	Rollatini
Arby's	$5 Combo of Summer
Pogo	Trivial Pursuit

Volkswagen	Autobahn for All
HSBC	Life Insurance
Comcast BusinessClass	8 People Fast
Bud Light	Tailgate
Trident Layers Gum	
Walmart	Christmas Roll-back
Bosch	Tassimo Home Brew
Subway	Chicken Melt - Lunchroom

All APA/Mixed Race Cast/APA Principal

Advertiser	Featured Spot
Garmin	Yao Ming Billboard
Sherwin Williams	He/She
Ford Fusion	Club
State Farm Insurance	Agent/Couple
eHarmony	Real Me
John Hancock	The Future is Yours
Walmart	Niece Gift Card
California Milk Board	Get the Glass
Quaker Cereal	Life
La-Z-Boy	President's Day Sale
E*Trade	Pull the Trigger Mr. Chang
Domino's Pizza	Brooklyn Style
VW Sign & Drive Sale	Honking horn
Washington Mutual	Rocket Car
Lowes	Every Day Low Prices
State Farm	Get Some Advice
Best Buy	Hancock Movie Promotion
Cisco Video Conference	Jelly Bean Cookies
Fiber One	Where's the Fiber?
Subaru Impreza	Boxer Engine
Subaru Forester	Flyout

Oreos
GE Biogas Technology
Healthy Choice
Tide to Go
Fiber One Yogurt
eHarmony
Wendy's
Priceline
Olay
La-Z-Boy
Microsoft Windows
GE Biogas Technology
Asics
Verizon Wireless Hub
Fidelity Funds
Red Bull
Sprint Data Plan
Armstrong Flooring
Olay
Jimmy Johns
Intel
Mutual of Omaha
US Postal Sevice
McDonalds
KY Intensive
Pledge Multi-Surface Cleaner
Tostitos
Acuvue Oasys
Fidelity
Starburst

Train Ride
Dragon Burp
Asian Inspired Dishes
MC Miko
Cardboard
Art & Dana
3conomics
Sweetlips
Crème Ribbons Bodywash
President's Day Sale
Kylie
Make the World Brighter
A Sound Mind in a Sound Body
Prom Dress
Guide
Welcome to My World
Leaf Blower
Cars
Professional Pro-X
Board Room
Our Rock Stars
Parents are People Too
Priority Mail Same Flat Rate
McCafe Coffee
Mr. & Mrs. Mark

Hint of Jalapeno

Freedom Funds
Pack of Contradictions-Scotch Korean

Frosted Mini-Wheats	Start the School Year Right
Target	Tetherball
Halls Refreshers	New Roommates
State Farm Insurance	Point of Know Return
Dove/Walmart	Home Salon
Tostitos Scoops	Surprisingly Simple
eBate.com	
Mass Mutual	Splash
Crayola	Color Wonder Magic Light Brush
Tylenol Cold	
Comcast	Shaq
Microsoft	Windows 7 – Kirsten
Walmart	Snickers Halloween
Yahoo	It's You
Minute Maid	Boost Juice

Who Is Selling to Whom?

The categories with the highest number of TV spots featuring APAs are, perhaps not surprisingly, Financial/Insurance (16% of above total) and High Tech Products (16.4%). These are closely followed by Food & Drink (including alcoholic beverages) at 14.7%, Health & Beauty Aids, Automotive and Miscellaneous Retail, all at 8.6%. Bring up the rear are Quick Service Restaurants at 7.8% and Travel-related Services at 4.3%.

Most surprising is not a product category, but instead, the number of TV commercials that feature either a Mixed-Race cast (usually a couple), an all-APA cast or an APA Principal. Over 28% of all the spots we tracked featured an APA Principal. While this is not an exhaustive study, the patterns of marketers recognizing the potential of APA consumers in specific product categories begins to emerge. We also suspect that more and more APA actors and actresses are showing up in casting sessions.

Implications for Marketers

Same Race/Same Face and Look-Like-Me are simple but powerful factors. And, as we experience an increasing diversity of tastes along with an increasingly diverse population, marketers will respond. This seems to be one of those times when doing good is good business.

XV. Media
How Do We Reach APAs?

The medium sends its own message.

At its most basic, media planning consists of finding the optimal solutions to two variables:

- which media to select to deliver your message to your chosen target, and
- how best to use the media you've selected.

Within these two areas come questions on the depth and breadth of your media vehicle list, the optimal number of times our message needs to be heard to take effect, validation of delivery of your message, the timing or flighting of the media plan, and affordability, among others.

In other words, planning media buys for the APA market is no different than planning for any other target. Naturally, you still need to go through a rigorous approach to developing Objectives, Strategies and Tactics tied to the objectives of the Marketing Plan. However, in the APA market, you may hear other concerns voiced, some based on fact, some based on fiction, that we brought up way back in Chapter 3.

"They're too hard to reach by mass media."

" We already reach them by mass media."

"We can't measure the media."

"There are no media for APAs."

The media landscape has changed more radically over the last ten years than all of the first fifty years of modern (read television) advertising combined. Not only are there more choices of media channels and media control than could ever have been imagined within the author's lifetimes, e.g. mobile messaging, social networking, TiVo, search engines, etc., but access to content is now global and available 24/7. Rather than attempt to cover the entire state of the media world, we'll stick to what affects your marketing and media plans to APAs the most.

The Large Media Agencies

As you're probably well aware, media planning and buying have been decoupled (or "unbundled") from the mainstream advertising agencies and are now combined into huge specialty shops – media agencies. The bulk of media planned and bought for the largest advertising agencies in the country is now done by only a few companies: Mindshare and MediaEdge: CIA owned by WPP, whose major agencies are Young & Rubicam, Ogilvy & Mather and J. Walter Thompson; OMD, owned by Omnicom, whose major properties are DDB and BBDO; Initiative, owned by Interpublic who also owns McCann Erickson and DraftFCB; and Starcom/Mediavest, controlled by Publicis, who also own Leo Burnett and Saatchi & Saatchi.

These companies are able to amortize the costs of syndicated research, planning/modeling systems and buying expertise across several agencies and multiple clients. This has been very attractive to major clients, who look for media buying efficiencies from these consolidations, in addition to the best media prices resulting from "buying in bulk."

The sheer size and specialization in the media arena has also allowed most of these media companies to look outside the traditional buying and planning functions to develop expertise in research, programming, and yes, ethnic specialty markets. Examples would be Starcom's Tapestry and SMG Multicultural units.

Aiming for the APA Target

Since its inception as a market, the APA target (in the Old Model, before the New Paradigm) has been caught between the proverbial rock and a hard place. Media planning and buying is, at its heart, a quantitative exercise that strives for measurable, objective results. APA "marketers" claimed that APA media plans, consisting primarily of in-language, unaudited print, was a qualitative decision-making process of buying and planning, something that was more art than science. What were marketers to do? All too often, it was light an incense stick and hope for the best.

Fortunately, those days are beginning to change. Let's focus on three areas:

- Do the APAs you're targeting tune into mainstream media or Asian language media? What's the "best" media for reaching APAs?
- How should we think of measuring media targeted at APAs? Is there a difference between targeting and reaching?
- What is "real" ethnic media?

Do APAs Tune into Mainstream Media or Asian Language Media?

The answer is simple. Yes. Both. While the APA market can be aggregated under many different variables, media consumption does not appear to be one of them – at least not to the exclusive degree that "experts" would have you believe. APAs consume a wide variety of media – from the Super Bowl to the local Vietnamese neighborhood newsletter.

We might add, with the fairly busy APA work and study agenda, media consumption might be slightly more purposeful. Aside from that, the other unique aspect, unsurprisingly, is a wide array of Asian language media. This media, again not surprisingly, skews toward the more recent immigrants – still a large and increasingly prosperous group.

That said, Asian language media is just part of the large picture. There is absolutely no logic in the theory promoted by some "experts" that APAs consume only Asian language media. If this were the case, Nielsen would never bother to capture APA TV ratings information. There would be no need. More on this later.

The range of media options is growing, just as the APA population is growing in size and prosperity. There has never been such a wide variety of media vehicles to choose from. Bill Imada of the IW Group writes:

> From 1990 to 2007, the number of media organizations addressing information needs of Asian American communities throughout the country more than quadrupled. Today, there are more than 640 Asian media outlets in the US (not including new media). A vast majority of these publications and broadcast-media organizations are in languages other than English. However, we should not discount the rise in English dominant and bilingual media, including well-established publications such as *AsianWeek* in San Francisco; the *Rafu Shimpo* in Los Angeles, and broadcast organizations such as AZN Television (Comcast) and ImaginAsian TV.[1]

The key point in this issue is to *not let Media Vehicle Options drive your Marketing Objectives!* In the matrix we presented in the previous chapter, note that there is only one combination of Creative Strategy, Ad Content and Media Strategy that *requires* that you use Asian-language-only media. If you've decided that the best way to reach your APA target is to create messages in Asian languages, then the media options are more or less decided for you. However, too many marketers *start* with Asian-language media options for a number of reasons. First, all of the myths they've been told and never bothered to investigate. Second, it's easy to get lost in all the subgroups in this market. Third, many of the pioneers in this area were offering translation services as a key part of their marketing. Finally, this world has a growing number of media vehicles targeting APAs – and, understandably, they have their own agenda. All too many are stuck with this collection of agendas as their input. So it's not surprising that they take that and *then* go backwards to develop their strategies.

Here's what some "experts" say on the subject:

> Some Asian American communities exhibit an insularity that is hard to penetrate, seeing other Americans of any ethnic or racial background as cultural outsiders. Many people who have lived in New York's self-sufficient Chinatown all their lives have had only rare encounters with people outside the Chinese community.

> But even this insularity can be a bonanza for marketers who take the time to target their ads properly. Many Asian American rely heavily on word of mouth and on the recommendations of their peer group.

> Dr. Diane Simpson, president of Simpson International of New York and an expert on the Asian market, explains that peer group influence is one example of collective behavior: "Research has shown that in an apartment building, it's not unusual for all Korean American occupants to use the same detergent."[2]

And just as naïve:

> Asian Pacific American print media are far more diverse than the print media of the African American communities. Unlike the African American communities, which have a number of widely read African American publications – *Black Enterprise, Vibe, Ebony* and so on – the Asian Pacific American communities don't have such vehicles. Even an established publication such as *AsianWeek* lacks the strength, reach and circulation of such publications as *Ebony*.[3]

And in the opinion of a Caucasian broadcast *finance* (not marketing) chief discussing *his* market:

> Q. The Asian market is not monolithic. We are talking about several different ethnic groups, right?

> A. Right. Each one is distinct. I don't believe that anybody calls themselves an Asian American. If you're Chinese, you're either Chinese or Chinese American. If you're Korean, you're a Korean American. Asian American is something that the press has created to talk about this group. It's different with Hispanic media. There are obviously different cultures, but the language is the same. In ours, the languages are different. So we program specifically to each language.[4]

And worst of all, as this was written by the head of an Asian American advertising agency:

> Assimilated Asian Americans tend to use little or no Asian specific media and are geographically dispersed, so they are hard to reach.[5]

If you've read the previous chapters of this volume, these observations barely require commentary. However, we can't let them pass without some judgment. So here are our comments on some of these comments.

"Many people who have lived in New York's Chinatown ... have had only rare encounters with people outside the Chinese community." Wait a minute. Not come into contact with people outside the Chinese community? In New York City? Even if Chinatown residents never leave the 'hood, what about the millions of people who come to eat and shop. APA teens and college kids are coming for fun and a bit of "home cooking." And let's not forget the comfort of the "same race" factor. Most of all, where do you think that next generation is going to school and getting established. Grandma may want to stay with her friends, but, generation by generation, the APA family is

expanding – without losing their roots.

> We're seeing an exodus among Asian Americans from estab-
> lished urban Asian communities. Marketers aiming to com-
> municate with Asian Americans are discovering that they're
> going to have to increasingly look outside the segregated
> confines of Asian-dominated neighborhoods in big cities. In
> Los Angeles, for example, 62% of Asians live in areas where
> they account for less than 10% of the population. Nation-
> ally, Asians live in a neighborhood that's 19% Asian, 58%
> white, 10% black, and 12% Hispanic.[6]

*"Unlike the African American communities, which have a number of
widely read African American publications … the Asian Pacific American communities don't have such vehicles"* If the writer means that there
is no dominant, national APA publication with a fifty year history,
then yes, this is certainly true. Though, for the moment, we'll avoid
discussion of the reach of *any* publication in this day and age.

However, this logic also assumes that ethnic media are the only way
to reach an ethnic audience. Remember from Chapter 6, the APA
market cannot and should not be modeled after any other ethnic
market. Oh, and by the way, if this statement is attempting to create the impression that any of the national publications targeted
towards the African American market guide the entire community, remember that *Black Enterprise* has a circulation of around 500
thousand, *Vibe* has a circulation of approximately 800 thousand
and *Ebony* has a circulation of 1.7 million. The black population in
the U.S. is over 36 million.[7]

We would add two more observations about this type of media.
First, across the board, consumption of this type of media tends to
be more *purposeful*. Second, advertisers in these media vehicles are
sending another signal – a signal of support for that community –
and that signal is received loud and clear.

"I don't believe anyone calls themselves an Asian American… is something the press has created… It's different with Hispanic media." We almost don't know where to start with this one. We need to break down almost every part of this statement. If this person would like an introduction to anyone calling themselves an Asian American, we'd be happy to have him meet one or two. Just as the "press" did not create an African American or Hispanic market, neither did it "create" the APA market. The press may latch onto phrases coined by marketers or sociologists, but it seldom creates labels themselves. Though it does popularize the ones that seem "catchy." Lastly, is the writer using language to define culture? Or is there something else we don't understand. If the market exists, sooner or later, there is media to serve the market. Growing market = growing media options.

"Assimilated Asian Americans tend to use little or no Asian specific media and are geographically dispersed, so they are hard to reach." We agree with every part of this statement – assimilated APAs use little Asian-specific media and are geographically dispersed, therefore hard to reach – *if you are only using Asian-specific media to try to reach them!* To say that a target segment is hard to reach because they don't use the media the way you want them to is another example of a Media Tactic trying to drive the Marketing Plan. The logical consequence of that is: Let's change our Target Market selection because we can reach another segment more easily!

Solving the APA media puzzle may not be the easiest problem to solve. But, actually, in many cases there are some surprisingly straightforward solutions.

Now for some opinions based on marketing principles and facts as opposed to myth or the rehashing of "conventional wisdom."

"I'm not Asian. I'm an American of Asian descent. I want to see programming that I can relate to."[8]

Thomas Teng, co-founder and principal of multicultural market research firm New American Dimensions argues that there is too much emphasis on Asian language media. "There is a slew of media reaching that immigrant but there aren't a lot of media reaching the American generation," he said. Tseng pointed to surveys his firm conducted this summer which find a sharp drop in Asian language fluency by the second generation.[14]

"For too many years we had advertisers believing they were doing 'Asian marketing' when what they were doing was Chinese marketing in San Francisco or Korean marketing in LA," he said. "The English language is a way to aggregate the Asian audience." [15]

English for everyone! That's what we mean by a straightforward solution.

e-Mail and Direct Mail

While most of our discussion has been focused on television and print, there are two additional media channels that can be used to target the APA consumer that deserve special attention – Online and Direct Mail – for two opposite reasons.

While all consumer groups use the internet for email, APAs are far more likely to use it for research, news gathering, and most importantly to marketers, for online shopping.

APAs are not only tech-savvy and more likely to buy high tech devices as early adopters, but they feel that tech is an essential part of their everyday lives.[10]

To each of these factors, let's add purposeful behavior. Think about it. The easy price comparison on the 'net plays to the "smart shopper" in every APA. And, with extra time for business and study, the time-saving component is one more plus for this already tech-savvy group.

Here is some research that might provide a bit more insight.[11]

Attitude	Total Respondents	Hispanics	African Americans	APAs
Technology helps make my home life more organized.	61%	61%	61%	73%
Before buying electronics, I do as much research as possible.	61	61	62	71
I'm fascinated by new technology.	59	62	65	73
When I find technology or electronics that I like, I typically recommend it to people I know.	55	56	59	60
I'm willing to pay more for top quality electronics.	53	53	55	62
I give others advice when they are looking to buy technology or electronic products.	33	41	43	46
I am among the first of my friends and colleagues to try new technology products.	27	33	41	35

We'll add one more factor. APAs are more likely than any other ethnic group to own not just technology, but the *latest* technology.

Percent who own:	Total Respondents	Hispanics	African Americans	APAs
Blu-Ray	3%	3%	2%	5%
Desktop Computer	61	53	50	64
Laptop computer	37	32	28	52
MP3 Player	29	32	23	45
LCD TV	24	18	16	28

Plasma TV	11	13	10	13
Cell Phone	84	82	79	89
Internet Service	73	63	57	88
Wireless Internet	15	12	10	22

Personal communications, e-commerce and entertainment/information are top uses of the Internet among APAs. Surprised? No.

Activity	Total Respondents	Hispanics	African Americans	APAs
Used email	65%	52%	49%	76%
Obtained latest news	42	30	29	53
Paid bills	36	30	27	48
Made purchase	33	23	19	41
Used IM	26	28	24	41
Shared photos	23	22	16	25
Watched video	22	20	18	32
Played game	22	30	23	21
Downloaded music	19	21	21	25
Visited TV Website	17	15	12	22
Visited blogs	10	7	7	19
Looked at TV listings	7	7	6	9
Watched TV program	5	5	5	11
Visited chat room	4	6	6	8
Uploaded video	4	4	4	6

This combination of embracing high-tech tools and using them to replace traditional forms of media and retailing will have major impact to marketers. And, of course, it's already happening. This may be another case of the APA market being a microcosm of what the general public will become. This is a target already comfortable with using the tools and means to global commerce, education, collaboration and innovation.

On the opposite end of the spectrum is Direct Mail. Direct Mail represents one of the oldest marketing technologies in contrast to today's electronic world in terms of speed of delivery, global vs. extreme local reach and costs per thousand reached.

The little data that exists on APAs and their response to direct mail look pretty good at first glance, if a bit outdated. Research tells us that APAs are more likely than any other group to open and read the direct mail pieces they receive (90%) and return offers at an extremely high average response rate of over 10%.[12] The assumption is that since they receive fewer pieces than Anglos, they read and respond at a higher rate because they feel "special" to receive the pieces at all. They are also more likely to use coupons received in the mail vs. Anglos, at 48% vs. 31%.[13]

The problems with APAs and Direct Mail are the same as with all DM targets, only magnified by several factors. The most important variable in all of Direct Mail is the accuracy of the target list. There exist few specialized "Asian" lists, as the methodology for capturing names is always suspect.

- Does a direct marketer simply scan the phonebook for Asian surnames?
- How does one factor in Spanish surnames for Filipino citizens?
- What about those who are of partial descent?
- How do you account for multiple generations of families living in the same dwelling?
- Given the overall younger age of the population with their propensity to move more frequently than older people, how long does the list last?
- How can you tell by the surname if a recipient speaks English or an Asian-based language? And if you can determine English fluency (or lack thereof) how do you know if someone named Chen speaks Mandarin, Thai, Tagalog or even Japanese?

The data derived from the upcoming Census may assist Direct Marketers in their quest to pinpoint APAs geographically, but as with other forms of media, the Americanization Dynamic, English as a Common Denominator and the embrace of High Tech may render the use of Direct Mail more and more ineffective and inefficient towards APAs in the next century.

The good news – the high incidence of computer usage and online commerce will make the group increasingly accessible and affordable as we move from direct mail to Internet-driven direct marketing.

Targeting the APA Market

For this market, we need to think "media targeted at APAs" and not "APA media." There is a significant difference between the two. It's a difference that will become clearer in the next section.

Targeting does not mean reaching. Just as aiming an arrow at a bulls-eye does not mean that the archer will hit it, targeting efforts towards the APA market does not guarantee that a company will reach them. Conversely, it's difficult to reach people unless you target them intentionally. And, of course, as we've discussed in the previous chapter, it's possible to reach people you don't intentionally target at all.

While we're at it, let's get on the same page regarding some media theory and terminology. The definitions listed below are taken from one of the author's texts on media planning written almost 35 years ago, but with the exception of tweaking for the internet and mobile-based vehicles, they still ring true.[14]

Reach – The number of different persons or homes exposed to a specific media vehicle or schedule at least once. Usually measured over a specific period of time, e.g., four weeks. Also known as cume, cumulative, unduplicated or net audience.

Frequency – The average number of times an audience unit is exposed to a vehicle. Usually referred to as Average Frequency.

Effective Reach – The level at which the number of persons reached is maximized between ineffectiveness (threshold effect of frequency) and a marked negative effect due to overexposure (wear out). The underlying basis for this concept is that each exposure to a medium and message has different values.

Ratings – The percent of households/individuals of a sample who have tuned in to a particular program.

Share – The audience of a program as a percent of all households using the medium at the time of a program's broadcast.

Circulation – In print, the number of copies of a vehicle distributed based on an average of a number of issues. In broadcast, the number of television or radio households that tune into a station a minimum number of times within a broad period. In outdoor, the total number of people who have an opportunity to see a given showing of billboards within a specified period.

Readership – The total number of people who read a publication as distinguished from the circulation or umber of copies distributed. This number takes into account pass-along audience, or the total readers of a publication beyond the original purchaser/subscriber.

Audit Statement – An independent, third-part verification of a publisher's/broadcaster's statement that the media vehicle in question actually attains the ratings, share, circulation and readership numbers claimed.

Coverage – A term used to define a medium's geographical potential. In newspapers, the number of circulation units of a paper divided by the number of households in the metro area. In magazines, the percent of a demographic market reached by a magazine. In radio-television, the percent of television households that can tune-in to a station (or stations) because they are in the signal area. In outdoor, the percent of adults who pass a given showing and are exposed in a 30-day period. In previous years, coverage meant the same as reach. Today, the meaning will depend on which medium is being discussed.

Composition – The characteristics of the people who make up the audience of a magazine, TV show, newspaper, radio show, etc., in terms of age, family size, location, income, education, product usage and other factors.

Media Message Response Function – An effect on target audience members caused by an association of those individuals with media vehicles and ads in those vehicles.

The Nielsen Approach

Nielsen Research is also giving this topic a bit of thought. In November of 2005, Nielsen Media Research, the television ratings service that defines the global standard in audience measurement, created the Asian Pacific American Advisory Council, consisting of 11 community, civic and business leaders. The Council's job is to advise Nielsen on a range of issues in the APA community involving sampling for television audience measurement. Jack Oken, general manager of local services at Nielsen Media Research states, "As viewing audiences evolve, Nielsen continues to strive to be at the forefront of that change by being as culturally sensitive and relevant to our viewing households as possible. The support of this council will greatly enhance Nielsen's ability to more accurately measure the television viewing behavior of APAs through out the US."[15]

In September 2006, Nielsen released its first report on APA demographics, building upon its previous reports which only included information on total APA households. These actions were foresighted, as the latest Nielsen Universe Estimates illustrate that the biggest year over year growth amongst US households is APA households, up 4.4 percent to 4.7 million, followed by Hispanic households, up 4.3 percent to 12.6 million, and black households up 2.2 percent to 13.9 million.[16]

Evolution and Exodus

As previously identified by the Market Segment Group: "We're seeing an exodus among Asian Americans from established urban Asian communities. Marketers aiming to communicate with Asian Americans are discovering that they're going to have to increasingly look outside the segregated confines of Asian-dominated neighborhoods in big cities. In Los Angeles, for example, 62% of Asians live in areas where they account for less than 10% of the population. Nationally, Asians live in a neighborhood that's 19% Asian, 58% white, 10% black, and 12% Hispanic." This data dovetails nicely with what we presented in Chapter 8.

The use of "Asian" (read in-language) media, particularly print media, automatically limits the number of the APA audience you will reach by definition, as the limited language proficiency and accessibility will cut off the bulk of the APA population. The fact that most in-language publications are un-audited additionally brings into question every definition listed above, especially circulation, readership, coverage and composition. Without proof of delivery, no media vehicle can be a part of a true measure of ROI. Further, as most local, in-language media vehicles are free, one must question the value of such publications. If it's free, how much is it really worth to the reader? Certainly these media have their place. Our country has a tradition of media that serves a recent immigrant population. But the APA market is now growing into something else – and these media vehicles are becoming a smaller part of a bigger picture.

The Evolution of APA Media

By now, you're familiar with the concepts we've been building – the APA Escalator, the Americanization Process, shared cultural values and, finally, the role of English in a market with huge variations in background and history.

Just as the market has evolved, so has the media. Let's look at the growing range of options

What Is "Real" Ethnic Media?

Is "real" ethnic media defined by a single ethnicity watching the programming? By program content? By ownership? Yes, all of the above. And no, none of the above. The "Melting Wok" is having its effect on old-fashioned Asian media. More and more, single ethnicity viewership, content and ownership are becoming outdated or artificial constructs when discussing ethnic media. That is why we always refer to the media vehicles used to reach the APA market as *targeted* media, rather than ethnic media. Let's look at each of these issues.

A New Generation of Media

When Michael Hong, founder of ImaginAsian Entertainment, was launching the network, his product was described by some as "a fusion between MTV and Black Entertainment Television in their early days." Unlike those networks that focused only on music fans or one ethnic group, ImaginAsian employs multiple media platforms, targeting an audience of all ethnicities who desire Asian-related film, video, music and web content. ImaginAsian features Korean soap operas, Japanese anime, Bollywood hits, Asian cooking and fitness shows and original APA content such as *Uncle Morty's Dub Shack*, a sitcom featuring APA rappers.

"We want a 'big tent' approach," Hong says. "We want to be accessible to all Asians and non-Asians." In building ImaginAsian, Hong didn't want to broadcast only in-language content, nor cater to one ethnic group. Today, more than sixty percent of ImaginAsian's audience is white and other ethnicities.[17]

We think that's fine. And, more and more, we think it's to be expected in the increasingly diverse country that is the United States of America.

A recent article in *Advertising Age* entitled "The Catch-22 of buying black media" seems to confuse media that reach an ethnic target with media that are owned by an ethnic group.

The request is always the same: Detailed data on where the brand this CMO manages spends its sizeable advertising budget – including black-owned media. And each year, the request for a breakdown of ad budget is politely declined by the marketing chief, who cites its proprietary nature.[18]

And so each year, the brand winds up with an F in the area of marketing and communications – along with 16 others – in the NAACP Annual Consumer Spending Guide. The stated goal is to measure corporate America's relationship with the African American community.

The survey's goal is to urge the black community to buy from marketers that support black media and to boost media ownership within the community, according to Richard McIntire, a spokesman for the organization. "Brands have these huge budgets, and less than 1% is reinvested back into African American media," Mr. McIntire said. "The black press does not see the advertising dollars coming from major corporations who will advertise in a market with two dailies, but won't in the smaller community papers."

Some of the biggest names in black media are actually owned by corporate titans. The most notable example is BET, which founder Bob Johnson sold to Viacom for $3 billion in 2000. Then there's *Essence*: Time Warner's publishing arm took full ownership of the legacy brand in January 2005.[19]

This is another bit of media evolution we're seeing. Once, the owners of ethnic media were from that group – almost exclusively. Now, that is less and less the case.

Henry Louis Gates Jr., director of the WEB DuBois Institute for African and African American Research at Harvard University and editor-in-chief of the Washington Post's *The Root*, a site intended to be a 'black version of *Slate*,' dismisses the notion that ownership is the crucial factor. 'There's a romantic, black-nationalist ideal that it's great if everything is all-black-owned. But what's all-black-owned? We are living in an era of a multi-national, multicultural environment. Diversity is the rule. Interrelationships are the rule.'"[20]

How does Mr. McIntire rationalize the millions of dollars companies spend on BET? Are they supporting black-owned media? Clearly not, by his definition. Are they targeting a black audience? Clearly, so. Like Mr. Gates, we do not see ownership as a crucial factor to effective use of targeted media.

Our Definition

We define "real" ethnic media by target, not by ownership. We define it as media that *your targeted ethnic market considers for them and is in their considered set of viewing choices.*

Mike Sherman, General Manager of KTSF-San Francisco, the country's largest Asian language broadcaster goes on to say:

> How do we define mainstream consumers when nearly 21% of the San Francisco DMA is now Asian? When San Francisco-based KTSF became the first broadcaster in the country to air Asian-language programming in 1976, it truly was a niche market. For many years, KTSF was labeled an "ethnic" broadcaster with minimal impact. That has changed.
>
> KTSF now is the only Asian-focused media outlet in the US that offers Nielsen viewership data to successfully track the viewing habits of the Asian community. KTSF continues to outperform some mass-market and Hispanic stations with its weekday prime-time dramas and news programs, seeing a 14.8% increase in household viewership ratings from 2006 to 2007.[21]

In the future, will there even be a need for "ethnic" programming? Good question. The latest information from Nielsen reports:

Once upon a time, the only top 10 TV show to appear on both the African American and Total US viewers list was *Monday Night Football*. In a landmark turn of events this year, black and white viewers both tuned in to the same seven shows in their respective listings. The top three were exactly the same. Some experts ascribe much of the change to less Afrocentric programming, the merger of the WB and UPN networks, and the rise of reality TV that erases racial boundaries. Perhaps it's a lack of choice. Or perhaps the increasing diversity of our culture is also having something of a unifying effect – something to think about. Here's a quick comparison of white and African American viewing patterns.

Rank	Program Originator	Program Name	African American Households Rating
1	Fox	American Idol	20.9
2	Fox	American idol	20.3
3	ABC	Dancing with the Stars	13.1
4	NBC	NBC Sunday Night Football	12.3
5	Fox	The OT	11.4
6	ABC	Dancing with the Stars	11.4
7	Fox	House	11.3
8	CBS	CSI: Miami	10.9
9	ABC	Dancing with the Stars	10.4
10	ABC	Grey's Anatomy	10.3
11	CBS	CSI: NY	10.3
12	CW	America's Next Top Model	10.0
13	CBS	CSI	9.9
14	CBS	Without a Trace	9.9
15	CW	Girlfriends	9.7
16	CW	America's Next Top Model	9.5
17	ABC	Dancing with the Stars	9.4
18	CBS	Shark	9.3

Rank	Program Originator	Program Name	White House-holds Rating
19	ABC	Day Break	9.3
20	CW	The Game	9.0
1	Fox	American idol	16.7
2	Fox	American Idol	16.1
3	ABC	Dancing with the Stars	13.8
4	ABC	Dancing with the Stars	13.4
5	ABC	Dancing with the Stars	13.3
6	CBS	CSI	13.2
7	ABC	Grey's Anatomy	12.5
8	ABC	Dancing with the Stars	12.5
9	ABC	Desperate Housewives	11.5
10	CBS	CSI: Miami	11.3
11	Fox	House	11.2
12	NBC	NBC Sunday Night Football	10.7
13	CBS	Two and Half Men	10.4
14	NBC	Deal or No Deal	10.0
15	CBS	NCIS	10.0
16	CBS	Without a Trace	10.0
17	CBS	Survivor: Cook Islands	9.8
18	CBS	Cold Case	9.7
19	CBS	Criminal Minds	9.4
20	CBS	60 Minutes	9.3

American Idol is the perfect storm exemplar of this type of programming, where the competitor roster accurately reflects the diversity that is America. Three finalists, including the ultimate winner Jordin Sparks and Melinda Doolittle, who many believe to be the finest voice ever to appear in the competition, were women of color. African Americans and other ethnic minorities find themselves mainstreamed on the airwaves thanks to featured players and producers responsible for current programming. True to historical precedent, the arts are once again proving to be the catalyst that bridges the cultural divide."[22]

Perhaps Nielsen is a bit too optimistic as well as a bit premature to predict that the desire for ethnic specific programming will go away as TV more accurately reflects the make-up of the American population. We also think a broadening of tastes is part of it. Sometimes we want a burger. Sometimes we want barbecue. Sometimes we want sushi. And don't forget the influences of the Cultural Connectivity and Look-Like-Me Needs.

Implications for Marketers

- Media planning has the potential to be the single most difficult part of an APA marketing program. As with Creative Strategy and all other variables in the Marketing Plan, do not ignore the basic rules of good media planning and buying.
- To paraphrase Marshall McLuhan, the medium sends its own message. The choice of language in which to communicate to your target determines the media vehicles and all of the pros and cons that go along with each choice. Do you want to communicate to the smallest, hardest-to-reach segments or the biggest, easiest-to-reach portions?
- APAs consume the same media, watch the same programs, read the same magazines, more or less, as everyone else. Much more and much less. Media measurement will remain the single most difficult part of the APA media equation, perhaps for years to come.
- The General Market decrease in old media such as newspapers in favor of new media such as online is reflected at an accelerated pace in the APA market.
- Look for additional Message Windows with events and community organizations.

XVI. APA Specialists
Who is going to do the work?

This chapter is not necessarily going to recommend that you hire a firm specializing in APA communications. Rather, it is going to explain the range of options available.

Certainly, a financial marketer serving a community with a large number of recent APA immigrants should consider some sort of "translation service" supplier for a range of collateral needs. And, just as certainly, there should be some in-house training for employees who interact with them – or even a dedicated expert.

That said, let's examine our options.

We're going to assume you've figured out a strategy for communicating with the APA market. You've figured out (sort of) how you want to reach your own particular subset of that. Now we get down to the executional nitty-gritty of who is actually going to do the work for you. Do you pick your general market ad agency – the one that says they can handle every sort of marketing communications? Do you pick an ethnic marketing specialist who states that they have the Rosetta Stone for reaching that market for you? Or do you throw you hands up in the air and say "This is just another issue that makes the APA market so difficult." You'd like to have the business, but you may wonder if the prize is worth the price.

As we've touched on in previous chapters, if you were trying to reach the African American or Hispanic markets, the social pressures alone may drive you to the quick conclusion of picking an African American or Hispanic agency. Not so in the APA market. In the APA market, the "demand" to use APA specialists does not exist to the degree it does in the African American or Hispanic markets.

Frankly, this social pressure may be one of the strongest reasons for choosing an ethnic market specialist in any ethnic category. Well, whether there's pressure or not, you do have a lot to choose from.

The *2009 Lexis/Nexis Advertising Redbooks – Agency Edition* lists over a hundred agencies that claim to specialize in, or have departments that specialize in communicating with the APA market.[1] These include recognized APA specialist agencies, major multi-national general market agencies, and as this listing is provided via a self-identification by the company, anyone who may want to claim expertise in the field. So how do you know who is qualified to do the work?

The Asian American Advertising Federation, a group made up of Asian American advertising agency principals, media, advertisers and other strategic partners, lists among its members about two dozen APA advertising agencies.[2]

The most consistent source for information on APA advertising agencies, at least as it pertains to size of revenues, is *Advertising Age* magazine, in its yearly Agency Report. In addition to listing the Top Agency Companies, Consolidated Agency Networks, Media Agencies and Specialists such as Digital, Search and Direct Marketing Agencies, *AdAge* lists the Top 10 Multicultural Agencies representing communications directed towards the Hispanic American, African American and Asian American markets.[3]

Here are the APA specialists.

2009 Rank	Agency	2009 Revenues (In millions)	% CHG
1	Kang & Lee	$16.5	26.9
2	InterTrend Communications	$12.1	51.5
3	Admerasia	$10.5	7.7
4	IW Group	$10.2	30.0
5	Time Advertising	$7.1	3.0

6	Apartnership	$7.0	-19.4
7	PanCom International	$5.9	-22.9
8	AdAsia Communications	$5.8	31.8
9	Ethnic Solutions	$4.7	16.6
10	Global Advertising Strategies	$4.5	80.0

It's interesting to note that the total revenues for 2009 represented by the Top 10 Asian American ad agencies is a little over $84 million. The African American list exceeds that total with only four agencies. The Hispanic American agency list surpasses that total by almost 29 percent with just the top three agencies.

Then again, each of these markets are twice the size.

Does size alone ensure that an APA advertising agency is the right company to launch your foray into the APA market? Of course, not. As with any search for partners, a rigorous vetting process must be undertaken to ensure that the company most likely to help with your success in the marketplace is chosen (the authors would be happy to assist you with this process). But how do you do that?

A Left Brain/Right Brain Process

We suggest a "left-brain/right-brain" approach to the agency search process, an objective/subjective series of questions that should give you all you need to know to be able to pick your marketing partner. While this screening phase should be no different than a search for a general market agency, it may be a slightly more difficult activity, due to the fact that there are fewer choices, shorter business histories, and different criteria used in the decision process.

First, using some guidelines established by the 4As (American Association of Advertising Agencies), the left-brain/objective questions:[4]

1. **Have they studied your industry, products or services or company?** There used to be a saying among old-time client service people to their trainees that "you have to know

more about your client's business than your client does." Of course, this is well-intentioned but impossible. You live your business every day. Your agency does not. However, do they know more about the *advertising business* and *how it pertains to your category or business* than you do? Can they talk about your industry or company on a relatively informed level?

2. **Do they have the abilities to analyze your marketing objectives and target audience?** Do they have experience with your product's usage, life cycles, seasonality, geography, trade or industry, technological and economic conditions?

3. **Do they understand your company's distribution and sales force?** All marketers are supposed to cut their teeth on the 4 Ps of price, product, promotion and place (distribution) but do they grasp point-of-purchase, packaging, personal selling, public relations, vendors, logistics, consumer contact points, retailers, wholesalers and jobbers as well?

4. **Can they analyze media choices and make the best recommendations?** Do they have the buying power to get you the best rates in ay chosen media category? Do they have local, regional and national contacts? Do they have the latest media modeling, tracking, and billing mechanisms?

5. **If necessary, can they write your marketing plan?** Many companies rely on their ad agencies to take on a role larger than just marketing communications, particularly when a company is strapped for manpower resources. Could your agency reps pinch-hit for your brand managers (as the authors have often been asked) if called on to do so?

6. **Once everything is written and finally agreed upon, can they execute the plan?** Can they go from creative research through concept development and into creative execution including printing/recording, planning and contracting for

media space and time, trafficking and distributing materials, checking on proper media insertions, and correctly billing you in a timely manner?

7. **Can they provide insight into revising or adapting your strategies?** Do they have the expertise to monitor marketing activities, track communications recall, recognition of your products and measure attitude changes amongst your potential consumers?

8. **Do they follow generally recognized industry standards for professionalism?** Do they avoid false or misleading advertising? Are they financially solvent? Are they active members of the industry e.g. are they members of the American Association of Advertising Agencies, the American Advertising Federation, the American Marketing Association, and, perhaps, the Asian American Advertising Federation? Are all generally recognized accounting principles in place?

Now to the much more difficult right-brain/subjective issues:

1. **Do they have the answer even before they think about the question?** Do they offer *real insight* in to your company's marketing situation, or do they just present the same old demographic information on income, education and buying power?

2. **Do they have real marketing credentials?** Once a company has decided to enter into the APA marketplace, the knee jerk reaction is to hire someone with an Asian name to lead the project. As with all minority-owned, operated or focused companies, there is big difference between an APA professional and a professional APA. Have they spent their entire career at one ethnic marketing company, or did they put in any time in the "real world?" Diversity and understanding marketing are not the same thing.

3. **What reasons do they offer to hire them, either in the absolute, or in competition with other APA agencies?** Is there a difference in what they do *functionally* versus a general market agency? Is the APA agency you're talking to primarily a translation service? Or do they bring other skill sets?

4. **Are they recognized as marketing professionals?** Who are their clients and what have they done for them that moved the client's business ahead? Historically, has their organic growth come from the quality of their work, or simply by being acquired by a large general market agency looking for an ethnic specialist?

5. **Are they truly experts in the APA category?** Everyone recognizes that there are differing opinions on the best ways to reach the APA market and even who that market is. Do they have the guts to take a stand on their opinions and, better yet, back them up with some hard data?

Take this Simple Test.

Here is another simple test for determining whether or not you may need an APA specialist.

	General Market Media	APA Targeted Media	Asian Language Media	Other, e.g. Events
General Content	No/No	No/Maybe	No/Yes	No/Maybe
Targeted Content + Asian Face	Maybe/No	Maybe/Maybe	Maybe/Yes	Maybe/Maybe
Targeted Content + Asian Face + Asian Language	Yes/No	Yes/Maybe	Yes/Yes	Yes/Yes

First pick a choice from the far left column. If the content of your marketing efforts to the APA market is not different from that used in the General Market, your answer is "General Content" and that gets a "NO" for choosing an APA marketing partner. Since your answer was General Content, stay in the top row to identify your media choices. If you will use only the media vehicles for the APA market that you use for everyone else, then your choice for this question is "General Market Media" and that also gets a "NO" in choosing a specialist partner. GIven your choices and subsequent direction of "NO/NO" you probably do not need an APA marketing partner to execute your efforts.

Likewise, if you identify the use of "Targeted Content with Asian Casting in Asian Languages" coupled with (obviously) "Asian Language Media," you'll almost certainly need an APA Specialist partner.

Two Points of View

As with everything in business, and the world for that matter, there is no single, definitive approach for choosing a general market agency versus an ethnic specialist as part of a program to reach the APA market. Let's take a look at two radically different viewpoints – and some of our own commentary on each.

Bill Imada, head of the IW Group, a $10 million APA specialist with clients like Comcast, Met Life and McDonald's and also a frequent contributor to *Advertising Age*, writes:

A General Market Agency for Ethnic work? It's a waste of money.

Is there really any value hiring a mass-market media firm to assist you with your multicultural media strategy? Not really. But why would you anyway? To save money? To consolidate your media planning and buying under one roof? Or, because your mass-market media agency is feeling the pinch of reduced corporate media budgets? Clearly the reasons aren't always that simple to explain.

Having worked with a few of these firms, I know first-hand that these large, often multi-national media firms don't offer the same level of strategic thinking, creativity, cultural awareness or even the promised savings that ethnic media experts offer and often guarantee.

And while most ethnic advertising firms offer a full array of media services as part of their primary business offerings, nearly all of the mass-market firms are simply trying to appear as if they can do it all – when they really can't.

If I were a marketer searching for an ethnic media expert, I certainly wouldn't trust the mass-market firms. But even if I didn't have a choice, I'd still demand some proof from the mass-market firms to support their claims of being ethnic media experts. And so should you.

Nearly all of the ethnic agencies have a team of dedicated media professionals at your service. And you don't have to pay extra for their cultural expertise because they make it a point to select, negotiate and offer the best strategic thinking when planning ethnic media buys for their clients. And oftentimes at better prices.

Marketers also need to know that mass-market firms are not certified as minority-owned and operated firms, which also places them at a disadvantage when dealing with community leaders and key influencers. These community leaders expect and occasionally demand that corporate marketers support bona fide minority-owned business owners.[5]

Let's take a look at some of Bill's points. Having worked at both general market and ethnic specialty agencies, the authors take a little umbrage at the suggestion that those in general market agencies "don't offer the same level of strategic thinking, creativity, cultural awareness…" Given the notion that marketers should "demand some proof from the mass-market firms to support their claims of being ethnic media experts," we'd suggest the same should be done for every company you may be vetting, ethnic specialists included.

Regarding media buying, we offer this observation, based on many years at both kinds of agencies, and seemingly shared by every media expert we've talked to. Ready? We've never seen "the promised savings that ethnic media experts offer and often guarantee" by ethnic specialists or anyone else for that matter. Then again, any media buying service that could *guarantee* savings for its clients would certainly have their doors beaten down by every major advertiser in the nation.

Of course, most mass-market communications companies are not certified as minority-owned and operated firms. But neither are they certified as female-, teenaged- or disabled-owned and operated. Yet, they continue to do business with and for all of these groups. The list of sponsors of major events in the APA community (e.g. State Farm Insurance, Pacific Gas & Electric, Ford, and J.C. Penney, among others) suggests that the APA community is more interested in getting their interests supported than dealing with "bona fide minority-owned business owners." For most APA groups, this is a non-issue with plenty of examples of second generation APAs finding their way in corporate America. As with the media examples shown earlier, the separation of business transactions and civil rights and "social fairness" is different in the APA community.

That said, when companies do support APA activities, there is a consistent pattern of the APA market responding with good will and, more often than not, positive impact on ROI.

Now, for a completely different viewpoint, let's hear from Alberto Ferrer, Managing Partner of the Vidal Partnership, currently the third largest Hispanic advertising agency in the US. They have revenues of $31 million and clients like Kraft, Mastercard and Nissan.

Why you don't have to be Hispanic to be a successful Hispanic marketer

Just in case you're saying to yourself: "Oh, no he didn't!" let me reiterate: I believe you don't have to be Hispanic to be an effective Hispanic marketer. There, I said it.

That's the short answer. However, it's not as simple as that. There are a fair number of caveats and a not-insignificant number of nuances in the long answer. I do believe that being Hispanic can make the job easier.

Hispanic marketing is not about speaking Spanish or being Hispanic or even being married to a Hispanic. In fact, non-Hispanics can be as effective (and in some cases more so) as Hispanics involved in Hispanic marketing.

It's about (among others):

- Having a passion for the Hispanic market
- Understanding the business imperative that the Hispanic market represents
- Being open to and on the lookout for the cultural differences that can make or break communications
- Recognizing that the market is different and, thus, different rules apply
- Asking questions to understand and learn

In my opinion, Hispanics who work in Hispanic marketing have it easier because they usually need fewer things explained to them (for example, they can read and understand creative that is in Spanish, and many of the idiosyncrasies of the market are second nature to them). They "get" the market and creative nuances right in their guts.

But it's not all fun and games. These marketers need to be mindful of their audiences and realize they themselves are not necessarily the target of the communications. They need to evaluate the work from the target's point of view and not their own.

Clearly, the more different a target population, the less it is fully understood by the general population and therefore more difficult it is to hit one out of the ballpark when it comes to developing communications. This applies even with a target as broadly defined as "women." Most men I polled, even some who have been married for years, admit they haven't figured out women even though they interact with them daily.

On the agency side, there is more of a debate, especially with the recent surge in general-market-agency interest in the Hispanic market. Agency folks, however, have an even greater responsibility and that is to represent the market, understand it, and bring it to life for clients.

The matter of nuances and insights doesn't apply just to creatives and account planners, by the way, but also to account management folks, the media team and every other agency department that has a hand in the conception, development and delivery of messages to the Hispanic consumer.

My rule of thumb is that the closer the work you do at the agency is to the end consumer of the communications, the more important and helpful it is that you are a part of that target population and deeply immersed in it.

So you don't have to be Hispanic to be effective in Hispanics marketing, but it's easier if you are. Whichever is the case, you need a passion for the market, a deep desire to understand it more than you do today and a drive to deliver insightful communications to the target.[6]

In addition to simply following Marketing 101 standards, one of the factors pointed out by Alberto is that all marketers, whether general market or ethnic specialist, need to go into the niche without bias, particularly, in this case, built-in ethnic bias. The review of work by *the target's standard and not my own* is a challenge all marketers need to embrace with every new assignment.

The Primary Concern is ROI

As we've said from the beginning, the biggest concern for market-ers should be ROI. Whether you're developing a program geared towards the general market or the APA market, the bottom line for planning for success is the same. Pick a partner who can provide an in-depth, insightful understanding of the target and then cre-ate great communications that connect with that target. Exploit the potential for profit and growth through business excellence. The color of skin or ethnic origin should not be the determining factor when making this decision, even though it does play a role in how the market itself responds.

Here is an excerpt from *Ad Age*'s "Big Tent" column. It's by Nils von Zelowitz, VP-Associate Director of Direct and Digital Marketing, who is also at The Vidal Partnership (a non-Hispanic at an Hispanic agency?!). He writes:

> For as long as anyone can remember, multi-cultural agen-cies have been subsisting on budgets left over after general-market initiatives are funded. A typical conversation might go as follows: "Now that we have the general-market budget established, we can narrow down on spending for multi-cultural (or Hispanic, Asian, African-American)." The sub-text is that the allocation to multi-cultural comes from the remaining budget.

> This leaves the multi-cultural agencies frustrated and dread-ing this conversation. However, the dread comes from the wrong place and for the wrong reasons. The focus needs to change from worrying about what leftovers clients can be persuaded to allocate outside of general market to under-standing how to most wisely invest the dollars that are in the marketing budget.

> Clients and agencies need to insist on a zero-based approach to prioritizing opportunities and allocating dollars. If there

was ever a moment to shed the "this is the way it has always been done" and take a fresh and unencumbered approach, it is now. It's doubtful anyone would dispute that the focus on ROI has increased exponentially in the last year. Partnership commitment is required to shift the conversation and concentrate on figuring out how to generate the best return for every dollar invested.

If it is more efficient to start with Hispanic, African American, Asian or general market, so be it. This is about doing the homework and making informed decisions vs. doing things the way they have always been done. And in today's world, that means doing less of the same."[7]

What continues to obfuscate the discourse is the fact that additional factors still drive the discussions: agency staff ethnic diversity, "big guys" vs. "little guys," and "civil rights marketing" vs. ethnic target marketing.

Even though these factors are, in the main, irrelevant to the APA discussion, they are still a factor in the overall ethnic marketing conversation.

In the *Advertising Age* series written for Black History Month, the writer states, "The fact of the matter is that diversifying the employee makeup of general-market agencies does not ensure that those agencies will have the expertise or experience to do segmented ethnic marketing. For starters, they do not have the resources or appropriate leadership at the top."[8] Perhaps, but is the reverse true? We think not.

She goes on to interview E. Morris CEO, Eugene Morris, who heads one of the leading African American agencies. He observes, "We think it is the general desire of general-market agencies to put us out of business. Unless African-American agencies become a part of the mainstream, our community would definitely suffer," noting that African-American businesses make an economic contribution to the African-American community – a critical capital boost that general-market agencies do not.

If, by economic contribution, Mr. Morris means jobs, then anyone hiring African-Americans makes contributions to the community. If he means monetary donations, we would hold up the good works of organizations like Chicago's *Off-the-Street Club*, supported in great part by the Chicago advertising community, against the donations of any single African-American business. Then again, don't feel like you're being singled out, Mr. Morris. Doesn't Young & Rubicam want to put Leo Burnett out of business? And vice versa.

Entering the Multicultural Mainstream

What we'd like to see happen in the marketplace was summed up most eloquently by *Advertising Age* columnist Jonah Bloom in his editorial piece entitled "Wish I may, wish I might: Fewer Swiffers, more soccer in '06, please."

> Ethnic-silo fans: Multicultural is mainstream or, perhaps more pertinently, the mainstream is multicultural. That means that minority-owned businesses "specializing" in multicultural marketing and siphoning off small, specially allocated "multicultural" budgets are a deeply inadequate solution. It's time for 'mainstream' agencies to make a serious commitment to staffing their shops with people of varied ethnicities and cultures, and likewise it's time "multicultural" agencies started pitching "general market" accounts. Whatever the hell they are.[9]

We endorse this approach not only for reasons of "social justice," but also because experience has shown that companies that have a broader outlook tend to have a healthier bottom line. Moreover, it seems to be protection against the unhappy results that too often come from a narrow business perspective.

Other avenues to consider: External and Internal

There's a lot more than advertising on the APA marketing menu. So it may very well be that you can't afford, or otherwise do not want to develop traditional media advertising to support your APA program? Note that we say traditional. For example, an entry-level foray into online marketing can be very inexpensive in terms of out-of-pocket costs. And, if you'll recall, the APA market is one of the most computer-savvy and online-friendly.

What if, right now, audience composition is more important to you than audience coverage and you can't afford the production costs of specialized in-language efforts? Suppose you have a brand that needs to understand APA reactions to a sampling program, or needs to stimulate first trial of the product or wants to test a new product launch on a limited basis? How, then, can you reach the APA market without media?

Event Marketing

One of the most successful ways in which we've been able to introduce some of our clients to the APA target is through Event marketing. There are literally thousands of APA events every year, ranging from a sponsorship of the Chinatown New Year Parade in San Francisco, broadcast all over the world and costing several hundred thousand dollars, to a local street fair where title sponsorship may be only a few thousand dollars. Perhaps some of the organizations listed at the end of this chapter can help you with this.

With Event Marketing, just as with previous strategic recommendations, we suggest a fairly rigorous process for weeding out the suspects from the prospects. This is particularly true with events falling into the "festival" category run by community volunteers. The exact return for your sponsorship support is often less than business-like, bordering on hyperbole e.g. "the biggest in the country," "attracting thousands of your customers," or "the best opportunity to reach X."

We suggest the following checklist as the "Criteria for Inclusion" of any event sponsorship.

- **Fit with Business Objectives** – Is your intent on using this event as a marketing tool to boost or develop your image with the APA market? To gain new business leads? To retain existing or win back lost business? To link local agents, representatives or retail outlets to neighborhood groups? To increase senior level contacts with civic, community or other groups? Will this event give you the opportunity to do any of these?

- **Types of Support Offered** – What sort of support is expected by the organization holding the event and at what out-of-pocket cost to you? Is there an opportunity for real programmatic support of an organization, or are you simply underwriting the costs of another chicken dinner? Are increasing levels of support by your company accompanied by increased offerings by the organization? Are these subject to customized negotiations? Is there an opportunity for your company to be a "title sponsor" or will you take a position secondary to other stakeholders? Do you want to be a big fish in a small pond or vice versa? How about a big fish in a big pond?

- **"Media" Measurement** – We often use paid media terms to measure the ROI surrounding Event marketing opportunities. Is the "reach" of the event sufficient in terms of getting to a critical mass for you? Is the "frequency" of reminders of your company sponsorship enough to get attendees to recognize your involvement? What is the "non-duplication" of attendees of this event versus similar ones?

- **P.R. Opportunities** – What are the public relations efforts surrounding the event? Will you be included in press releases, information to constituents, and paid advertising? Are there other variables your company can use to gauge the success specific to your plans e.g. sales leads, local representative satisfaction, attendee awareness increases of your brand, return on "intent?" Have you or has the organizing body planned for any pre- and post-measurement on your image among attendees, how it can be enhanced through marketing, how well your Tactics directed towards the APA market are working vis-à-vis thought leaders or new/old customers?

- **Profile** – There is always a trade-off in high profile versus low profile and high reach versus low reach. The Committee of 100 Conference includes the top business, government, education, social service and entertainment luminaries in the Chinese American community, but your immediate message only reaches the thousand or so people attending the event. It's an important group but it's small. Then again, you may be targeting the Los Angeles Lotus Festival, which reaches almost a hundred thousand visitors interested in Asian and APA culture, and is open to anyone who wants to drop by. Which fits better with your marketing plan?

- **Collateral Materials** – Do you have or will you need informational materials that attendees will take with them? Particularly for mass reach events like the Lotus Festival listed above, do you have materials that show no favoritism towards any group via language, message or offerings? Note that in most major urban areas, this would include not offending other ethnic groups such as Latinos or African Americans as well. What about company logo giveaways? If appropriate, your logo on a T-shirt – particularly in kid sizes – can be a winner. Remember, family is important across the board – and that T-shirt with your logo can become a friend of the family.

- **Staffing** – Will you need trained staff that knows your business to field questions or complaints about your company, or do you just need spokesmodels to hand out product while sporting your logo? Are there APAs who are part of your company? They should be there.

- **Attendees** – Who is coming to the event? Are the attendees national thought leaders or community grassroots activists? Are groups represented, or just individuals? Is the event purposefully segmented towards a specific Asian ethnic group or nationality, or is it geared towards the general APA population? Are most of the attendees APA or non-APA? This may sound ridiculous at an APA–oriented event, but as in the case of the Los Angeles Lotus Festival above, while thousands of APAs attended, the majority of visitors were Latino. Does this surprise, or do you remember the information we covered in Chapter 12 on non-APAs as a bonus?

- **Geography** – How does fit in with your sales area or distribution? Is the event national, regional, local or multi-site?

- **Follow-up** – How are you going to follow up on your experiences and learnings of the event? What are you going to do with sales leads, team reports, consumer feedback or new contacts? Do you have their e-mail addresses? Will there be any impact on company policy as a result? Will you continue your new relationship with APA event groups as an ongoing partner, or was this a one-off? Is there an opportunity for you to become a key player in the organization or market based on your event involvement?

If you can address every one of the variables listed above based on your Marketing Plan, then the opportunity for a good return on investment and a good return on intent is probably pretty high.

Housekeeping

As with every idea in this book, we ask you to first look at your company's objectives, processes and structure before you venture out into the realm of the APA market. So what can you do *internally* to set yourself up for the best possible return on investment? What can you do in your own backyard before you even present your program to the public?

First and foremost, don't treat it like a hobby. If you are going to venture into a market that's new to your company, you must formalize the role of your marketing staff within your organization. We've seen countless examples of companies that set up an "ad hoc committee on APA marketing" or a "skunk works" program on multiculturalism and failed miserably. As we've said from the start, if you're going to enter the market, do it as an active participant, not as a hobbyist. If your Marketing Plan has an APA element in it, it should also have staff that is dedicated to making sure it's a success. But who else can you get to help these people?

We've seen several companies, with great success, set up internal "advisory boards." These are people working for the company with an interest in the APA market, but who are not part of the marketing staff charged with carrying out the plan. Often, they are APAs who work for the company or key suppliers – and they are pleased to participate. In addition to adding company expertise from outside the marketing department, these employee groups can act as corporate cheerleaders for the entire APA program. Often, they will merchandise your marketing efforts through internal communications.

Is your Human Resources department aware of your marketing program? Can they assist you in finding current or future hires with an interest in your APA program, cross- disciplinary interests, or by promoting positive hiring practices? Does HR actively recruit from colleges and universities that would assist you with geographic concentrations, ethnic marketing specialist needs or contacts with APA student organizations?

Does your company have a network of Minority- or Gender-based suppliers and business partners that may be interested in assisting your efforts? Are they involved with any APA Chambers of Commerce or other business and community groups that would promote your record of involvement with the APA communities?

Are you training your people to better market to the APA target?

Are you sending them to conferences and seminars? Are you developing internal training programs, customer service workshops, issues management policies and most important, rewarding your staff for marketplace successes?

Large Scale/High Profile APA Events

We think you'd like to know about some of the largest and most significant APA events in the US. While there are hundreds of smaller, local events, you should know that some of these attract crowds in excess of 100 thousand and the most prominent APAs and non-APAs in the country. Here are the big ones:

Los Angeles Lotus Festival
San Francisco Cherry Blossom Festival
APAICS Conference in Washington DC
San Francisco Nihonmachi Street Festival
Asian Pacific Women's Leadership Initiative in Washington DC
Los Angeles Nisei Week
Asian American Coalition Lunar New Year in Chicago
National Association of Asian American Professionals Conference
Committee of 100 Conference in New York
Asian American Journalists Association Conference
Organization of Chinese Americans Conference
Leadership Education for Asian Pacifics Conference
New York and San Francisco Chinatown New Year's Parade

National APA Groups

Here is a list of some of the biggest, oldest, most influential national APA groups. These are groups you may wish to consider as marketing partners.

Asian American Journalists Association
Asian Pacific American Institute for Congressional Studies
Committee of 100
Japanese American Citizens League
Korean American Coalition

Leadership Education for Asian Pacifics
National Asian Pacific American Bar Association
National Association of Asian American Professionals
Organization of Chinese Americans

Almost all of these organizations have local chapters to contact, and almost all can lead you to a group that covers your area of interest.

The Organization of Chinese Americans, sponsored by Philip Morris, used to publish what was probably the most complete directory of APA organizations ever compiled. The directory covered Arts, APA Studies, Civil Rights Advocacy, Health, Legal, Media, Cultural/Educational/Historical, Service/Community, Political, Professional, Women's, and Student groups. It's worth checking to see if a back issue or update is available.

Implications for Marketers

- Marketing to APAs is not a genetically transferred skill. As with any target market, employ Marketing 101 questions and guidelines, such as those set forth by the 4As, to determine who is best to assist you in your efforts. It's not a matter of skin color or language proficiency. Do you want to go after the smallest, hardest-to-reach segment, or the largest, easiest-to-reach?
- Often, the best place to test the APA waters is via event marketing and organization partnerships. Remember that partnerships, in the APA sense, need (and are expected to be) a give and take on both sides, not just funds thrown at social problems in hope of reaping community support as a reward. In general, you will find a concern with delivery value and an entrepreneurial spirit.

XVII. Conclusions

The premise of this volume is, first, that the Asian Pacific American market is a very unique 4% of the larger U.S. market – one that behaves as a single market despite its wide-ranging origins.

Second, we note that this market can be targeted, reached, and understood in fairly simple terms provided that basic marketing principles are applied to the process.

As we said in the beginning, this is not a "how-to" book. Anyone wanting to enter into the APA market will still have to do a considerable amount of work – just as they would with any other target group. However, those adopting the current conventional wisdom of the bulk of the APA "marketing experts" are bound to experience the same anxieties felt by those who have entered and exited the market out of frustration.

While we know you will draw your own conclusions based on your own specific marketing situation, we want to leave you with a few of our own.

- **There really *is* an Asian Pacific American Market**
  A true Pan-Asian culture is emerging. As shown in previous chapters, historical ethnic differences aside, APAs are finding more in common with other APAs than not. Some of the strongest identifiers that would allow a marketer to reasonably approach APAs as a true market are based on psychographic commonalities rather than national or ethnic differences. APA values are very overt. Respect for parents, education, drives towards success are all worn on the sleeves. We see common cohorts of sacrifice for the group, family respect and other characteristic traits. The ethnic enclaves of the 19th and 20th centuries are both reinforcing themselves via a Pan-Asian sen-

sibility while breaking out in the most unlikely of places due to expertise in specific job markets. The "place of first landing" has become and is becoming less and less important. No longer are immigrants relegated to being ghetto-ized in Chinatowns for generations. Intermarriage and outmarriage amongst APAs places less value on purity of bloodline (and historical differences) and the changing biological definitions are creating attitudinal shifts for future generations.

- **There is no *single* marketing model that can be applied to all ethnic groups**
  Marketers cannot reach the APA market merely by taking a program used to reach African American or Hispanic markets and simply changing a face or a language. Civil rights activities have not shaped and driven marketing efforts towards APAs as they have with African Americans and Hispanic Americans. The APA history in the U.S., immigration patterns, status, acculturation process, demographic make-up and psychographic tendencies all demand a different approach for marketers to be successful in reaching an APA audience.

- **Stress *marketing fundamentals* in reaching out to APAs**
  The "deep dive" and "Marketing 101" disciplines should be required no matter who you want to reach. The APA market should be entered by companies with a single focus – ROI. It's not about social causes, civil rights or corporate goodwill. The discipline used to approach your mainstream market is no different than what should be used to reach the APA market. Building your APA marketing plan into your overall plan allows you to define goals, establish metrics and evaluate results right from the start. If you trust any professional to do your mainstream marketing work, the same rules and structure apply to working within the APA market, and in fact, all your target markets. Develop your APA plan and ask the tough questions at the beginning rather than as an add-on. Be wary of the "genetic ex-

perts" who pass themselves off as marketing experts. Sound use of marketing fundamentals nuanced to the APA market trumps who is actually doing the work.

- **The APA Market is *not* impenetrable**
  There exists a simple, rationale approach in reaching the APA market if you are ready to accept the New Paradigm. Assimilation is not a zero-sum game, and APAs are here to stay and become "American" whether they are recognized as such or not. The Americanization Dynamic overrides almost all boundaries for APAs. APAs, along with everyone else, react strongly via the Look-Like-Me Need. When representing APAs in communications, the differences among APAs are less important than presenting a recognizable Asian face. Most important of all, English is the Common Denominator that can be used to reach the largest number of APAs. This unifying factor is the single strongest argument for erasing most of the conventional wisdom for not racing out to the APA marketplace.

- **The APA Market has some inherent "extras"**
  By identifying what drives your consumers, not only from a product use perspective, but from ethnographic measures, marketers can evaluate the "bonus" received when reaching out to APAs. Just as APA groups are tied more closely via psychographic similarities than separated via national origin, so are non-APAs tied in via "gateways." The importance of hapas as part of both the APA and non-APA communities further extend the sphere of reach when addressing the APA target.

Finally, the APA escalator is still in good working order. As you've been reading this book, all the trends, all the dynamics are still moving forward. Immigration is still going strong, and the next generations are honoring their families' winning traditions.

So, whether you're looking to connect with the APA market as a source of business or as a resource for your on business, we wish you the best in applying *fuseki* to your *gambit* in the Asian Pacific American marketplace.

Endnotes

I: Introduction

1. Mintel Reports USA. *Multicultural America, Asian American Lifestyle*, U.S. (November,2009).

2. Marlene Rossman, *Multicultural Marketing: Selling to a Diverse America*, (AMACOM, 1994), 103.

3. Ibid., 101.

4. Ibid., 97.

5. Alfred L. Schreiber, *Multicultural Marketing: Selling to the New America*, (NTC Business Books, 2001), 88.

6. U.S. Census Bureau. http://www.census.gov/.

7. Chris Rock, *Rock This!*, (Hyperion, 1997), 165.

8. U.S. Census Bureau. http://www.census.gov/.

II: Background

1. Rod Paige, *Remarks by U.S. Secretary of Education Rod Paige Before the States Institute on International Education in the Schools*, http://www2.ed.gov/news/speeches/2002/11/11202002.html, (November 20, 2002).

2. *National Geographic.* "Roper Public Affairs 2006 Geographic Literacy Study," May 2006.

3. Ibid., 6.

4. Ibid.

5. Ibid., 8.

6. *U.S. Department of Education.* "Teaching Language for National Security and American Competitiveness," http://ed.gov/teachers/how/academic/foreign-language/teaching-language/, (October 26, 2007).

7. Lucinda Branaman, Rhodes Branaman, and Nancy Branaman, "Foreign Language Instruction in the United States: A National Survey of Elementary and Secondary Schools," *U.S.*

Department of Education, Office of Post-Secondary Education, International Research and Studies Programs, Center for Applied Lingusitics, (December 1997).

8. Max Weber, *The Protestant Ethic and the Spirit of Capitalism,* London & Boston: Unwin Hyman, 1930.

9. Wikipedia contributors, "Fork," *Wikipedia, The Free Encyclopedia,* http://en.wikipedia.org/wiki/Fork

10. Wikipedia contributors, "Languages of Asia and infoplease. com/The Indo-European Family of Languages," *Wikipedia, The Free Encyclopedia,* http://en.wikipedia.org/wiki/Languages_ of_Asia_and_infoplease.com/The_Indo-European_Family_of_ Languages

11. Parag Khanna, "Waving Goodbye to Hegemony," *New York Times Magazine,* January 2008, 34-41, 62-67.

12. R.G. Ratcliffe, "Lawmaker defends comment on Asians," *Houston Chronicle,* April 9, 2009.

III: Blind Spots

1. Advertising Age. "Asian-American Agencies Link to 'Validate Market'," *Advertising Age,* March 8, 1999, 24.

2. Direct Marketing News. "Targeting Asian Americans, the Fastest Growing Ethnic Group," *Direct Marketing News,* September 7, 1998, 59.

3. Al Gore, *An Inconvenient Truth,* DVD, directed by Davis Guggenheim (Paramount Classics, 2006).

IV: History

Generally:

*   Eric Lai and Dennis Arguelles, editors, *The New Face of Asian Pacific America: Numbers, Diversity & Change in the 21st Century,* AsianWeek & UCLA Asian American Studies Center Press, 2003.

*   Ronald Takaki, *Strangers From a Different Shore: A History of Asian Americans,* Little Brown & Co., 1989.

- Asian American Institute (AAI), *Asian American Compass: A Guide to Navigating the Community*, 3ʳᵈ ed., 2006.
- Lan Cao and Himilce Novas, *Everything You Need to Know About Asian American History*, Plume Penguin Books, 1996.

1. Cao, 39.
2. Helen Zia, *Asian American Dreams: The Emergence of an American People*, (Farrar, Straus & Giroux, 2000), 31
3. Takaki, 417.
4. U.S. Senate, *Subcommittee on Immigration and Naturalization of the Committee of the Judiciary*, (Washington D.C., February 10, 1965), 65.
5. Ibid.
6. AsianWeek. "Killers Stalked Vincent Chin," *AsianWeek*, April 28, 1983; "1,000 Detroit Asians Protest Sentences," *AsianWeek*, May 12, 1983; "Killer Goes Free," *AsianWeek*, May 8, 1987.
7. Clarence Page, "Profiling Hits Asians Both Ways," *Chicago Tribune*, June 14, 2000.

V: Cultural Snapshots

1. Frank Wu, "Speaking as an Asian American...," *AsianWeek*, April 27, 2000.
2. Zia, 42.
3. Wikipedia contributors, "German American Bund," *Wikipedia, The Free Encyclopedia*, http://en.wikipedia.org/wiki/German_American_Bund
4. Takaki, 80.
5. Ibid., 81.
6. Ibid.
7. Ibid., 82.
8. Ibid., 84-86.
9. Ibid., 488.
10. Ibid., 12.
11. Ibid., 488.
12. Jennifer 8 Lee, *The Fortune Cookie Chronicles: Adventures in the*

World of Chinese Food, (Twelve-Hachette Book Group, 2008), 15-16.

13. Takaki, 318.
14. Ibid., 324.
15. Ibid., 332-333.
16. Zia, 303.
17. Ibid., 200.
18. Takaki, 446.
19. Zia, 210.
20. Ibid.
21. Ibid.
22. Howard M. Sachar, *American Jewry*, http://www.myjewishle-arning.com/history/Modern_History/1948-1980/America.shtml, (1992).
23. Lai, 52.
24. Zia, 209.
25. Ibid., 205.
26. Ibid., 171-172.
27. Ibid., 172.
28. Ibid., 172-173.
29. Lai, 61.
30. Takaki, 449.
31. Ibid., 454.
32. Ibid.
33. Zia, 46.
34. Takaki, 455-458.
35. Lai, 79.
36. Ibid., 3.
37. Ibid., 80.
38. Ibid., 81-82.
39. Ibid., 83.
40. David Henry Hwang, *M Butterfly*, (Plume Penguin Books, 1986), 17.
41. Philip Kan Gotanda's *Yankee Dawg You Die* in his book: *Fish*

Head Soup and Other Plays, (University of Washington Press, 1991), 97-98.

VI: Getting Started

1. Advertising Age. "Multicultural 'Not a Fad'," *Advertising Age's Multicultural Guide,* November 3, 2003, M3.
2. Advertising Age. "Niche-market Focus Takes Multicultural Ad Spotlight," *Advertising Age,* November 16, 1998, S6.
3. Ibid., S10.
4. Schreiber, 72.
5. Aol.com. "IW Group, InterTrend Tap into the Fast-growing Asian-American Market," *Aol.com,* October 24, 2006.
6. Rossman, 86.
7. Christine Bunish, "Marketers Explore Opportunities in Multicultural Area," *Advertising Age's Multicultural Guide,* November 2, 2003, M1.
8. Julie Liesse, "The Latino Identity Project: Understanding a Market," *Advertising Age Special Section,* February 19, 2007, A8.
9. Ibid., A8.
10. Lee, 9.
11. Peggy Noonan, "Declarations: We Need to Talk," *Wall Street Journal,* July 7, 2007, P12.
12. Bunish, M1.
13. SiTV.com
14. Advertising Age. November 3, 2003, M3.
15. Beth Snyder Bulik, "Marketers: We Don't Get How to Do Diversity," *Advertising Age,* February 25, 2008, 25.
16. Advertising Age. November 16, 1998, S18.
17. Advertising Age. February 25, 2008, 25.
18. Ibid., 1.
19. Ibid., 25.
20. Advertising Age. November 16, 1998, S10, S12.
21. Advertising Age. November 2, 2003, M2.

22. Ibid., M3.

23. Orlando Patterson, "Ecumenical America: Global Culture and the American Cosmos," *World Policy Journal*, June 22, 1994.

24. David Bernstein, "Lessons from the Jewish Experience," *AsianWeek*, June 22, 2000, 5.

25. Clarence Page, "A Dream Dies at the NAACP: Gordon's Departure Puts Focus Squarely on Ideological Schism," *Chicago Tribune*, March 7, 2007, 25.

26. Leonard Pitts, "Who Made Sharpton the Official Spokesman?: No Individual Can Speak on Behalf of 36 Million People," *Chicago Tribune*, November 13, 2007, 17.

27. Judy Ching-Chia Wong, "Victims of Both Sides," *New York Times*, May 28, 1992, A23.

28. Alex Kotlowitz, "Our Town," *New York Times Magazine*, August 5, 2007, 37.

29. Ibid., 37.

30. Ibid., 37.

31. U.S. Department of Education, Office of English Language Acquisition, Language Enhancement and Academic Achievement for Limited English Proficient Students, (2002).

32. Lisa Moran, "Right on Target: The Industry Responds to Changing Demographics with Cultural Marketing," *Market Watch*, May, 1993, 32.

33. *Global Language Monitor.* "The Top Politically Incorrect Words for 2006," http://www.languagemonitor.com/?s=the+top+politically+incorrect+words+for+2006, (December 13, 2006).

VII: Demographics

Generally:

- U.S. Census Bureau. http://www.census.gov/.
- *U.S. Census Bureau.* "American Community Survey," http://www.census.gov/acs/www/Site_Map.html, (2005-2007).
- *U.S. Department of Labor, Bureau of Labor Statistics.* "Consumer

Expenditure Survey," http://bls.gov/CEX/.

- *U.S. Department of Labor, Bureau of Labor Statistics.* "American Time Use Survey," http://bls.gov/TUS/.
- *National Opinion Research Center (NORC).* "General Social Survey," http://norc.org/GSS.
- *Ronin Group.* "18-49 Year-Old APAs and Non-APAs," Online Survey, (2006).

1. Daniel Moynihan and Nathan Glazer, *Beyond the Melting Pot: The Negroes, Puerto Ricans, Jews, Italians and Irish of New York,* MIT Press, 1963.

2. Population Reference Bureau. http://prb.org/.

3. Stephen Thernstrom and Abigail Thernstrom, *America in Black & White: One Nation Indivisible,* Simon & Schuster, 1995.

4. Vivek Wahhwa, "Are Indians the Model Immigrants?," *BusinessWeek.com,* September 14, 2006.

5. Malcolm Gladwell, *Outliers: The Story of Success,* Little, Brown & Company, 2008.

VIII: Diversity

Generally:
- U.S. Census Bureau. http://www.census.gov/.
- *U.S. Census Bureau.* "American Community Survey," http://www.census.gov/acs/www/Site_Map.html, (2005-2007).
- *U.S. Department of Labor, Bureau of Labor Statistics.* "Consumer Expenditure Survey," http://bls.gov/CEX/.
- *U.S. Department of Labor, Bureau of Labor Statistics.* "American Time Use Survey," http://bls.gov/TUS/.
- *National Opinion Research Center (NORC).* "General Social Survey," http://norc.org/GSS.
- *Ronin Group.* "18-49 Year-Old APAs and Non-APAs," Online Survey, (2006).

1. AAI, 6.

2. June Kronholz, "Racial Identity's Gray Area: The Definition of Whiteness Continues to Shift," *Wall Street Journal,* http://

online.wsj.com/article/SB121322793544566177.html?KEY
WORDS=Racial+Identities+Gray+Area.

3. *Center for Immigration Studies.* "Three Decades of Mass Immigration: the Legacy of the 1965 Immigration Act," (September, 1995).

4. Malcolm Collier, "Demographics of Asian Americans," *San Francisco State University,* http://google.sfsu.edu/search?q=malcolm+collier&x=0&y=0, (2006).

5. TPA Realty Services. http://tparealtyservices.com/john-screek/

6. Wikipedia contributors, "Spring Valley, Nevada," *Wikipedia, The Free Encyclopedia,* http://en.wikipedia.org/wiki/Spring_valley,_nevada

7. Wikipedia contributors, "Cary, North Carolina," *Wikipedia, The Free Encyclopedia,* http://en.wikipedia.org/wiki/Cary,_north_carolina

8. Thernstrom & Thernstrom, (1995).

9. Jennifer Rubin, "The New Jews: Asian Admissions at the Ivies," *Weekly Standard* 13, no. 47 (September 9, 2008).

10. Moynihan & Glazer, (1963).

11. Anthony Daniel Perez & Charles Hirschman, "The Changing Racial and Ethnic Composition of the U.S. Population: Emerging American Identities," *Population & Development Review,* March, 2009.

12. C.N. Le, "Asian-Nation: Asian American History, Demographics & Issues," *Asian Nation,* http://www.asian-nation.org/

13. Sharon Lee and Barry Edmonston, "New Marriages, New Families: U.S. Racial & Hispanic Intermarriage," *Population Bulletin,* June, 2005.

14. Ibid.

15. Pew Global Attitudes Project. "Publics of Asian Powers Hold Negative Views of One Another," *Pew Global Attitudes Project,* 2006.

16. Perez & Hirschman, (2009).

17. Joseph White, "What Really Makes an American Car?" *Wall Street Journal*, January 27, 2009, D6.

IX: Lifestyle

Generally:

- U.S. Census Bureau. http://www.census.gov/.

- *U.S. Census Bureau.* "American Community Survey," http://www.census.gov/acs/www/Site_Map.html, (2005-2007).

- *U.S. Department of Labor, Bureau of Labor Statistics.* "Consumer Expenditure Survey," http://bls.gov/CEX/.

- *U.S. Department of Labor, Bureau of Labor Statistics.* "American Time Use Survey," http://bls.gov/TUS/.

- *National Opinion Research Center (NORC).* "General Social Survey," http://norc.org/GSS.

- *Ronin Group.* "18-49 Year-Old APAs and Non-APAs," Online Survey, (2006).

1. Barry A. Kosmin and Ariela Keysar, "American Religious Identification Survey 2008," *U.S. Census Bureau,* http://www.americanreligionsurvey-aris.org/.

2. *U.S. Census Bureau.* American Time Use Survey, https://ask.census.gov/cgi-bin/askcensus.cfg/php/enduser/std_adp.php?p_faqid=1022&p_sid=g-K9nn*j&p_created=1133377016&p_sp=cF9zcmNoPSZwX3NvcnRfYnk9JnBfZ3JpZHNvcnQ9JnBfcm93X2NudD0mcF9wcm9kz0mcF9jYXRzPSZwX3B2PSZwX2N2PSZwX3BhZ2U9MQ!!&p_search_text=American%20Time%20Use%20Survey

3. *New American Media.* "Deep Divisions, Shared Destinuy – A Poll of Black, Hispanic and Asian Americans on Race Relations," http://news.newamericamedia.org/news/view_article.html?article_id=28501933d0e5c5344b21f9640dc13754, (December 12, 2007).

4. Daniel Golden, *The Price of Admission: How America's Ruling Class Buys Its Way into Elite Colleges – and Who Gets Left Outside*

      the Gates, Random House, September 5, 2006.

5.   Rubin, Ibid.

6.   Ruben G. Rumbaut and Alejandro Portes, *Ethnicities: Children of Immigrants in America*, University of California Press, September 2001; "The Children of Immigrants Longitudinal Study (CILS-III)," *Princeton University*, http://www.princeton.edu/main/tools/search/?q=The+Children+of+Immigrants+Longitudinal+Study&x=0&y=0, (2003); *Immigrant America: A Portrait*, University of California Press, December, 2006.

7.   NORC GSS, Ibid.

8.   Gladwell, Ibid.

9.   NORC GSS, Ibid.

10.   ScienceDaily. "Culture Influences Brain Function, Study Shows," Massachusetts Institute of Technology: *ScienceDaily*, January 13, 2008.

11.   Ibid.

12.   ScienceDaily, (July 15, 2007).

13.   ScienceDaily. "Americans Trail Chinese in Understanding Another Person's Perspective," University of Chicago: *ScienceDaily*, July 15, 2007.

14.   Kosmin and Keysar, Ibid.

15.   ScienceDaily. "Face Recognition: Nurture Not Nature," Public Library of Science: *ScienceDaily*, August 22, 2008.

16.   Survey Sampling International. "Business-to-Business," http://www.surveysampling.com/en/samplingsolutions/business-business, (2010).

17.   Clotaire Rapaille, *The Culture Code: An Ingenious Way to Understand Why People Around the World Live and Buy as They Do*, (Broadway Books, 2006), 146.

X: Products and People

1.   Christopher Borelli, "The Knives Are Out at Sun Wah," *Chicago Tribune*, February 11, 2010.

2. Market Segment Group. "Multicultural Snapshot," *Market Segment Group*, May 11, 2001.

3. Ibid., (November 17, 2000).

4. Ibid., (August 31, 2001).

5. Ibid., (July 12, 2001).

6. Ibid.

7. Ibid., (July 20, 2001).

8. Ibid., (March 15, 2002).

9. Ibid., (January 26, 2001).

10. Ibid.

11. CTAM Pulse. "The Multicultural Marketplace: Insights on Technology and Media Behavior," *CTAM Pulse*, August/September, 2009.

12. Mike Collins, *Saving American Manufacturing: Growth Planning for Small and Midsize Manufacturers*, (First Flight Books, 2006), 247-260.

13. C.N. Le, "Asian Small Business," *Asian Nation*, http://www.asian-nation.org/small-business.shtml.

14. Market Segment Group. "Multicultural Snapshot," *Market Segment Group*, November 02, 2001.

15. Le, Ibid.

XI: One Market

Generally:

• *Ronin Group*. "18-49 Year-Old APAs and Non-APAs," Online Survey, (2006).

1. Market Segment Group. "Multicultural Snapshot," *Market Segment Group*, March 1, 2002.

2. *U.S. Census Bureau*. "American Community Survey," http://www.census.gov/acs/www/Site_Map.html, (2005-2007).

3. U.S. Census Bureau. "Population Estimates," *U.S. Census Bureau*, http://www.census.gov/popest/estimates.html, (2006).

4. Market Segment Group. "Multicultural Snapshot," *Market Segment Group*, June 7, 2002.

5.	Carol Hymowitz, "Marketers Focus More On Gobal 'Tribes' Than on Nationalities," *Wall Street Journal*, December 10, 2007, B1.

6.	Noreen S. Ahmed-Ullah, "Chinatown Now Trendy for Young: Embracing Their Roots, Chinese-Americans Are Bringing New Life to the Old Neighborhood," *Chicago Tribune*, July 26, 2007, 1, 20.

7.	John Steinbeck, *East of Eden*, (Viking Press, 1952), 162.

8.	Hymowitz, B1.

9.	Xiaoguang Lu and Anil K. Jain, "Ethnicity Identification from Face Images," *Michigan State University: Department of Computer Science & Engineering*, 2002.

10.	S. Sangrigoli, C. Pallier, A.-M. Argenti, V.A.G. Ventureyra, and S. de Schonen, "Reversibility of the Other-race Effect in Face Recognition During Childhood," *Psychological Science*, June 2004.

11.	Nolo contributors, "Peremptory challenge," *Nolo's Plain English Law Dictionary*, http://www.nolo.com/dictionary/peremptory-challenge-term.html

12.	*New York Federal Criminal Practice*. "Second Circuit Affirms Government's Reverse-Batson Challenge," nyfederalcriminalpractice.com/jury-selection, (June 6, 2008).

13.	Dirk Olin, "Jury Selection, Peremptory Challenges," *Sheridan: Con-Law*, http://sheridan_conlaw.typepad.com/Sheridan_conlaw/jury_selection_peremptory_challenges/, (December 22, 2004).

14.	Gary Thorne, "Study Puts Umpires Under Even Greater Microscope," *USA Today*, September 10, 2007;"Batter Out: Umpires Likely to Favor Pitchers of Same Race or Ethnicity; Game Attendance and Electronic Monitoring Mitigate Behavior," *The University of Texas at Austin*, utexas.edu/news, 2007/08/13/economics, (August 13, 2007).

15.	Aol.com. "IW Group, InterTrend Tap into the Fast-growing Asian-American Market," *Aol.com*, October 24, 2006.

16. *U.S. Census Bureau.* "American Community Survey," http://www.census.gov/acs/www/Site_Map.html, (2005-2007).

17. Ibid.

18. U.S. Census Bureau. http://www.census.gov/.

19. *U.S. Census Bureau.* "American Community Survey," http://www.census.gov/acs/www/Site_Map.html, (2005-2007).

20. Ibid.

21. Market Segment Group. "Multicultural Snapshot," *Market Segment Group*, April 5, 2002.

22. Scott Jaschik, "The SAT's Growing Gaps," *Inside Higher Ed,* http://www.insidehighered.com/news/2008/08/27/sat, (August 27, 2008).

23. Grace Tzeng, "Asians Score Higher Than Whites in English," *AsianWeek*, August 29, 2008; California Department of Education. "2008 Standardized Testing and Reporting Program", http://star.cde.ca.gov/star2008/.

24. AsianWeek. "Why Asians Speak English," *AsianWeek*, August 29, 2008, 4.

25. Michael Erard, "Anyone Here Speak Chinglish?," *Wired*, July 2008, 23,26.

26. Fareed Zakaria, *The Post-American World*, (W.W. Norton & Company, Inc. 2008), 79-80, 170.

27. AsianWeek. "The ABCs of Language and Health," *AsianWeek*, July 25, 2008, 4.

XII: Bonus

1. Philip Kotler, *Marketing Management: Analysis, Planning and Control*, 2nd ed., (Prentice-Hall, Inc., 1972), 165-166.

2. Rajeev Batra, John G. Myers, David A. Aaker, *Advertising Management*, 5th ed., (Prentice-Hall Inc., 1996), 189-190.

3. J.K. Yamamoto, "Kikkoman Celebrates 50th Anniversary in U.S. Market," *Sushi & Sake*, sushiandtofu.com/business/200707kikkoman, (June 11, 2008); "Kikkoman Announces $100 Million Expansion in Wisconsin," *Busi-*

ness Wire, May 30, 2003; "Heinz Reports Third-quarter EPS Rose 12% to $0.76, Net Income Grew 11%," *Heinz*, http://www.heinz.com/our-company/press-room/press-releases/press-release.aspx?ndmConfigId=1012072&newsId=20090224005703, (February 24, 2009); "Eleven Ketchup Facts," *Fooducate*, http://www.fooducate.com/blog/2009/02/24/eleven-ketchup-facts/, (February 24, 2009); "Heinz Ketchup Unveils New Personality: 'Talking Labels' Target Teens with Fun Messages," *ProcessingTomato.com*, http://www.seedquest.com/processingtomato/news/heinz/p1001.htm, (October 25, 1999).

4. Wikipedia contributors. "Anime," *Wikipedia, The Free Encyclopedia*, http://en.wikipedia.org/wiki/Anime

5. RZA, *The Wu-Tang Manual*, Riverhead Trade, 2005; "Popularity of the Martial Arts," *Winstonstableford*, http://winstonstableford.com/popularity

6. Ellie M. Hisama, "Afro-Asian Crosscurrents in Contemporary Hip Hop," *ISAM Newsletter*, http://depthome.brooklyn.cuny.edu/isam/2002/hisama1.html, (Fall 2002).

7. Jeff Yang, "Forever and Ever, Ramen," *Asian Pop, San Francisco Chronicle*, http://articles.sfgate.com/2007-01-18/entertainment/17225108_1_momofuku-ando-instant-ramen-noodles, (January 18, 2007); Rich Whittle, "Upstart Aims to Soup Up Ramen Noodles," *The Wall Street Journal*, http://www.business-opportunities.biz/2007/01/31/upstart-aims-to-soup-up-ramen-noodles/, (January 31, 2007); Wikipedia contributors. "Campbell Soup Company," *Wikipedia, The Free Encyclopedia*, http://en.wikipedia.org/wiki/Campbell_soup_company

8. NCCAM. "Backgrounder: An Introduction to Acupuncture," *National Center for Complementary and Alternative Medicine, National Institutes of Health*, http://nccam.nih.gov/health/whatiscam/chinesemed.htm

9. S. Ranjan, "Yoga – A Spiritual Commodity!" *Central Chronicle*,

centralchronicle.com, (June 19, 2007); Yoga Journal. "The Yoga Journal Story," *Yoga Journal*, http://www.yogajournal. com/global/34; Melissa Hill, "Yoga Industry Growing in the U.S.," *Renew's Insidethespa.com*, http://www.insidethespa.com/articles/content/cat/24/item/256, (April 10, 2008).

10. Lee, Ibid.

11. Mutiny.wordpress.com. "Bollywood vs. Hollywood – the Complete Breakdown," *Mutiny.wordpress.com*, http://mutiny. wordpress.com/2007/02/01/bollywood-vs-hollywood-the-complete-breakdown/; Anita N. Wadhwani, "Bollywood Mania Rising in United States," *U.S. Department of State*, http://www.america.gov/st/washfile-english/2006/August/20060 809124617nainawhdaw0.8614466.html, (August 9, 2006); Wikipedia contributors. "Bollywood," *Wikipedia, The Free Encyclopedia*, http://en.wikipedia.org/wiki/Bollywood

12. "Adopted Asian Americans," *Asian-Nation,* Ibid.

13. Janet Stilson, "Nets Tightly Focused, Stay Engaging," *Advertising Age*, April 10, 2006, S-4.

XIII: Hapas

1. Pearl Fuyo Gaskins, *What are you?: Voices of mixed-race young people*, (Henry Holt & Company, 1999), 4.

2. *U.S. Census Bureau.* http://www.census.gov/population/soc-demo/race/

3. Loving et.ux v. Virginia, 388 U.S. 1 (1967), No. 395, (Argued April 10, 1967, Decided June 12, 1967).

4. U.S. Census Bureau, Ibid.

5. Donna Jackson Nakazawa, "A New Generation is Leading the Way," *Parade*, July 6, 2003, 5.

6. U.S. Census Bureau, Ibid.

7. Ibid.

8. Steven A. Holmes, "True Colors: The Confusion Over Who We Are," *New York Times*, June 3, 2001, sec. 4, 1.

10. Janet Dang and Jason Ma, "HAPAmerica: The Coming of Age

of Hapas Sets the Stage for a New Agenda," *AsianWeek*, April 13, 2000, 17.

11. Ibid.

XIV: Messages

1. Rossman, 89-90.
2. Sarah Patterson, "Creativity in a Multicultural Environment," *AAAA Account Planning Conference*, Chicago, August 3, 2005.
3. Jason Carroll, "Will Obama suffer from the 'Bradley effect'?," *CNN.com*, http://www.cnn.com/2008/POLITICS/10/13/obama.bradley.effect/, (October 14, 2008); Wikipedia contributors. "Bradley Effect," *Wikipedia, The Free Encyclopedia*, http://en.wikipedia.org/wiki/Bradley_effect
4. Judy Cohen, "White Consumer Response to Asian Models in Advertising," *Journal of Consumer Marketing*, (Spring, 1992) vol. 9, no. 2.

XV: Media

1. Bill Imada, "Forget the Asian-American-market Myths – But Remember These Truths," *Advertising Age*, November 5, 2007, 14.
2. Rossman, Ibid., 85-86.
3. Schreiber, Ibid., 89.
4. TVNewsday. "DTV May be Key to LA's Asian Community," *TVNewsday*, July 15, 2008.
5. Leon Wynter, "Marketplace: Business & Race," *Wall Street Journal*, June 10, 1998.
6. Market Segment Group. "Multicultural Snapshot," *Market Segment Group*, June 22, 2001.
7. *Bacon's Magazine Directory*, 56th ed., Chicago: Cision, 2008.
8. Ronin Group, Ibid.
9. Luis Clemens, "Lack of Data, Lot of Promise for Asian-American Media," *Multichannel News*, December 18, 2006.
10. CTAM Pulse, Ibid.

11. Ibid.

12. Market Segment Group, Ibid., (May 11, 2001).

13. Ibid., (March 16, 2001).

14. Jack Z. Sissors and E.R. Petray, *Advertising Media Planning*, Crain Books, 1976.

15. Nielsen. "Nielsen Media Research Establishes Asian Pacific American Advisory Council," *Nielsen*, nielsenmedia.com/nc/portal/site/Public.

16. Katy Bachman, "Nielsen: TV Households to Increase 1.5% for 2008-09 Season," *MediaWeek*, August 28, 2008.

17. Edward Iwata, "ImaginAsian Tries to Capture Imagination of Many Groups," *USA Today*, January 22, 2007.

18. Mya Frazier, "The Catch-22 of Buying Black Media," *Advertising Age*, April 7, 2008, 1.

19. Ibid., 28.

20. Ibid., 30.

21. Mike Sherman, "Auspicious Year for Asian Programming," *TelevisionWeek*, February 2, 2008, 8.

22. Todd Hale, Patricia McDonough, and Patricia Andrews-Keegan, "Influence - The African American Consumer: Is the Cultural Divide Breaking Down?," *Nielsen Consumer Insight*, nielsen.com/cosnsumer_insight/issue4/ci_story.

XVI: APA Specialists

1. *The Advertising Redbooks - Agencies*, Lexis Nexis, 2009.

2. http://3af.org/roster

3. Advertising Age. "Top U.S. Multicultural Agencies," *Advertising Age*, December 29, 2008, 49.

4. Allen Gardner, "A Client's Guide to Conducting an Agency Search," *American Association of Advertising Agencies*, 1994.

5. Bill Imada, "A General Market Agency for Ethnic Work? It's a Waste of Money," *Advertising Age*, http://adage.com/bigtent/post?article_id=122997, (January 10, 2008).

6. Alberto J. Ferrer, "Why You Don't Have to be Hispanic to be

a Successful Hispanic Marketer," *Advertising Age*, February 4, 2008, 16.

7. Nils von Zelowitz, "Will the Recession Put Multicultural and General Market on a Level Playing Field?" *Advertising Age*, http://adage.com/bigtent/post?article_id=136140, (April 20, 2009).

8. Marissa Miley, "Do Ethnic Shops Have a Future?", *Advertising Age*, February 16, 2009, 21.

9. Jonah Bloom, "Wish I May, Wish I Might: Fewer Swiffers, More Soccer in '06, Please," *Advertising Age*, January 16, 2006, 14.

Index

A

About the Authors

Bob Kumaki is Principal of the Ronin Group, a marketing communications consulting firm.

Bob has over two decades of marketing experience in numerous categories including packaged goods, consumer durables, insurance, automotive, sporting goods, entertainment, telecommunications and retail for clients like Procter & Gamble, Sears, Allstate Insurance, E.J. Brach, adidas AG, Amoco Oil Co., Tribune Companies, Comcast Networks and the Government of Canada.

Bob has held management positions at some of the world's largest marketing communications organizations including Young & Rubicam, Ogilvy & Mather, the Publicis Groupe's Burrell unit, and has run his own consulting firm for ten years. He has an extensive background in strategic planning, new market/new product development, positioning, and strategic alliances with a long list of turnaround successes.

Bob has served as Adjunct Professor of Advertising at the University of Illinois as well as an Instructor in the University's International Executive Development Program. A strong believer in ongoing executive education, he has been a training program instructor at each of the major ad agencies where he has worked.

Well-known in Asian Pacific American community-based organization circles, Bob has served as an Officer, Director or Member of over a dozen APA groups including the Asian American Institute (Founder), the Asian American Coalition, the Japan America Society, the Heiwa Terrace Housing Corporation, the

Japanese American Citizens' League, the National Association of Asian American Professionals, the Japanese American Service Committee, the Organization of Chinese Americans, and Sister Cities International (Osaka). He has been a conference guest of major national APA organizations including Leadership Education for Asian Pacifics (LEAP), the Asian Pacific American Institute for Congressional Studies (APAICS) and the Committee of 100 as well as being invited as a guest lecturer at the University of Illinois, the University of Michigan, Northwestern University, the Asian American Bar Association, the Marcus Evans Asian American Conference, the Broadcast Cable Financial Management Conference, and Comcast Networks, among others.

Bob lives in Wilmette, IL, with his wife and daughter.

Jack Moran, PhD is President of the Moran Group, an independent market research company. Over the past 25 years, Jack has held various senior research positions at DDB Needham, working on Kraft, General Mills and Anheuser Busch; Young & Rubicam, where he pioneered the use of ethnographic studies and wrote a proprietary correspondence analysis program for positioning studies for clients like Jacobs Suchard, G. Heileman Brewery, Navistar and Terminex; and NFO Research, heading the office where he created the Ameriscope portfolio of consumer insight and strategic planning products for Frito Lay, Visa, United Airlines, KGF, RJ Reynolds and Oscar Meyer. Since 1992 the Moran Group has serviced such Fortune 500 clients as Allstate Insurance, Citibank, Hewlett Packard and Quaker Oats, among others.

Jack lives in Evanston, IL, with his wife and two children.